Manufacturing Happy Citizens

To Jara, for her boundless love, her clear mind, and her exemplary sense of justice

Edgar Cabanas

To the memory of my father, Emile-Haim, who preferred justice over happiness

To my children, Nathanael, Immanuel and Amitai, who give me much more than happiness

Eva Illouz

Manufacturing Happy Citizens

How the Science and Industry of
Happiness Control Our Lives

Edgar Cabanas
Eva Illouz

polity

First published in French as *Happycratie*, © Premier Parallèle, 2018
This English edition © Polity Press, 2019

Polity Press
65 Bridge Street
Cambridge CB2 1UR, UK

Polity Press
101 Station Landing
Suite 300
Medford, MA 02155, USA

Edgar Cabanas co-financed by the Talent Attraction Research Fellowship [2017-T2/SOC-5414], Community of Madrid, Spain.

ISBN-13: 978-1-5095-3788-4
ISBN-13: 978-1-5095-3789-1 (pb)

A catalogue record for this book is available from the British Library.

Library of Congress Cataloging-in-Publication Data

Names: Cabanas, Edgar, author. | Illouz, Eva, 1961- author.
Title: Manufacturing happy citizens : how the science and industry of
    happiness control our lives / Edgar Cabanas, Eva Illouz.
Description: Medford, MA : Polity Press, [2019] | Includes bibliographical
    references and index.
Identifiers: LCCN 2018056641 (print) | LCCN 2019005414 (ebook) | ISBN
    9781509537907 (Epub) | ISBN 9781509537884 (hardback) | ISBN 9781509537891
    (pbk.)
Subjects: LCSH: Happiness. | Positive psychology.
Classification: LCC BF575.H27 (ebook) | LCC BF575.H27 C33 2019 (print) | DDC
    158.1--dc23
LC record available at https://lccn.loc.gov/2018056641

Typeset in 10.75 on 13.5 pt Janson Text by
Servis Filmsetting Ltd, Stockport, Cheshire
Printed and bound in Great Britain by TJ International Ltd, Padstow

For further information on Polity, visit our website: politybooks.com

Contents

What apocalypse has ever been so kindly?

Philip Rieff, *The Triumph of the Therapeutic*

Introduction

The Hollywood movie *The Pursuit of Happyness* was an international hit in 2006, raking in a total revenue of $307,077,300 at the box office. The movie is based on the best-selling memoirs of Christopher Gardner, a lower-middle-class African-American who went from living in poverty to become a successful businessman, stockbroker and inspirational speaker. Set in the early 1980s, the film begins with Ronald Reagan delivering bad economic news on television. The timing of the announcement could not be worse for Gardner and his wife, Linda, both of whom struggle to keep themselves and their five-year-old son out of poverty. Gardner's family situation is indeed dire: they can barely afford their rent, bills or his son's day care. Persistent and talented, Gardner is a go-getter with a deep longing for a better career and, in spite of everything, he remains optimistic.

One day, while standing in front of one of the most prestigious stockbrokerage firms in the country, Gardner stares at the faces of the brokers leaving work: 'They all look so damn' happy', he thinks; 'Why can't I be like them?' This thought inspires him to become a stockbroker at that very same company. His charm and social skills get him admitted into a highly competitive yet unpaid internship programme at the company. His wife, Linda, however, does not support his dreams. When Gardner tells her about his intention of becoming a broker, she sarcastically counters, 'Why not an astronaut?' Depicted as Gardner's foil, she represents the whiner, the pessimist and the quitter, abandoning the family just when things seem that they could not get any worse. Without the economic support of his wife, Gardner finds himself destitute. He and his son are forced to move to a homeless shelter after being kicked out of their apartment and then a motel.

Nevertheless, Gardner does not allow himself to be overcome by the circumstances: he maintains the outward appearance of success in front of the programme's CEOs and his Ivy League competitors. He works day and night, combining two jobs while studying hard for the final internship test, and still takes good care of his son. But Gardner is driven: 'Do not ever let somebody tell you that you cannot do something. You got a dream, you have to protect it. If you want something, go get it. Period', Gardner tells his son while they play basketball. Gardner finishes at the top of the programme and finally gets his dream job. 'This is happiness', he declares at the end of the movie.

An interesting aspect of the international success of the movie is that it says a lot about the extent to which both the ideal and pursuit of happiness are omnipresent in our daily lives. Happiness is everywhere: on TV and the radio, in books and magazines, at the gym, in food and diet advice, in hospitals, at work, at war, in schools, in universities, in technology, on the web, in sports, at home, in politics and, of course, on the market's shelves. Happiness has haunted our cultural imaginary, becoming *per diem* and *ad nauseam* present in our lives, so rarely does one go a day without hearing or reading about it. Indeed, a simple search on the web for the word 'happiness' yields hundreds of thousands of results. For instance, whereas Amazon listed no more than 300 books with the word happiness in the title before the turn of the century, today that list includes more than 2,000; and the same increase goes for the weekly number of tweets, Instagram and Facebook posts that people exchange every day. Happiness has grown into a fundamental part of our commonsensical understanding of ourselves and the world, a concept so familiar that we take it for granted. It feels and rings so natural today that to call happiness into question is odd if not audacious.

Nevertheless, it is not only the frequency and pervasiveness with which happiness shows up that have radically changed in the past few decades. The way in which we have come to understand happiness has radically transformed as well. We no longer believe that happiness is somewhat connected to fate or circumstances; the absence of ailment, the valuation of a whole life, or a petty consolation for the foolish. In fact, happiness is now generally seen as a mindset that can be engineered through willpower; the outcome of putting into practice our inner strengths and authentic selves; the only goal that makes life worth living; the standard by which we should measure the worth of our biographies, the size of our successes and failures, and the magnitude of our psychic and emotional development.

Most importantly, happiness has come to be presented as the very epitome and incarnation of today's ideal image of the good citizen. Gardner's story becomes especially interesting in this regard. Indeed, one of the most appealing aspects of the movie *The Pursuit of Happyness* is not what it says about the notion of happiness *per se*, but what is reveals about the kind of citizen that rightfully achieves it.[1] What Gardner's story actually proposes is that happiness is not a thing as much as a particular kind of person: individualistic, true to himself, resilient, self-motivated, optimistic and highly emotionally intelligent. In this sense, the movie simultaneously renders Gardner as the ideal embodiment of *the* happy person and presents happiness as an exemplary narrative of how to organize and mobilize the self around certain ideological values, anthropological assumptions and political virtues.

Gardner's story, though, goes beyond the movie. The story of the real Christopher Gardner continued in the media, which was interested in Gardner's life and how it could inspire millions with the idea that wealth and poverty, success and failure, happiness and unhappiness are actually choices. In 2006, Will Smith, who played Gardner in the movie, said in a series of interviews that he loved Gardner because, 'he personified the American Dream'. On the *Oprah Winfrey Show*, Smith also mentioned that 'America was such a great idea' because it was 'the only country in the world that Chris Gardner could exist' (*sic*). Nevertheless, Smith forgot to mention that cases like Gardner's are actually as exceptional in North America as they are in the rest of the world. He disregarded that North America is one of the nations with the highest income inequality and social exclusion rates in the world,[2] so wealth and upward mobility are actually very hard to achieve for the majority of the population. Smith also failed to mention that North America is one of the countries where the belief that, whether winners or losers, individuals are the only ones accountable for their own success or misery is deeply embedded in the cultural and national unconscious – a meritocratic assumption that extends to Western countries at large, where there is an increasing tendency to see one's particular situation in terms of individual deservingness rather than in terms of structural processes.[3] The movie is a very representative instance of this, with Gardner depicted as the quintessential self-made individual, and his life as a sort of Social Darwinist struggle for upward mobility which ends with the key message that meritocracy works because persistence and personal effort are always rewarded.

The film's success brought the real Christopher Gardner immense global fame in the years that followed. He gave hundreds of interviews during which he shared his secret to happiness and explained why 'happyness' was spelled with a 'y': 'the "y" is there to make us all mindful that it is YOU and YOUR responsibility to make the life you want for you. The cavalry ain't coming. It's about you.' Gardner, a successful stockbroker turned motivational speaker, found his true mission in life: sharing with the world his hard-won wisdom about the power of people pulling themselves up by their own bootstraps and turning adverse circumstances into opportunities for growth and success. Named ambassador of happiness in 2010 for AARP, a non-profit organization with more than 40 million members worldwide, Gardner was fully devoted to spreading a simple message: just as selves can be moulded, shaped and transformed through willpower and the right know-how, happiness can also be engineered, taught and learned.

Gardner's message, though, was at the very least paradoxical as well. At the same time that he claimed that happiness was about 'YOU, YOUR responsibility, and only yours', he nevertheless argued for the necessity of experts like him to guide people in this endeavour. Undoubtedly, Gardner was trapped in the everlasting paradox embedded in the myth of personal reinvention, to wit that even self-made individuals need instructions and guidance, after all. Gardner's thinking, indeed, was not new. On the contrary, it comes out of a deep-seated tradition of mixed ideological, spiritual and popular features that have long fed a powerful market built on the commodification of life-stories of self-change, redemption and personal triumph – a sort of 'emotional pornography' aimed at shaping the way people should feel about themselves and the surrounding world. Indeed, turning these stories into exemplary biographies aimed at teaching people what to become to be happy has been a constant in American culture, one which traces back via Oprah Winfrey in the 1990s and Norman Vincent Peale in the 1950s to Horatio Alger in the late 1880s and Samuel Smiles in the 1850s.[4]

The pursuit of happiness is actually one of the most distinctive exports and chief political horizons of North American culture that has been spread and pushed forward with the help of a wide array of non-political actors, including self-help writers, coaches, businesspeople, private organizations and foundations, Hollywood, talk-shows, celebrities and, of course, psychologists. Nevertheless, only recently did the pursuit of happiness cease to be a mainly North American political horizon to become a multibillion global industry operating alongside (and with the complicity of) hard, empirical science.

Had it been released in the 1990s, *The Pursuit of Happyness* would have gone relatively unnoticed amongst the vast array of stories of personal triumph that filled the market, especially the non-fiction bookstore shelves and Hollywood's catalogue of cheesy drama movies. But in the 2000s, the situation was different. Founded in 1998 and handsomely financed with North American funds, the emergent science of happiness or positive psychology had already taken over the task of explaining why the pursuit of happiness should be self-evident not only for North Americans – as written in to their constitution – but also for the rest of the world. According to these psychologists, all individuals are driven by an inherent urge to be happy, so the pursuit of happiness should be seen not only as natural, but as the highest expression of their realization as human beings. Psychological science, it was claimed, had already hit on some of the key factors that would help people to lead happier lives, and anyone could benefit from such discoveries by just following uncomplicated, albeit proven, expert advice. Certainly, the idea did not sound new, but coming from the headquarters of psychological science it nonetheless seemed worthwhile to take it seriously. In a matter of years, the movement had achieved what no other had achieved before: it introduced happiness at the top of the academic priorities and set it high on the social, political and economic agenda of many countries.

Thanks to positive psychology, happiness was no longer considered a nebulous concept, a utopian goal or an inaccessible personal luxury. Instead, it became a universal objective, a measurable concept around which these scientists claimed to have finally spotted the psychological features that defined the healthy, successful and optimally functioning individual. It turned out, though, and to a great extent unsurprisingly, that these features almost perfectly matched those embodied by people like Gardner himself. According to positive psychologists, high levels of emotional intelligence, autonomy, self-esteem, optimism, resilience and self-motivation were the typical psychological features of self-managed, authentic and flourishing people who displayed higher levels of happiness, health, and personal success. Indeed, the profile of the happy individual bears such close resemblance to Gardner's that it was claimed that the movie qualified as a high-quality positive psychological film.

The appearance of positive psychology at the turn of the century was a game changer. Gardner's inspirational sermons no longer appeared to be mere mottoes about the power of individuals to lift themselves up, but rather, a scientific truth. Positive psychologists indeed provided the lofty legitimacy of science to powerful institutions, Forbes Top 100 multinational companies, and a multibillion global industry widely interested in promoting and selling the same simple idea that Gardner touts in his talks: anyone can reinvent their life and become the best version of themselves by simply adopting a more positive outlook on themselves and the surrounding world. To many, the pursuit of happiness had become a serious issue whose scientific approach would yield enormous social and psychological benefits. To many others, however, the science behind all these rosy promises of personal realization and social amelioration, both in theory and in practice, cast too much of a shadow over many of its most apologetic claims, disquieting uses and contentious effects.

Time has proved the sceptics and critics right: sure enough, all that glitters in happiness is not gold, so we should approach its science and enticing promises with caution.

All that glitters is not gold: misgivings and disbeliefs

The question then arises: is happiness the most important goal we should all strive towards? Perhaps. But, if we consider the discourse of happiness scientists, then we must remain critical. This book is not against happiness, but against the reductionist, albeit widespread view of 'the good life' that the science of happiness preaches. Helping people feel better is a commendable intention. That really goes without saying. But in the light of what the science of happiness has to offer in this regard, we are not so sure that its idea of happiness – henceforth, only 'happiness' – is without serious limitations, controversial claims, contradictory results and ill consequences.

Our reservations about happiness are based on four main critical concerns: epistemological, sociological, phenomenological and moral. The first might be called epistemological because it is concerned with the legitimacy of the science of happiness as science – and by extension, of its concept of happiness as scientific and objective. To put it bluntly, the science of happiness is a flawed science – and, as such, so too is the rationale behind the notion of human happiness that this movement posits. The pragmatist Charles Pierce once said that a chain of reasoning is no stronger than its weakest link, and the science of happiness relies on several unfounded assumptions, theoretical inconsistencies, methodological shortfalls, unproven results, and ethnocentric and exaggerated generalizations. This makes it difficult to uncritically accept everything this science claims as true and objective.

The second concern is sociological. Irrespective of how good or bad as science the science of happiness might indeed be, it is essential to interrogate and examine which social agents find the notion of happiness useful, what and whose interests and ideological assumptions it serves, and what the economic and political consequences of its broad social implementation are. In this regard, it is noteworthy that the scientific approach to happiness and the happiness industry that emerges and expands around it contribute significantly to legitimizing the assumption that wealth and poverty, success and failure, health and illness are of our own making. This also lends legitimacy to the idea that there are no structural problems but only psychological shortages; that, in sum, there is no such thing as society but only individuals, to use Margaret Thatcher's phrase inspired by Friedrich Hayek. The notion of happiness as formulated and socially implemented by happiness scientists and experts works too often as little more than the handmaiden of the values which brought about the radical revolution of the world formulated by Chicagoan and other neoliberal economists, who, from the 1950s onwards, convinced the world that the individual search for happiness was the most worthwhile and the only realistic substitute for the search for the collective good – as Thatcher herself remarked on the occasion of an interview for the *Sunday Times* in 1981: 'What's irritated me about the whole direction of politics in the last 30 years is that it's always been towards the collectivist society. People have forgotten about the personal society [. . .] Changing the economics is the means of changing that approach [. . .] Economics are the method; the object is to change the heart and soul.'[5] In this regard, we argue that the pursuit of happiness as devised by happiness scientists does not represent the unquestionable and supreme good that we should all seek but epitomizes the triumph of the personal society (therapeutic, individualist, atomized) over the collectivist one.

The third concern might be called phenomenological. It relates to the fact that too often happiness science not only fails to deliver, but also breeds a great many unacknowledged, undesirable and paradoxical outcomes. Certainly, the science of happiness builds its proposal of well-being and personal fulfilment upon the very same therapeutic narratives of deficiency, inauthenticity and un-self-realization for which it promises solutions. As happiness is established as an imperative albeit moving goal with no clear end, it produces a new variety of 'happiness seekers' and 'happychondriacs' anxiously fixated with their inner selves, continuously preoccupied with correcting their psychological flaws, and permanently worried about their own personal transformation and betterment. Thus, whereas this makes happiness a perfect commodity for a market that thrives on normalizing our obsession with mental and physical health, this obsession easily turns against the very same people who pin their hopes on the many types of happiness products, services and therapies offered by scholars, professionals and so-called wellness experts.

Lastly, the fourth concern is moral and involves the relationship between happiness and suffering. In identifying happiness and positivity with productivity, functionality, goodness and even normality – and unhappiness with the exact opposite – the science of happiness places us at the major crossroads of a choice between suffering and well-being. This assumes one always has a choice – positivity and negativity are two diametrically opposed poles – as well as the possibility of ridding our lives of suffering once and for all. To be sure, tragedies are unavoidable, but happiness science insists on suffering and happiness as a matter of personal choice. Those who do not instrumentalize adversity into a means for personal growth are suspected of wanting and deserving their own misfortune, regardless of their particular circumstances. So in the end, we are not given much choice: the science of happiness not only obliges us to be happy, it blames us for not leading more successful and fulfilling lives.

Introduction

Outline structure

Chapter 1 tackles the relationship of happiness to politics. The chapter begins with an overview of the rise and expansion of the most influential fields in the scientific study of happiness since the turn of the century: positive psychology and happiness economics. The chapter focuses on the foundational aims, methodological assumptions, social and academic reach and the institutional influences of both fields. It then argues that happiness research has wormed itself into the very fabric of government. The presentation of happiness as an objective and measurable variable allows happiness as a chief, legitimized criterion to steer first-order political decisions, assess social and national progress, and settle controversial ideological and moral issues (e.g., inequality) in a rather technocratic and non-moral fashion.

Chapter 2 addresses the relationship of happiness to neoliberal ideology. We argue that happiness proves useful in legitimizing individualism in seemingly non-ideological terms through the neutralizing and authoritative discourse of positive science. The chapter first reviews positive psychology's literature to show the extent to which the movement is characterized by strong individualist assumptions as well as by its narrow sense of the social. Then the chapter shows that whereas positive psychology might capture people's longing for solutions, especially in times of social uncertainty, happiness recipes might themselves contribute to sustaining and creating some of the dissatisfaction which they promise to remedy. The chapter ends with a critical note on the introduction of happiness into the sphere of education.

Chapter 3 focuses on the organizational realm. It deals with the extent to which investing in one's own happiness has come to be rendered as a *conditio sine qua non* for workers to navigate the emerging conditions and requirements of the world of labour.

Introduction

We argue that by displacing previous psychological models of work behaviour, the science of happiness articulates a renewed discourse for the construction of workers' identities that allows for organizations to better adapt workers' behavioural patterns, sense of worth and personal prospects to the emerging needs and demands of organizational control, flexibility and power distribution within corporations. The chapter also discusses the extent to which happiness repertoires and techniques facilitate workers' acquiescence and conformity to corporate culture; exploit positive emotions as productive assets for corporations; and facilitate the displacement of the burden of market uncertainty, scarce employment, structural powerlessness and increased work competition onto workers themselves.

Chapter 4 analyses happiness as a commodity. It develops the idea that in twenty-first-century capitalism happiness has become the fetish commodity of a global and multibillion industry including things such as positive therapies, self-help literature, coaching services, professional counselling, smartphone applications and self-improvement tips. Here we argue that happiness has become a series of 'emodities' – namely services, therapies and products that promise and enact emotional transformation,[6] circulating and exchanged in a market. These emodities follow a circuitous route – they may start as theories in university departments but quickly follow different markets, such as corporations, research funds or consumer lifestyles. Emotional self-management, authenticity and flourishing are not only ways of making the self constantly produce itself but a way for various institutions to make emotional commodities (or emodities) circulate in the social body.

Chapter 5 picks up on previous chapters to argue that the scientific discourse of happiness is progressively hijacking the language of functionality – to wit the language that defines what it is to perform, act and feel within psychological and social standards and expectations – thus establishing itself as the yardstick to measure what is considered healthy, adaptive and even normal. The chapter first analyses the strong divide that happiness scientists posit between what they consider positive and negative emotions, which they draw upon when revisiting the notion of the 'average person'. We challenge this division by highlighting some of its pitfalls from a sociological perspective. The chapter then hinges on the relationship of happiness to suffering and ends with a critical reflection on the perils of rendering suffering as something instrumental, evitable and ultimately useless.

Manufacturing Happy Citizens: How the Science and Industry of Happiness Control our Lives aims to contribute to the lively debate on happiness from a critical sociological perspective. It builds on our previous works in the fields of emotions, neoliberalism, happiness and therapeutic culture,[7] articulates and expands some of these arguments, and introduces new ideas on the relationships between the pursuit of happiness and the ways in which power is wielded in neoliberal capitalist societies. The term 'happycracy' – the title of the original edition – is here coined to emphasize the particular interest of the book in showing the new coercive strategies, political decisions, management styles, consumption patterns, individual obsessions and emotional hierarchies that, together with a new notion of citizenship, have emerged in the age of happiness. The book concludes with a more personal reflection on happiness and its truncated promises.

In recent years, sociologists, philosophers, anthropologists, psychologists, journalists and historians have published an abundance of works dealing with happiness from a critical perspective. Prominent among these are the works of Barbara Ehrenreich[8] and Barbara Held[9] on the tyranny of positive thinking, Sam Binkley's[10] and William Davies'[11] analyses of the relationships between happiness and the market, and Carl Cederström's and

Introduction

André Spicer's[12] exploration of wellness as ideology, to name only a few that also inspire this book. Since happiness remains a rather controversial concept of notorious cultural, social, political and economic impact, we expect further publications.

I

Experts on your well-being

We live in an age consumed by worship of the psyche. In a society plagued by division of race, class, and gender we are nonetheless bound together by a gospel of psychological happiness. Rich or poor, black or white, male or female, straight or gay, we share a belief that feelings are sacred and salvation lies in self-esteem, that happiness is the ultimate goal and psychological healing the means.

Eva S. Moskowitz, *In Therapy We Trust*

When Seligman had positive dreams

'I have a mission',[1] declared Martin Seligman a year before running for president of the American Psychological Association (APA), the largest professional association of psychologists in the United States, with more than 117,500 members.[2] Seligman was not sure what his mission was exactly, but he believed that he would find out once elected.[3] He already had some things in mind, amongst them doubling research funding for mental health, further expanding the scope and reach of applied psychology to the field of prevention, and turning away from the dull, negative, disease model of clinical psychology. 'But at bottom', he said, 'that's not it.'[4] He had a more ambitious goal in mind.

Seligman was looking for a new psychological perspective on human nature that could rejuvenate psychology and extend its scope and influence.

Seligman's 'eureka' moment came only a few months after being 'surprisingly' elected president of the APA in 1998. While weeding his garden with his five-year-old daughter, Nikki, he yelled at her for throwing weeds into the air and she replied: 'Daddy, do you remember before my fifth birthday? From the time I was three to the time I was five, I was a whiner. I whined every day. On my fifth birthday, I decided I wasn't going to whine anymore. That was the hardest thing I've ever done. And if I can stop whining, you can stop being such a grouch.'[5] According to Seligman, 'Nikki hit the nail right on the head' and he suddenly 'realized that raising Nikki was not about correcting whining', but about amplifying her 'marvelous strength'.[6] As with parenting, he said, the problem of psychology was to focus on fixing what is wrong with people rather than nurturing what is right with them to help them develop their fullest potential. 'This was an epiphany for me, nothing less',[7] claimed Seligman in the inaugural manifesto, 'Positive Psychology: An Introduction', published in *American Psychologist* in 2000. Seligman stated that he did not have a 'less mystical way' to explain the genesis of positive psychology. Indeed, offering the same epiphany narrative that religious leaders tell their followers, Seligman stated 'I did not choose positive psychology. It called me [. . .] Positive psychology called to me just as the burning bush called Moses.'[8] Thus, as if descended from heaven, Seligman claimed to have finally found his mission: the creation of a new science of happiness to inquire about what makes life worth living and to discover the psychological keys to human flourishing.

But as is often the case with revelations, the picture of positive psychology presented in the inaugural manifesto was vague. Cherry-picking from evolutionary, psychological, neuroscientific and philosophical claims and concepts, the rubric of positive psychology was rather eclectic and poorly delineated. The manifesto resembled more a declaration of intentions than a solid scientific project. 'Like all selections, this one is to some extent arbitrary and incomplete', claimed the authors of the manifesto, who rushed to clarify that the special issue was intended only to 'stimulate the reader's appetite' regarding the 'offerings of the field'.[9] But, what did the field really offer? For many, nothing new: old, scattered claims on self-improvement, happiness and deeply rooted American beliefs on the power of individuals for self-determination, clothed in positivist science, and whose history could be easily traced back via the adaptability psychologies and self-esteem movements of the 1980s and 1990s, the humanistic psychology of the 1950s and 1960s, and the consolidation of the self-help culture and 'mind cure' movements throughout the twentieth century.[10]

Indeed, it might be well said that, very much like the main character from F. Scott Fitzgerald's short story *The Curious Case of Benjamin Button*, the newborn positive psychology seemed to have come into existence quite aged. Not for its fathers, though. In Seligman and Csikszentmihalyi's own words, the newborn field offered 'a historical opportunity [. . .] to create a scientific monument – a science that takes as its primary task the understanding of what makes life worth living'.[11] This included positive emotions, personal meaning, optimism and, of course, happiness. In this guise, positive psychology was optimistically announced at the highest levels of academic psychology as a new scientific enterprise able to expand its results 'to other times and places, and perhaps even to all times and places'.[12] Nothing less.

The idea raised eyebrows and sparked scepticism, to say the least, but Seligman was determined to push his mission forward. While in his 1990 book *Learned Optimism*, the former behaviourist and cognitive psychologist said that 'optimism may sometimes keep us from seeing reality with the necessary clarity',[13] the epiphany changed him – as he put it, 'in that moment, I resolved to change'.[14] Seligman did not want to label his proposal as behaviourist or cognitivist, or even as humanistic, but to start a brand-new scientific field that could gather as many adherents as possible. After all, the road to a more positivist orientation towards the scientific study of happiness had already been paved: although timidly, it had already begun to be outlined in psychology in the early 1990s with the works of Michael Argyle, Ed Diener, Ruut Veenhoven, Carol Ryff and Daniel Kahneman, all of whom claimed that previous attempts to understand happiness had a meagre impact, lacked theoretical consistency and credible assessment procedures, and were excessively value-laden. Thus, perhaps aware that there was something fanciful about the new-born field of positive psychology – 'you might think that this is a pure fantasy', the founding fathers admitted – the manifesto concluded with a rather encouraging and confident statement: 'the time is finally right for positive psychology [. . .] We predict that positive psychology in this new century will allow psychologists to understand and build those factors that allow individuals, communities and societies to flourish.'[15]

In the weeks following his election as president of the APA, cheques started 'appearing' on Seligman's desk, as he put it. 'Grey-hair, grey-suited lawyers' from 'anonymous foundations' that only picked 'winners' called Seligman for meetings in fancy buildings in New York, wondering 'what is this positive psychology?' and asking him for 'ten-minute explanations' and 'three-pager' proposals: 'a month later, a check for $1.5 million appeared', said Seligman. 'Positive psychology began to flourish with this funding.'[16] The field, indeed, expanded to unprecedented levels in a very short time. Already in 2002 the field had amassed around $37 million in funding. It seemed to be the right time to publish the first *Handbook of Positive Psychology* that would declare the 'independence of the field'. The chapter entitled 'The Future of Positive Psychology: A Declaration of Independence' concluded that it was time to 'break away' from 'traditional psychology' based on 'weakness' and a 'pathological model' of human behaviour. The editors claimed that the handbook 'simply had to happen', finishing with the remark that 'it is our view [. . .] that the first stage of a scientific movement – *one that we would characterize as a declaration of independence from the pathology model* – has been completed.'[17] Thus, with the help of worldwide press coverage and media hype, positive psychologists successfully disseminated amongst academics, professionals and the lay public the idea that a new science of happiness capable of finding the psychological keys to well-being, meaning and flourishing had finally arrived.

An expensive monument

In a matter of a few short years, positive psychologists had swiftly created a broad and global institutional network, widely propagated through PhD and Master's programmes; prizes, scholarships and specialized courses in applied positive psychology; symposiums and workshops all over the world; an increasing number of handbooks, textbooks and monographs; blogs and websites for information dissemination and data collection on life satisfaction, positive emotions and happiness through online questionnaires; and numerous academic journals exclusively devoted to carrying out research in the field, such as the *Journal of Happiness Studies*, founded in 2000, the *Journal of Positive Psychology*, founded in 2006, and the *Journal of Applied Psychology: Health and Well-Being*, founded in 2008. As Seligman foresaw, positive psychology had built itself a monument. But scientific journals, global academic networks and media hype alone could not explain its expeditious construction. Lots of money was needed, too.

Grants and funding did not stop with the first cheque that

appeared on Seligman's desk. Big investments would keep coming from a wide array of private and public institutions interested in the field in the months and years after. As early as 2001, the ultra-conservative and religious institution the John Templeton Foundation, which Seligman praised in his APA presidential address, endowed the father of positive psychology with $2.2 million to establish the Positive Psychology Center at the University of Pennsylvania. Apparently, Sir John Templeton was thrilled by the project, given his interest in how individuals can control their minds to master their circumstances and shape the world at will. In fact, Templeton wrote the 2002 preface for the very same *Handbook of Positive Psychology* that would go on to declare the independence of the field: 'I am hopeful that as current and future researchers catch the vision of a positive psychology, and as foundations and governments initiate programs to support this ground-breaking and beneficial work, we will all forge ahead', wrote Templeton. The foundation would later fund several projects studying the relationship between positive emotions, ageing, spirituality and productivity. For instance, in 2009 the foundation gave Seligman another grant, this time of $5.8 million, to conduct further research on positive neuroscience and the role of happiness and spirituality in successful living.

The John Templeton Foundation was not the only institution funding research on positive psychology. Numerous major and minor private and public institutions, including the Gallup Organization, the Mayerson Foundation, the Annenberg Foundation Trust and the Atlantic Philanthropies, had provided positive psychologists with handsome funding and numerous grants, prizes and scholarships. For instance, the Robert Wood Johnson Foundation funded Seligman in 2008 with $3.7 million with the aim of exploring the concept of positive health. Similarly, institutions such as the National Institute on Aging (NIA) and the National Center for Complementary and Alternative Medicine

(NCCAM) funded positive psychology's research on the effects of well-being, life satisfaction and happiness on health and mental illness prevention. Companies such as Coca-Cola also chipped in, investing in positive psychology with the objective of finding out cheaper and more efficient methods to increase productivity, reduce stress and anxiety at work, and promote workers' engagement in corporate culture. One of the latest and most substantial investments, and perhaps the most resounding, comes from the $145 million initiative Comprehensive Soldier Fitness (CSF), a psychological programme conducted by the US Army since 2008 and in close collaboration with Seligman and the Positive Psychology Center. Having introduced the programme to the general public in a special issue published in *American Psychologist* in 2011, Seligman made the point elsewhere that instructing soldiers and military personnel on positive emotions, happiness and spiritual meaning would help 'create a force as fit psychologically as it is physically'[18] – or, as he also put it, to create 'an indomitable army'[19] (we will explore this further in chapter 5). Investments were not limited to the United States. Since the founding of the field in 2000, an increasing number of private and public institutions from European and Asian countries now fund research on happiness and positive psychology, China, the United Arab Emirates and India being some of the latest countries attracted to the field.

Interestingly, although it was not amongst his stated priorities, Seligman had soon achieved notably rising public and private investment in positive mental health and mental illness prevention. Happiness provided a rather fertile and allegedly uncharted field to explore from a scientific point of view: why are positive emotions so important? How can people lead happy lives despite difficulties? What is the relationship between optimism and health, productivity and performance? Can science discover the keys to human flourishing? Such questions started to fill the introductions of thousands of scientific papers and specialized magazines, many of which replicated each other's questions, findings, arguments, foundational myths, references and so on, thus giving readers a sense of theoretical and conceptual consistency and consensus that the field lacked.

In 2004, perhaps in an effort to create said consistency, Peterson and Seligman published *Character Strengths and Virtues: A Handbook and Classification*. This 'manual of the sanities', as they called it, presented a positive counter-version of the *Diagnostic and Statistical Manual of Mental Disorders* (DSM) and *International Classification of Diseases* (ICD), the two most relevant references for psychologists, psychiatrists and therapists around the world. Instead of diagnosing and measuring mental disorders, the manual offered a universal classification of human strengths and virtues 'to help people evolve to their highest potential' and guide researchers and professionals in measuring, diagnosing and nurturing what was right, authentic and empowering for individuals: 'this handbook focuses on what is right about people and specifically about the strengths of character that make the good life possible. We follow the example of the DSM and ICD [. . .] The crucial difference is that the domain of concern for us is not psychological illness but psychological health.'[20] The manual also aimed at providing positive psychologists with a 'common vocabulary' that the field was lacking:

> Positive psychology as a whole would be benefited – indeed, shaped and transformed – by agreed-upon ways for speaking about the positive, just as the DSM and ICD have shaped psychiatry, clinical psychology, and social work by providing a way to speak about the negative. We believe that the classification of character presented here is an important step toward a common vocabulary of measurable positive traits.[21]

Still, the authors acknowledged that *Character Strengths and Virtues* was just a classification and not a taxonomy of positive human traits, since that was beyond their actual 'ability to specify a reasonable theory' on happiness.[22] The manual, however, moved the field one step forward towards consolidation, having a special impact on the political, organizational, educational, and therapeutic spheres in the years to follow.[23]

An alliance foretold

In less than a decade, the size, reach and impact of academic research on happiness and related topics, such as subjective well-being, strengths and virtues, positive emotions, authenticity, flourishing, optimism and resilience, multiplied by ten, engaging not only psychology, but also disciplines such as economics, education, therapeutics, health, politics, criminology, sports science, animal welfare, design, neurosciences, the humanities, management and business.[24] The widespread success of positive psychology had finally invalidated previous scepticism of the scientific study of positivity and happiness. Concepts such as optimism, positive thinking, positive emotions, flourishing and hope, commonly seen with suspicion as products of wishful thinking and mere self-help quackery, were now rendered credible and legitimate. Positive psychology made scepticism seem like retrograde negativity that prevented scholars from a clear understanding of the good life and from unleashing withheld human potential. Progressively, more and more psychologists and social scientists, either by conviction or for convenience, started to jump on the bandwagon of the new scientific field of happiness, especially as the economic, organizational, therapeutic, educational and political interest in the topic gathered momentum and its advocates gained academic authority, social power and cultural influence.

Academics were not the only ones who benefited from the success and expansion of the field. The vast array of non-academic 'psy' professionals who had been making their way in the therapeutic market – and simultaneously making and disseminating the therapeutic market on their way – for the previous decades, including self-help writers, coaches, motivational speakers, management trainers and learning consultants, greatly benefited, too. In charge of shaping lifestyles and facilitating emotional, psychological sensibilities and habitus, all these cultural intermediaries and 'need merchants'[25] were deeply embedded in numerous therapeutic, health, educational and organizational contexts in the 1980s and 1990s. They were all equally fascinated by selves, spirituality, the individual's capacity for self-improvement, and the power of the mind over body. Lacking a rigorous and common body of knowledge, these professionals underpinned their practice by appealing to a half-baked, eclectic mixture of heterogeneous sources, ranging from psychoanalysis and religion to behaviourism, medicine, occultism, neuroscience, conventional oriental wisdom and personal experience.

In this regard, as Barbara Ehrenreich has noted,[26] positive psychology seemed no less fallen from heaven to these professionals than it had seemed to Seligman himself. The emergent science of happiness provided these professionals with a common set of repertoires and techniques that appeared to scientifically prove the relationship between positive thoughts, positive emotions, self-development, health and economic success. Ideas already popularized by authors such as Norman Vincent Peale, with his 1959 book *The Power of Positive Thinking*, and Daniel Goleman (emotional intelligence), which had initially had a cold, critical reception within the scientific community, now moved from counselling rooms, self-help shelves, lifestyle magazine pages and popular science books into psychotherapeutic clinics, scientific publications, university departments and academic curricula. Suddenly, scientists and professionals were speaking the same language. Further, positive psychologists allowed these professions to shake off the stigma of being frivolous and opportunist.

The hopeful, the extrovert, the cheerful, the healthy, the rich and the successful were now as entitled to and in need of receiving a psychologist's attention as the desperate, the lonely, the depressed, the ill, the poor and the failed. There it was a matter of one's turning away from psychic misery. Everyone, with no exception, could (and should) now use an expert to guide them on their path to finding the best part of themselves.

Since its foundation, positive psychology has established powerful and profitable synergies with what Eloise Swan has called 'personal development workers', that is, 'psy' professionals who already targeted healthy people and used 'therapeutically based practices with the aim of helping someone work better, become a "better" person or get a "better life"'.[27] On the one hand, these workers began gaining legitimacy following the popular success and psychological platform of positive psychologists. On the other, positive psychologists benefited from the dissemination of positive psychological teachings by these professionals, who took the teachings into virtually any sphere of everyday life, including marriage, sex, eating, work, education, interpersonal relationships, sleep, addictions and so on. Indeed, although positive psychologists have always resorted to a hostile rhetoric of hard, positive science in the attempt to draw a clear line between the 'experts' and non-experts – e.g., Seligman himself has emphasized claims such as 'in contrast to pop psychology and the bulk of self-improvement, my writings are believable because of the underlying science'[28] – this distinction remained, for the most part, a pious wish.

Soon enough, positive psychologists began to make a few concessions to lucrative movements such as coaching – imaginably because they were also well aware of the fact that the coaching business alone accounted for an industry that generates $2,356 billion a year worldwide, according to the International Coach Federation (IFC).[29] Indeed, already in 2004 and 2005 titles such as 'Toward a Positive Psychology of Executive Coaching' and 'Positive Psychology and Coaching Psychology: Perspectives on Integration' could be read in chapters and papers published by positive psychologists. In 2007, Seligman himself published the paper 'Coaching and Positive Psychology', where he remarked that 'coaching is a practice in search of a backbone, two backbones actually: a scientific, evidence-based backbone and a theoretical backbone. I believe that the new discipline of positive psychology provides both those backbones.'[30] In 2011, he would further insist that positive psychology should be the field in charge of providing coaches with 'adequate credentials to be a coach'.[31] Not surprisingly, in his latest and perhaps most influential book on happiness to date, *Flourish: A New Understanding of Happiness and Well-Being – and How to Achieve Them*, Seligman would explicitly borrow from the characteristic tone of coaching and self-help writers, as evident from its opening:

> This book will help you flourish. There, I have finally said it [. . .] Positive psychology makes people happier. Teaching positive psychology, researching positive psychology, using positive psychology in practice as a coach or therapist, giving positive psychology exercises to tenth graders in a classroom, parenting little kids with positive psychology, teaching drill sergeants how to teach about post-traumatic growth, meeting with other positive psychologists, and just reading about positive psychology all make people happier. The people who work in positive psychology are the people with the highest well-being I have ever known.[32]

Make psychology great again

Over time, the founding manifesto of positive psychology put forward a win–win deal for psychologists. Happiness research breathed oxygen into a discipline perpetually looking for its object of study and in constant need of conceptual reinvention in order to maintain its social status, keep attracting funds and remain fashionable. Furthermore, the field finally blurred the thin, porous line that differentiated mainstream psychology from its commercial and professional counterpart. Positive psychologists borrowed from the influential albeit scattered activity of personal development workers as much as these professionals borrowed from the positive, scientific language of positive psychologists. There was no longer reason to be ashamed of psychology's tight-knit relationship with the market of 'psy' services and commodities promising to deliver the keys to happiness and self-realization: positive psychology would take over the task of distinguishing mere gossip on human happiness from proven statements that could be safely marketed as scientific and legitimate advice. In addition, positive psychology provided psychologists with a promising new career strategy, including a new market for workshops, training courses, organizational advice, semi-academic books and so on, as well as the appeal of having to deliver tons of new publications that opened new possibilities of surviving and thriving in the publish-or-perish culture of academia, especially for younger scholars.

One of the keys to positive psychology's success inside academic psychology is that it suggested an expansion of the discipline without theoretical, internal friction with different schools of thought. In this regard, Seligman proposed not so much a new psychological approach as a new positive attitude that moved basic and applied psychology away from stagnation and focused scholars and professionals on the unexploited market target of healthy, normal people. Arguably, Seligman did not want to repeat the history of psychology and start a competition for what theoretical framework was stronger within the discipline. Contrary to the aim of humanistic psychology some decades ago, which eventually lost the internal battle against behaviourism and cognitive psychology, Seligman's proposal did not seek to antagonize any well-established faction in psychology. Instead, he sought to turn as many psychologists as possible on to the new, positive faith, and the manifesto was vague and eclectic enough to leave enough room for everyone to join and chip in regardless of previous academic psychological training. The 'intellectual zoo' of psychology, to use George Miller's harsh characterization of the discipline,[33] could hence expand without internal competition.

While positive psychologists had soon argued for a certain independence of the field in its own right and presented themselves as a necessary alternative to what they called 'traditional', 'business-as-usual' or 'negative' psychotherapy, they did not seek to burn all their bridges with clinical psychologists, or to challenge widely held theoretical and methodological foundational views. According to positive psychologists, traditional psychology was still necessary, both for studying psychological illnesses and for palliating psychological deficiencies. However, positive psychologists argued that uprooting problematic conditions and learning coping strategies to deal with the hardships of everyday life were insufficient for building normal, fitting and adaptive behaviour and personalities – as coaches and self-help writers had long maintained. Positive psychologists insisted that people need to increase their happiness not only when things go wrong, but also when things go well, thus introducing a fundamentally new role to academic psychology: not only correcting suffering but maximizing selfhood. New experts and trained scholars of the brand-new positive endeavour of psychology were therefore claimed to be needed both for studying the psychological keys to human happiness and for instructing individuals in how to scientifically develop their full potential and live meaningful and worthy lives.

Their strategy, indeed, worked perfectly, and the need to move towards a more positive view struck a chord not only in psychology but in academia as well. It is no wonder that the father of positive psychology was elected president of the APA by three times as many votes as the next candidate. Seligman took both a conservative and an innovative step forward, convinced that some things in psychology had to change so it could not only stay the same, but also grow and keep expanding. After all, optimism – which Seligman finally resolved to adopt for himself – is not only a conservative attitude, as Henry James remarked:[34] it is also a typical feature of successful entrepreneurs, as positive psychologists usually claim. It is worth noting, though, that Seligman and many other psychologists leading the expansion of the field were neither mere intellectuals nor casual professionals, but well-positioned scholars who already operated within the state system and who held privileged posts in powerful political, economic and academic institutions. It is therefore no coincidence that immediately after Seligman secured the pulpit of the APA, the newborn field of positive psychology grew and spread to such unprecedented levels and forged such powerful alliances.

A great number of critiques have been levelled against the field over the past decades. Important critics have argued against the field's foundational assumptions, including decontextualized and ethnocentric claims;[35] theoretical oversimplifications, tautologies and contradictions;[36] methodological shortcomings;[37] severe replicability problems;[38] exaggerated generalizations;[39] and even its therapeutic efficacy and scientific status.[40] It seems clear that positive psychology could not have thrived on the basis of its science alone. The field is characterized by its popularity as much as its intellectual deficits and scientific underachievement. Indeed, after almost twenty years and over 64,000 research studies devoted to the scientific study of what makes life worth living, positive psychology has achieved little more than scattered, ambiguous, inconclusive and even contradictory results. Depending on their design and methodology, there are studies to show that a particular feature, aspect or variable reveals a key to happiness and other studies and methodologies that point to the exact opposite.[41]

What these studies have unmistakably revealed is the ideological agenda of many of those who fund, promote and implement happiness in organizations, schools, health institutions, the entertainment business, public policy or the army. It could be argued that positive psychology is little more than ideology recycled in the form of charts, tables and number-filled diagrams; an easily marketable pop psychology touted by scientists in white coats. And yet, this was one of the sources of its tremendous success. Positive psychology cleverly captured deep-rooted cultural and ideological assumptions about the self and reformulated them as objective, empirical facts. This strategy allowed positive psychology to grow internally vis-à-vis the expansion of the happiness industry, the increasing institutionalization of happiness in the public and private spheres, and the increasing number of alliances the field forged outside, including the fields of politics, education, labour, economics and, of course, therapy in its multiple varieties. We will focus on each of these fields throughout the book, starting with the close relationship between positive psychologists and happiness economics, another influential movement within academia well connected to politics.

Experts know best

As positive psychology grew, it not only strengthened its alliances with its professional, non-academic counterparts but also developed powerful synergies with happiness economists. Although this sub-field in economics had been growing progressively since the 1980s, it was not until the early 2000s that Sir Richard Layard gave the field the influence and reach that it has today. Layard had been an advisor to Tony Blair's government from 1997 to 2001; member of the House of Lords since 2000; director of the Centre for Economic Performance at the London School of Economics from 1993 to 2003; and founder and director of the Wellbeing Programme at that same centre since 2003. Known as the 'happiness tsar', Layard has been a well-known advocate of positive psychology ever since the field made its debut in academia. As early as 2003, Layard pointed out in a series of lectures given at the London School of Economics that to fully understand happiness, economists and psychologists should work together: 'Fortunately,' he said, 'psychology is now moving rapidly in the right direction and I hope economics will follow.'[42] Like the English philosopher Jeremy Bentham, one of the fathers of utilitarianism, Layard was convinced that the primary and most legitimate objective of politics was to maximize the sum of happiness in society. Like the utilitarians before him, he was also convinced that happiness was a matter of maximizing pleasure, and that happiness could be accurately measured. And like Seligman in his view on traditional psychology, Layard was convinced that traditional economics needed to change. According to him, one of the main problems was that traditional economics was so busy linking money to utility that it forgot that happiness was actually a better and more accurate measure of economic value. Thus, Layard claimed, focusing on happiness would provide the needed reform of the field, emphasizing that economists could use some of the key 'findings of the new psychology of happiness'[43] – which they would soon start doing.

In fact, in the 1990s, a large group of psychologists and economists interested in the topic of happiness and how to scientifically study it had already begun cooperating. Previous interest in the topic from a scientific point of view had been scarce and dominated by the idea that happiness was a relative, elusive concept. Studies purporting to accurately measure happiness were still faced with scepticism within positivist science. A good example of this relativist approach is that of the economist Richard Easterlin. Already in 1974, many psychologists and economists had been bitten by the happiness bug thanks in large part to Easterlin and his famous paradox. Easterlin argued that whereas within-country comparisons at a certain moment in time showed that higher incomes were related to higher levels of happiness, both inter-country comparisons and within-country comparisons over time, on the contrary, suggested that the wealth of nations (as measured by their Gross National Product) was not linked to higher aggregated levels of happiness amongst their citizens. Easterlin concluded, among other things, that relative considerations were the real determinants of happiness, since people always adapt to their circumstances: 'in judging their happiness, people tend to compare their actual situation with a reference standard or norm, derived from their prior and ongoing social experience'.[44]

This entailed two difficulties. First, for economists, the problem was that if happiness was relative, then objective economic improvements and incentives seemed to yield no real benefits for people. How could they explain the disturbing fact that modern societies, carriers of progress, wealth and prosperity, were failing to provide people with higher levels of happiness? Second, for psychologists, the problem was that if happiness was relative then the very possibility of an objective science of emotions and feelings was called into question. It was at this point these economists and psychologists had an epiphany: what if the actual problem was that people were not good at assessing their own emotional states, after all? What if people did not really understand such a complex concept as happiness and were simply lousy at evaluating it, in the same way they were lousy at making rational decisions? These questions seemed to point to the answers they were looking for. Indeed, in the late 1980s, the psychologists Daniel Kahneman and Amos Tversky had already defended the idea that people usually draw upon a sort of intuitive psychology on a daily basis that made them rely on a set of incorrect, poor cognitive heuristics and biases.[45] These studies had an enormous impact in the field of economics and eventually garnered Kahneman the Nobel Memorial Prize in Economics in 2002. First, psychologists and economists agreed that more accurate methodologies able to overcome excessive introspection and to objectively measure feelings were needed. Second, they granted that new, specialized experts on happiness who nudged individuals on the right path towards happiness, and who told people the correct standards by which they should measure up their lives, were also necessary.

Throughout the 1990s, psychologists and economists collaborated to develop new questionnaires, scales and methodologies in the attempt to objectively measure concepts such as happiness, subjective well-being and the hedonic balance between positive and negative affect. The Oxford Happiness Inventory (OHI), the Satisfaction With Life Scale (SWLS), the PANAS (Positive Affect, Negative Affect Schedule), the Experience Sampling Method (ESM) and the Day Reconstruction Method (DRM) are some of the most famous examples. Apparently, psychologists and economists had proved two things with these methodologies: first, that the hedonic quality of happiness had objective anchors, since levels of happiness could be empirically compared and accurately measured as a function of the relative quantity of pleasure over pain, so it was not entirely relative; and second, that happiness was a matter of frequency rather than intensity.[46] Intensity, though, would not be entirely ruled out. On the contrary, to scientifically devise the role it played in happiness and how to objectively ground it in bodily measures – e.g., heart rate, blood pressure, glucose consumption, serotonin levels, facial expressions, etc. – would open a new field for exploration by psychologists, neuroscientists and psychophysiologists.

Experts on your well-being

In 1999, the book *Well-Being: The Foundations of Hedonic Psychology*, edited by Daniel Kahneman and Ed Diener, would summarize the decade's breakthroughs in the field[47] and corroborate the interdependence between psychologists and economists. The book both considered the supposedly fundamental relationship between the concepts of happiness and utility, and had its sights fixed on policy makers as it encouraged nations to begin monitoring pleasure and pain through new methodologies which could complement already existing social indicators in the assessment of public policies. These were central ideas that Layard and the field of happiness economics would successfully push forward in the subsequent years.

A measurable, self-evident good
In 2014 crowds flocked to an unlikely book written by economists, led by Richard Layard: *Thrive: The Power of Psychological Therapy*. The book was presented as a convincing case for the need for increasing public investment in cost-effective, positive therapies to get rid of the plague of mental illness that ravages modern societies.[48] Daniel Kahneman endorsed the book and dubbed it an 'inspiring success story' with a 'compelling message'. Seligman heaped excessive praise on it as well: 'this is simply the best book on public policy and mental health ever written'. However, the book did not introduce anything new: by the time the book was published, happiness and positive mental health were already high on the political agenda of many countries around the globe, including the United States, Chile, the United Kingdom, Spain, Australia, France, Japan, Denmark, Finland, Israel, China, the United Arab Emirates and India.[49]

Happiness economists and positive psychologists have played a fundamental role in this ever since both fields started gaining academic and political traction in the early 2000s. The global economic crisis of 2008 did the rest. After the global economic

34

meltdown, more and more countries taking advice from psychologists and economists thought that they could well use happiness indicators to check whether, despite the continuing decline of objective indexes of quality of life and equality, people were still nonetheless feeling well. Happiness scholars offered answers to policy makers' concerns, claiming that happiness was an accurate measure of citizens' felt and perceived well-being. Thus, against hard, objective indexes of economic and social progress, it suddenly seemed a good idea that softer, more subjective indexes such as happiness could provide a more comprehensive and accurate look at society. If people claimed to be happy, then there was nothing much to worry about – after all, wasn't happiness the real and ultimate objective of politics, a priority over justice or equality?

Chile was one of the first countries to join this initiative, perhaps to test whether the 'shock doctrine'[50] – the dramatic application of neoliberal economic and political reforms carried out by Augusto Pinochet as advised by Milton Friedman and other Chicago economists – was still bearing its 'good fruits'. The conservatives David Cameron and Nicholas Sarkozy would follow next, both of whom ordered their respective national statistics bureaus to start gathering information on people's happiness. The idea was to introduce the concept of Gross Happiness Product (GHP) as an indicator that went beyond Gross National Product (GNP) – and extensions of it such as the 'Measure of Economic Welfare', 'Economic Aspects of Welfare', 'Index of Sustainable Economic Welfare' or 'Human Development Index' – to measure political efficiency and national progress. From 2008 all the countries interested in happiness and positive mental health would start to progressively introduce, to a greater or lesser extent, these kinds of initiatives.

Most of these countries joined in when prominent global institutions and forums started to recommend happiness as an index of national, social and political progress. One such example comes from the United Nations, for which Layard coedits the annual *World Happiness Report*, a global study on the happiness of nations issued in collaboration with Gallup, Inc. In 2012, the UN declared 20 March the 'International Day of Happiness', proclaiming 'happiness and well-being as universal goals and aspirations in the lives of human beings around the world' and defending 'the importance of their recognition in public policy objectives' of nations. Another good example comes from the Organisation for Economic Co-operation and Development (OECD). This influential worldwide institution, which advocates economic policies and coordinates statistics between more than thirty of the wealthiest nations, issues its own happiness-based tools, databases and intervention projects, such as 'Your Better Life Index' and 'Better Life Initiative'. It also counts as advisors several positive psychologists, happiness economists and other happiness scientists including Ruut Veenhoven, Ed Diener and Bruno Frey. Since 2009, the OECD has strongly recommended national accounting systems to adopt well-being indexes 'for monitoring and benchmarking countries' performance, for guiding people's choices, and for designing and delivering policies'[51] in multiple policy domains, such as public resource allocation, education, urban design, unemployment or tax structures. Important multinationals such as Coca-Cola also contributed to these initiatives, opening branches of the Coca-Cola Institute of Happiness in all of these countries to issue an annual international report on happiness – called the 'happiness barometer' – with the collaboration of happiness economists and positive psychologists. Until 2017, this institute had dozens of branches in several countries, including Pakistan.

Different fields notwithstanding, since their early alliance positive psychologists and happiness economists have shared the conviction that happiness was not an ill-defined or speculative

construct with more than fifty shades of historical and philosophical grey, but an objective, universal concept that can be
unbiasedly and accurately measured. Measurement has been one
of the crucial agreements between both disciplines, even in the
absence of further theoretical consensus – somehow, though, it
could be quantified. Indeed, happiness was presented as a brutally
empirical concept that revealed itself in big databases rather than
in theoretical and philosophical speculation: 'Happiness is just
like noise', said Layard in his series of lectures in 2003: 'There
are many qualities of noise, from a trombone to a caterwaul. But
they can all be compared in terms of decibels.'[52] Two years later,
in his most important and influential book on the relationship
between happiness and politics, *Happiness: Lessons from a New
Science*, he would claim that happiness is not only measurable, but
self-evidently good. Layard coincided with positive psychologists in stating that happiness should be understood as a natural,
objective goal that all human beings inherently pursue:

> We naturally look for the ultimate goal that enables us to judge
> other goals by how they contribute to it. Happiness is that ultimate
> goal because, unlike other goals, it is self-evidently good. If we
> are asked why happiness matters, *we can give no further, external
> reason*. It just obviously does matter. As the American Declaration
> of Independence says, it is a 'self-evident' objective.[53]

It is worth noting, though, that this claim should be understood as posited rather than proven, as ideological rather than
scientific; a tautological affirmation that, as Layard himself men-
tions, lacks further, external reasons that can justify it.

The absence of solid theoretical underpinnings notwithstanding, self-reliance in the accurate and unbiased measurement of
happiness has indeed been one of the most significant charms
with which the scientific discourse of happiness has wormed
itself within the individualistic, technocratic and utilitarian

soul of neoliberal politics. According to happiness economists, Bentham's dream has come true. Utilitarianism has ceased to be an abstract utopia of social engineering, to instead become a scientific reality in which the good life is amenable to technocracy by integrating moods and feelings, meanings, development and even the most intimate nooks and crannies of the psyche into a mass-scale calculus of consumption, efficiency, productivity and national progress. As these economists assure: 'researchers have [already] succeeded in doing what Bentham could not accomplish: to devise a way of measuring how happy people are and how much pleasure or pain they derive from the ordinary events and conditions of their lives'.[54]

Affective thermometer

Thanks to the continuous development of research methods, as well as the advances of brain imaging, mood-tracking technologies, smartphone applications and social networks to monitor and retrieve real-time personal information on our body signals, day-to-day activity, personal relationships, language use, frequent whereabouts and so on, happiness economists claimed to have overcome the methodological problems associated with self-report in the measurement of happiness, such as introspection or cultural relativism. Happiness economists asserted that happiness was a strong scientific construct with which to measure economic and social progress. The objective was to introduce positive psychological science and happiness research into the fabric of government, where, today, it most certainly is.

Perhaps nowhere is the introduction of happiness into technocrat governmentality clearer than in big data, where data analysis, which *Harvard Business Review* has called 'the sexiest job of the 21st century',[55] gets along perfectly with what might said to be 'the hottest topic of the 21st century'. Happiness, indeed, works well with mass-scale statistics and the personal data economy.

The Fifth World Congress on Positive Psychology, celebrated in 2015 at the Walt Disney World Resort in Orlando, revolved around the relationship of happiness with big data and politics. It was also a main concern in the last World Government Summit in 2017, in Dubai. By studying Facebook profiles, tweets, Instagram messages, the use of Google's search engine, or the display and presence of the amount of positive versus negative lexicon on social media, happiness researchers and data analysts work together to gather massive amounts of data with which to draw geographical happiness maps, establish cross-cultural comparisons, conduct research on behavioural patterns and digital identities, or study how happiness can be used to understand and shape public opinion regarding any social or political issues, amongst others. In parallel, new trends in happiness measurement such as 'sentiment analysis' or the 'quantified self' also use data mining from the internet, mobile phones and social networks to calculate positive and negative moods as a way to forecast market trends, make electoral predictions, or personalize the marketing of certain products to encourage consumption, amongst many others.

To be sure, researchers on data mining have yet to offer any significant breakthrough regarding human happiness – that people prefer weekends to Tuesdays, that rain affects moods, that depressed individuals prefer darker colours and hues, and that Christmas is one of the happiest days of the year are amongst their earth-shaking findings. Yet the important side of mass-scale data mining is not what big data can say about happiness, but how this data can be used to act on it and influence the way we understand happiness and the relationship with ourselves and the world through it, without us being aware of the process. By digging into what we do and like, when we do it, how often and in what sequence of events, experts, institutions and corporations come to possess invaluable information that can not only hold sway over the smallest aspects of particular individuals' lives – such as affecting the news we read, the advertisements we should watch, the music we might like depending on our mood, or the advice on health and lifestyle that we should see – but also influence the larger behavioural patterns of the social collective by shaping what should or should not be valued as contributing to our happiness.

In 2014, Facebook revealed that it had conducted an experiment in which it manipulated 689,000 users' homepages to make people feel more positive or negative about themselves and their virtual friends.[56] The study said that the manipulation of the content was 'consistent with Facebook's data use policy, to which all users agree prior to creating an account on Facebook, constituting informed consent for this research'.[57] A huge scandal was soon sparked. The controversy was not only that Facebook failed to gain informed consent to conduct the research or that the algorithms used to manipulate moods are not shared with the public. The problem was the extent to which a single corporation such as Facebook was able to influence people's mood and thoughts on a massive scale by manipulating personal and social information. A member of the House of Commons Culture, Media and Sport Select Committee worried about the power of these companies to manipulate people's thoughts in politics or other areas.[58] Facebook's study emphasized two main issues: first, happiness has become a main concern for corporations and politicians in order not only to understand how people feel, react and value certain aspects of their lives and the lives of others, but mainly to influence the way they should feel, react and value them. Second, happiness has been strongly inscribed as a first-order quantitative measurement to inform and have an impact on politics, economics and public as well as private decision-making processes.

Measurement and quantification of social phenomena (or,

more precisely, what sociologists Wendy Espeland and Mitchell Stevens call 'commensuration'[59]) are indeed fundamental to understanding how happiness has become so prominent in modern, neoliberal societies. The measurement of happiness is essential for selling happiness as an objective, precise concept that could be studied under the aegis of the scientific rigour of the natural sciences. It is also key in turning happiness into a commodity whose market value and legitimacy are highly dependent upon the quantification of its efficiency, as we will later show (chapter 4).

Measurement also allows the use of the concept in several ways, both scientifically and politically. First, measurement allows its segmentation into calculable and weighted units or variables to be used as a common metric by which disparate, different and often incongruent information – biological, emotional, behavioural, cognitive, social, economic and political – can all be put together, compared and assessed with regard to their contributory effect on the happiness of individuals. Second, the quantification of happiness is decisive for happiness researchers to make causative reasoning and to carry out empirical research on the basis that quantification does not alter the meaning and properties of the concept. Third, commensuration is also decisive in classifying and ordaining happiness-related variables under a common metric, hence establishing which aspects, events or actions are allegedly more contributory and decisive to the well-being of individuals – be it sleeping well, buying a new car, enjoying an ice cream, spending time with the family, getting a job, visiting Disneyland, meditating four times a week or writing thank-you letters, all these aspects are somehow potential contributors to increasing people's happiness. Relatedly, and most importantly, commensuration allows happiness to be established as both a communicable social phenomenon and a legitimized, neutral criterion for guiding a wide array of political and economic decisions and interventions according to the demands of neutrality and objectivity characteristic of techno-scientific and neo-utilitarian politics.

The measurement of happiness has allowed happiness economists and political institutions to introduce individual satisfaction with life into local and global political cost–benefit analyses, thus challenging the traditional economic approach: where once costs and benefits were both measured in money units, it was now suggested benefits should be measured in units of happiness instead. Layard indeed recommended that the correct approach to assessing political decisions in democratic countries was 'to rank all possible policies in terms of the extra happiness which they generate per dollar of expenditure'.[60] Taking happiness as a unit of benefit, it now could be related to expenditure on a global scale in several ways. For instance, it allows for a monetary price to be put on happiness – e.g., experts claimed to have found £7 million to be the amount Brits claimed they would need to be happy;[61] for information about the economic returns and losses derived from the increase or decrease of happiness – e.g., Gallup reported that the unhappiness of employees cost the US economy $500 billion a year;[62] or for an assessment of the efficiency with which the policies of different countries contributed to the happiness of their citizens.

Thus, once turned into an apparently value-free and objective number able to cross cultural borders and operate within mass-scale cost–benefit calculations, happiness is postulated as one of the chief economic, political and moral compasses in neoliberal societies. In this regard, happiness economists claimed that research evidence was already solid enough: countries could be unbiasedly compared by their levels of happiness, so nations and institutions should adopt it as a value-free and objective 'affective thermometer' to measure economic utility, assess social progress and guide public policies.[63]

Techno-happycracy

Happiness aggregate measures have not been without their critics. To start with, some authors have contested that there actually are validated and consensual methods to measure happiness.[64] In this regard, even the OECD has issued a series of guidelines to tackle this problem, warning about the fact that many happiness measures 'lack the consistency needed for them to be used as the basis for international comparisons'.[65] Some other authors have expressed concerns over the excessive individual orientation of these measures. The claims of happiness economists notwithstanding, it is not clear that happiness measurements are comparable between individuals. For instance, how can we know that someone's score of 7 out of 10 in a happiness questionnaire is equivalent to someone else's score of 7 out 10? How can we know whether a score of 7 from someone in Ireland is higher or lower than someone else's score of 6 or 8 in Cambodia or China? How much happier is someone with a score of 5 than someone with a score of 3? What does a score of 10 in happiness actually mean? Another concern is that this methodology severely limits the range of informative responses that people can provide when assessing their own happiness. This is important because close-format responses might not only favour a self-confirmatory bias by researchers,[66] but also disregard important information to make political decisions. For instance, a recent study showed that when compared to life narratives obtained via interviews, quantitative self-assessments neglect important social issues in the way people assess their lives, including particular and specific circumstances, negative evaluations and mixed feelings. In this regard, the study concludes by pointing out that 'a major disaster' of happiness research 'would be that people do not do well, but researchers fail to recognize'.[67] Indeed, adopting these sorts of quantitative, narrow measures of happiness to learn about what is and is not important for people's lives involves the serious risk that many important issues for individuals will be underrepresented in the public debate – despite happiness advocates' claim that happiness is a reliable measure for seizing more subjective information that other indexes do not take into account.

But methodological concerns are not the only or the most crucial ones. It is also important to question the uses derived from raising happiness as a first-order political criterion. For instance, it is legitimate to wonder whether happiness-based policies might often work as smoke screens hiding important and structural political and economic deficiencies. This alarm, indeed, was already triggered during the tenure of Britain's Conservative prime minister David Cameron. In 2010, straight after announcing the greatest economic cutbacks in the history of the country, Cameron declared that the UK should adopt happiness as a national index of progress. The Conservative put aside economic issues to instead focus on promoting amongst Britons the brand-new idea that 'it's time we admitted that there's more to life than money and it's time we focused not just on GDP but on GWB – general wellbeing'. Focusing on individual and aggregate happiness was here, for everyone with eyes to see, an obvious strategy to side-line and deflect attention from more objective and complex socio-economic indicators of welfare and the good life, such as redistribution of income, material inequalities, social segregation, gender inequity, democratic health, corruption and transparency, objective vs perceived opportunities, social aids or unemployment rates. Israelis, for another example, like to proudly exhibit their very high ranking in world indicators of happiness, as if these rankings could conceal the fact that their country has one of the highest levels of inequality in the world and lives with an ongoing Occupation.

A similar concern can be expressed today, when countries characterized by widespread poverty, constant human rights violations, and high rates of malnutrition, infant mortality and suicide, such as the United Arab Emirates and India, have resolved to adopt happiness measures to assess the impact of their national policies. In 2014 the prime minister and ruler of Dubai, Sheikh Mohammed bin Rashid al-Maktoum, ordered the installation of several touchscreens around the city to retrieve real-time feedback on people's satisfaction with the aim of constructing the 'happiest city in the world'. Following this measure, in 2016 there was announced the most far-reaching government reorganization in the country's forty-four-year history, which included, as a star measure, the opening of a 'Ministry of Happiness' to create 'social good and satisfaction'. In this regard, the new Minister of Happiness, Ohood Al Roumi, told CNN that the role of the country was 'to create an environment where people can flourish – can reach their potential – and choose to be happy', further adding that 'for us in the UAE, happiness is very important. I am a very happy and positive person and I choose to be happy every day because this is what pushes me, this is what motivates me, this is what gives a sense of purpose to my life, so I always choose to see the glass half full.' Something similar happened in India, where Mr Chouhan, a yoga enthusiast and member of Prime Minister Narendra Modi's ruling BJP party, claimed 'happiness does not come into the lives of people merely with materialistic possessions or development, but by infusing positivity in their lives'.

But perhaps one of the important implications of happiness measurement is that it allows delicate political and economic issues to be settled in a seemingly non-ideological and purely technocratic manner. Whether to evaluate a vaccination programme, a school intervention or a new tax measure, aggregate happiness is postulated as an objective criterion. Regarding taxes, for instance, Adler and Seligman claim that happiness should be used to 'help policy makers design optimal tax structures that maximize tax revenue without reducing societal wellbeing.

The loss of wellbeing may be calibrated for different levels of taxation to find an efficient taxation structure that will maximize national wellbeing.'[68] Thus, taxation should not be a matter of political or social thinking but a technical issue sorted out by the amount of happiness that it produces in people. These authors also claim that this logic should apply to moral as well as to political issues:

> How can societies make legal decisions about morally controversial issues, such as prostitution, abortion, drugs, punishment, and gambling? Internally consistent arguments can be made for and against these issues. However, the values of individuals or small groups are rarely aligned. One of the advantages of wellbeing measures for advising public policy is the subjective nature itself of self-report instruments. In these cases, subjective indicators of preferences – which reflect people's own values and life goals – provide policy makers with one democratic and fair (from a utilitarian perspective) tool to make decisions on morally-charged issues.[69]

Inequality is one of the latest and most striking examples. According to recent studies, and contrary to the claims of many other economists that the idea of a social floor, redistribution and equality are indispensable for social prosperity, dignity, recognition and welfare,[70] research on large databases seems now to prove that income inequality and capital concentration have a positive relationship to happiness and economic progress, especially in developing countries. Apparently, inequality is accompanied not by resentment, but by a 'hope factor' according to which the poor perceive the success of the rich as a harbinger of opportunity, thus raising hope and happiness related to a higher motivation to thrive. This shift is not surprising, though. The meritocratic and individualistic values underlying happiness disguise the fundamental differences of class and endorse competition in unequal systems rather than promoting the reduction of economic inequality. In this regard, new economic studies on happiness claim that the deeper the inequality, the more opportunities individuals will see for themselves in the future, so the more happiness it brings. Kelley and Evans, for instance, recently concluded that 'income inequality is associated with greater happiness'. This 'key fact', they continue, would mostly apply to developing countries, whereas inequality in developed countries would be 'irrelevant' to individuals' happiness, 'neither harming nor helping'.[71] The policy implications concerning efforts to reduce inequality seem clear: there should be none.

> Tremendous efforts have been made, both now and in the past, towards reducing income inequality. *There is a widespread willingness to sacrifice economic growth in order to suppress inequality. Our results suggest that these efforts are largely misguided*: They are misguided because, in the world as we find it, societal income inequality does not in general reduce individual subjective well-being. *In developing countries, inequality if anything increases happiness*. This suggests that current efforts by such agencies as the World Bank directed towards reducing income inequality are potentially harmful to the well-being of the citizens of poor countries.[72]

Resorting to happiness is quite convenient from a technocratic point of view. Happiness seems to provide a humanizing varnish to the dehumanizing worldview of technocracy. The idea is that aggregate happiness reflects popular feelings and opinions in a rather accurate way, so there is no need to really ask people what they think about political measures, but just to ask them to assess how satisfied they are with life by filling out a five-item questionnaire. Opinions, contrary to happiness valuations, are messy, confusing and hard to interpret. Whereas at the beginning of their report on world happiness Layard and O'Donnell emphasize that aggregate happiness should be the criterion of good policy in any democracy, they also emphasize that asking people questions about how they value certain policies 'produces nonsensical answers', so data on happiness is a more reliable and a 'powerful new method of evidence-based policy making'.[73] Nevertheless, the idea of treating people as data but not asking them for their real opinions, on the premise that these might be nonsensical, seems more despotic than democratic. As William Davies[74] has suggested, a problem for neo-utilitarian, technocratic approaches is indeed democracy itself; perhaps the reach of democracy has extended too far and beyond manageable boundaries, so that concepts such as happiness, which are amenable to quantification, able to homogenize judgements and beliefs, and reminiscent of the idea of social welfare – increasingly untenable – have become a useful strategy for offering crumbs of democracy but without having to deal with the unruly outcomes and political challenges that real democratic decisions would involve.

Undoubtedly, happiness is currently a highly political concept, and has been in Anglo-Saxon cultures since at least the advent of modernity. This is acknowledged by happiness economists and positive psychologists alike, who both recognize that happiness has political as well as economic and social consequences. As Ashley Frawley shows, almost 40 per cent of positive psychologists' papers draw conclusions pointing to implications for policy interventions.[75] What they are reluctant to acknowledge, though, is that both happiness research and implementation might also be politically and culturally motivated; that is, that there might be an ideological agenda as well as a cultural bias behind its scientific study and its political, economic and social applications. Happiness researchers try to escape any cultural, historical or ideological questioning by holding on to the science/value dichotomy, insisting that their scientific approach prevents their definition of the happy individual from being laden with moral principles, ethical prescriptions and ideological values. This, nevertheless, plainly contrasts with the tight relationship that happiness holds with the main individualistic assumptions and ethical demands characteristic of neoliberal ideology, as the next chapter develops.

2

Rekindling individualism

Separated from family, religion, and calling as sources of authority, duty, and moral example, the self first seeks to work out its own form of action by autonomously pursuing happiness and satisfying its wants. But what are the wants of the self? By what measure or faculty does it identify its happiness? In the face of these questions, [. . .] individualism seems more than ever determined to press ahead with the task of letting go of all criteria other than radical private validation.

Robert Bellah et al., *Habits of the Heart*

Happiness and neoliberalism

Neoliberalism should be regarded as something wider and more fundamental than just a theory of political economic practices. As mentioned elsewhere,[1] neoliberalism should be understood as a new stage of capitalism characterized by the relentless expansion of the field and scope of economics to all cultural strata;[2] the rising demand for technical-scientific criteria to account for political and social decision-making;[3] a renewed emphasis on utilitarian principles of choice, efficiency and profit maximization;[4] the exponential increase of labour uncertainty, economic instability, market competition, risk-taking behaviour, and organizational flexibilization and decentralization;[5] the increasing commodification of the symbolic and immaterial, including identities, feelings and lifestyles;[6] and the consolidation of a therapeutic ethos that places both emotional health[7] and the need for individual self-realization at the core of social progress and institutional interventions.[8] More fundamental than these characteristics is the fact that neoliberalism must be grasped as an individualist social philosophy whose main locus of attention is the self, and whose main anthropological assumption, as Aschoff argues, is that 'we are all independent, autonomous actors meeting in the marketplace, making our destinies and in the process making society'.[9] In this sense, neoliberalism should be understood not only in terms of its structural features and consequences but also in terms of its infrastructural assumptions; that is, in terms of its ethical and moral maxims according to which all individuals are (and should be) free, strategic, responsible and autonomous beings who are able to govern their psychological states at will, fulfil their interests and pursue what is understood to be their inherent objective in life: the achievement of their own happiness.

Thus, it should not be surprising that the drastic shift to happiness at the turn of this century[10] began immediately after the consolidation of what authors such as Gilles Lipovetsky identify as 'the second individualistic revolution',[11] a pervasive cultural process of individualization and psychologization which deeply transformed the political and social orders of accountability within advanced capitalist societies. This revolution allowed the structural deficits, contradictions and paradoxes of these societies to be rendered in terms of psychological features and individual responsibilities. Aspects such as work became progressively understood as a matter of personal projects, creativity and entrepreneurship; education a matter of individual competences and talents; health a matter of habits and lifestyle; love a matter of interpersonal likeness and compatibility; identity a matter of choice and personality; social progress a matter of individual growth and thriving; and so on.[12] The consequence was a widespread collapse of the social in favour of the psychological,[13] with Politics being gradually replaced by therapeutic politics,[14] and with the discourse of happiness progressively replacing the discourse of individualism in the definition of the neoliberal model of citizenship (we will develop this idea in chapter 4).[15]

In this sense, happiness should not be seen as an innocuous, well-meant abstraction for wellness and satisfaction. Nor should it be conceived as an empty concept devoid of profound cultural, moral and anthropological biases and assumptions. Otherwise, it would be hard to understand why happiness and not any other value – e.g., justice, prudence, solidarity or loyalty – has come to play such a prominent role in advanced capitalist societies, or why it has come to organize in powerful ways how we explain human behaviour. Instead, we argue that one of the reasons accounting for why happiness has become so prominent in neoliberal societies is that happiness is saturated with individualist values – defining the individual self as a paramount value, conceiving of groups and societies as an aggregate of separate and autonomous wills. More specifically, we argue that if happiness has come to be so prominent in neoliberal societies, it is because it has proven a very useful concept for rekindling, legitimizing and re-institutionalizing individualism in seemingly non-ideological terms through science's neutral and authoritative discourse.

As Michel Foucault and many others have stated, instead of directly appealing to morality or politics, neutral discourses appealing to the natural properties of human beings are always more persuasive and easy to institutionalize.[16] Many happiness scientists under the umbrella of positive science have made the notion of happiness morph into a potent, ideologically aligned instrument that stresses personal responsibility for one's fate and conveys strong individualist values disguised as psychological and economic science.[17] Indeed, numerous scholars have critically and extensively analysed the strong individualistic bias underpinning the theoretical, moral and methodological foundations of the scientific study of human happiness.[18] Yet, whereas the tight relationship between happiness and individualism has been widely demonstrated, it is important to understand that the notion of happiness has not succeeded *in spite of* being a deep individualist notion, but rather, *because of* its underlying individualism. In a way, part of the widespread success of happiness actually lies in that it delivers a legitimate, universalizing and apolitical discourse for individualism[19] – a discourse that conceives one's life as separate from community and which sees the inner self as the cause and root of all behaviours.

Positive psychologists, together with happiness economists and other happiness experts, have played a key role in this regard. Indeed, positive psychology is the discipline that has related happiness to individualism most tightly, to the extent of making the two concepts strongly dependent on each other – and even interchangeable. To be sure, individualistic biases and assumptions are not particular to positive psychology and its notion of happiness. They are in fact a characteristic feature underlying mainstream psychology at large.[20] Yet we subsequently illustrate that the main difference lies in the remarkable circularity and explicitness with which positive psychology conceives of and links happiness to individualism, either morally or conceptually.

Positive psychology and individualism
Regarding morality, for instance, positive psychologists do not recognize any normative anchor other than the individual itself: happiness is good insofar as it is good and self-realizing for individuals themselves. For instance, Seligman states that any

action or pleasure derived from the application of one's signature strengths should be called happiness, even if we are talking about a 'sadomasochist who comes to savor serial killing and derives great pleasure from it [. . .] a hit man who derives enormous gratification from stalking and slaying [. . .] [or] a terrorist who, attracted to al-Qaeda, flies a hijacked plane into the World Trade Center'.[21] Thus, whereas Seligman adds that he 'condemn[s] their actions, of course', he nevertheless claims to be able to do so only 'on grounds independent of [positive psychological] theory'.[22] According to Seligman, positive psychology, like any other science, is descriptive and hence neutral, so there is no moral judgement involved in his claim. To be sure, this is a profound contradiction: indeed, the moral subjectivism underlying positive psychology's justification of the goodness of happiness is as moral as any other justification.[23] Seligman nevertheless insists on his position: 'It is not the job of positive psychology to tell you that you should be optimistic, or spiritual, or kind or good-humored; it is rather to describe the consequences of these traits [. . .] What you do with that information depends on your own values and goals.'[24]

Regarding conceptualization, positive psychologists maintain a strong happiness–individualism association, making individualism a cultural and ethical precondition for achieving happiness, and making happiness the scientific justification for individualism as a morally legitimate value.[25] The strong relationship between the two concepts frequently results in the espousal of tautological rationales. In this regard, positive psychologists assume, and often put it rather bluntly, that just as happiness is a natural goal that all human beings inherently pursue, individualism and the autonomous and independent pursuit of goals are the most natural way of living a happy life.[26] Relatedly, numerous positive psychology publications claim to offer empirical evidence that individualism is the variable that most consistently and robustly relates to happiness – and vice versa – regardless of any other sociological, economic and political factors.[27] Cross-cultural studies conducted within the discipline are very illustrative of this. For instance, positive psychologist Ed Diener and colleagues stated that despite other socio-economic and political factors, individualism was the variable that most strongly related to happiness. This explains why individualistic cultures tend to produce citizens with higher levels of life satisfaction than non-individualistic or collective cultures. The main reason advanced by Diener and his colleagues is that citizens in individualistic cultures have 'more freedom to choose [their] own life course', are 'more likely to attribute success to themselves' and enjoy more chances 'to pursue their individual goals'.[28] Ruut Veenhoven also subscribes to this claim, further adding that individualist and modern societies strongly contribute to the higher levels of happiness among their citizens by providing them with 'a challenging environment that fits an innate human need for self-actualization'.[29] Similarly, Oishi states that individualism defined as a cultural emphasis on independence and individual self-worth is the strongest feature associated with well-being and life satisfaction, thus explaining why citizens of Australia and Denmark are happier than those of Korea and Bahrain.[30] According to Steele and Lynch, individualism would also explain the rise of happiness in countries such as China, where the increase in happiness among its citizens would be closely related to the increasing acceptance of the ethic of personal responsibility in the country, even among those in socially disadvantaged positions.[31] Positive psychologists such as Ahuvia have also pointed out that the economic development of nations leads to higher happiness not by raising living conditions or improving the purchasing power of their citizens, but mainly by creating individualistic cultures that encourage people to pursue their own personal advancement.[32] Fischer and Boer conclude that, all these things considered, 'the overall pattern strongly suggests that greater individualism is consistently associated with more well-being'.[33]

Whereas working out which variables contribute more to the well-being of nations is still an ongoing and controversial debate,[34] the majority of positive psychologists side with the claim that the more individualistic the nation, the happier its citizens. Nevertheless, the fact that these scholars recurrently find evidence supporting the happiness–individualism association should not be surprising. The way positive psychologists conceptualize and measure happiness is highly individualistic in the first place. Indeed, to play down – when not simply neglecting – the role that circumstances might play in determining people's happiness has been one of the hallmarks of the discipline since its very foundation. This is evident in many of their cross-cultural studies and in the measuring instruments used to quantify happiness – e.g., see the popular Satisfaction With Life Scale (SWLS)[35] as an example of how these questionnaires tend to overemphasize individual and subjective factors to the detriment of other social, economic, cultural, political or more objective ones – as well as in the theoretical underpinnings of the movement. With regard to the latter, perhaps no case better illustrates the individualistic bias and narrow sense of the social than Seligman's famous 'happiness formula'.

The happiness formula

In his 2002 book *Authentic Happiness: Using the New Positive Psychology to Realize Your Potential for Lasting Fulfillment*, Seligman formulated what he calls the 'happiness formula': H (Happiness) = S (genetically determined set point of happiness) + V (volitive, intentional activity devoted to increasing one's happiness) + C (circumstances affecting happiness).[36] According to Seligman, this simple equation condenses breakthrough findings on the nature of human happiness, namely that genetics account for about the 50 per cent of individuals' happiness; volitive, cognitive and emotional factors account for 40 per cent; and life circumstances and other factors, such as income, education and social status, account for the remaining 10 per cent – 'circumstances' that, according to Seligman, can be grouped together 'because, surprisingly, none of them much matters for happiness'.[37]

Seligman's happiness formula, although scientifically questionable, summarizes the three key assumptions positive psychology's conception of happiness would subsequently be based on. The first is that 90 per cent of human happiness is attributable to individual and psychological factors. The second, which contradicts the first, is that happiness can be acquired, mastered and engineered to a great extent through choice, willpower, self-improvement and the proper know-how. And the third is that non-individual factors play a rather insignificant role in the well-being of any person. Regarding circumstances, Seligman hurries to clarify that what actually makes a difference to happiness is the individual, subjective perception of those circumstances, not the circumstances themselves. For example, concerning money, Seligman insists on 'how important money is to you, more than money itself, influences your happiness'.[38] Thus, although objective circumstances might exert some effect on people's happiness, Seligman concludes that their limited influence is not worth the effort of trying to change them: '[t]he good news about circumstances is that some do change happiness for the better. The bad news is that changing these circumstances is usually impractical and expensive.'[39]

The 40 per cent solution

Positive psychologists soon established the happiness formula as an important theoretical guideline to follow. For instance, in her popular book *The How of Happiness: A Scientific Approach to Getting the Life You Want*, positive psychologist Sonja Lyubomirsky claimed this formula to be a simple but evidence-based explanation of the causes that really determine people's happiness. She claimed that 'if we can accept as true that life circumstances are *not* the keys to happiness, we'll be greatly empowered to pursue happiness for ourselves'.[40] In this regard, Lyubomirsky encourages people to focus on themselves rather than on their personal circumstances as the key to improving their happiness. She called this 'the 40% solution'. According to Lyubomirsky, focusing on changing the way we feel, think and behave in our daily lives proves much more effective in improving people's happiness than any other solution – not only because neither genetics nor circumstances seem to be either feasible to modify or worth modifying, but also because in the absence of personal change, no matter how fortunate or unfortunate people are in life, everyone seems to rapidly return to their happiness set point (S) – the levels of happiness that each one would have by genetic predisposition. In this regard, after claiming the scientific virtues and breakthrough findings made by positive psychology since the field was founded, Lyubomirsky devotes most of her book to teaching readers several 'happiness activities' for taking advantage of their 40 per cent margin of happiness enhancement, including exercises about expressing gratitude, cultivating optimism, avoiding overthinking, managing stress, living in the present and savouring the small pleasures of life.

One of the severest criticisms levelled at the happiness formula was raised by Barbara Ehrenreich in her book *Smile or Die: How Positive Thinking Fooled America and the World*. Ehrenreich raised serious concerns about the dubious statistical basis and lack of scientific logic behind Seligman's 'misbegotten equation', as well as about the social and moral implications of reducing circumstances to a minor role in determining people's happiness.[41] Ehrenreich wondered, if what positive psychologists claim is true, why advocate for better jobs and schools, safer neighbourhoods or universal health insurance if any of these measures will do little to make people happy? Should we then just accept arguments that income does not contribute much to people's happiness? How about the many families who struggle to make ends meet, save for old age, support their unemployed relatives or pay the mortgage? Wouldn't higher and fairer salaries lessen the social exclusion and daily unrest of these low- and middle-class families?

Income has been the one of those so-called 'circumstances' that has attracted the most debate regarding its effects on people's happiness. For positive psychologists, when it comes to income there is not much reason for hesitation: money does not significantly relate to happiness (this poses the question of understanding why so many people appear to believe the contrary). A similar albeit slightly more nuanced claim has been supported by happiness economists such as Richard Layard, who argues that whereas money might be important for those whose income is 'low', beyond a certain threshold income would hold a null relationship with happiness and emotional well-being.[42] This threshold, however, has never been clearly set; depending on the study it ranges from an annual salary of $15,000[43] to $75,000.[44] Nevertheless, authors such as Stevenson and Wolfers have questioned the assumption that income and happiness are not related. As these authors point out, 'there is no major well-being dataset that supports this commonly made claim',[45] arguing that, contrary to the 'fragile and incomplete evidence about this relationship',[46] their studies show 'that the estimated subjective well-being-income gradient is not only significant but also remarkably robust across countries, within countries, and over time', so the claim 'that economic development does not raise subjective well-being' should be 'put to rest'.[47] Like Ehrenreich, Stevenson and Wolfers emphasize that although unfounded, arguments undermining the role that income and other socio-economic conditions play in determining people's happiness have important social and political consequences: 'the conclusion that absolute income has little impact on happiness has far-reaching policy implications. If economic growth does little to improve social welfare, then it should not be a primary goal of government policy.'[48]

> In its strong form this hypothesis suggests that people (and public policy) are powerless to deliver lasting gains in happiness, because individual happiness returns inexorably to one's set point of happiness. Our findings clearly falsify this strong form of adaptation: we find that those enjoying materially better circumstances also enjoy greater subjective well-being and that ongoing rises in living standards have delivered higher subjective well-being.[49]

Relatedly, if what positive psychologists claim is true and circumstances do not have a significant effect on people's happiness, why then blame social structures, institutions or poor living conditions for people's feelings of depression, distress or anxiety about their futures? Why even acknowledge that privileged living conditions help explain why some people do and feel better than others? Would that be another way to justify the meritocratic assumption that, in the end, everyone gets what he or she deserves? After all, with non-individual variables completely factored out of the equation, what else but individuals' own merit, effort and persistence could be held accountable for their happiness or lack thereof? This position has indeed been recurrently and severely criticized for its short-sightedness as well as for its disruptive social and moral consequences. Authors such as Dana Becker and Jeanne Marecek have summarized well the common uneasiness with positive psychologists' claims:

> The good life is not readily or equally available to all. Disparities in status and power resulting from social class, gender, skin color,

race, nationality, and caste, markedly influence wellbeing. These structural differences dramatically affect one's access to healthcare, educational and economic opportunity, fair treatment in the criminal justice system, safe and secure living conditions, a promising future for one's children, and even mortality. What kind of fulfillment is possible in the absence of these basic conditions? To suggest that self-help exercises can suffice in the absence of social transformation is not only short sighted but morally repugnant.[50]

Kahneman himself has also shown a belated scepticism with regard to positive psychology's understanding of circumstances, claiming that 'in positive psychology, it seems to me they're trying to convince people to be happy without making any changes in their situation [. . .] That fits well with political conservatism.'[51] But even in the face of all these criticisms, positive psychologists have nevertheless stuck to their guns, be it by ignoring the subject – it is actually hard to find any significant analysis on the role that social factors such as power relations, authority, disparities in status, migration, justice or coercion might be playing in people's happiness within the positive psychology literature – or by minimizing the importance that these factors would play in favour of psychological ones, as we have seen. Positive psychologists still emphasize that whereas the claim that people's circumstances roughly account for 10 per cent of people's happiness might seem like a 'counterintuitive finding',[52] their studies consistently find no significant link between structural, political and economic conditions – including inequality rates, public education, population pressure and social expenditure – and personal well-being.[53]

The silver lining, Lyubomirsky and other positive psychologists would say, is that the 40 per cent solution still leaves a large margin for anybody to craft their own well-being. So no matter how troublesome our living conditions or the times we live in might be, the keys to happiness and personal improvement will always lie mainly within ourselves. Whereas trying to change our unchangeable circumstances only brings about needless frustration, as Seligman indicates,[54] changing ourselves would yield sound and long-lasting results for our well-being. This message, although quite objectionable, has had great resonance in the last few years, especially because in times of uncertainty, powerlessness, and political and social turmoil, the promise that we can find well-being by just looking inwards might offer empowerment to some and an outlet for venting anxieties to some others. Yet, as we develop in this next section, we should question whether this individualist conception of human happiness is not itself doing more harm than good by contributing to sustaining and creating some of the dissatisfaction that it promises to solve.

The retreat to the inner citadel

In the years following the financial crisis of 2008, it became quite common to solicit the views of coaches and other personal development workers. Media, internet sites and blogs wanted to provide self-care tips and advice on how to personally deal with one's feelings in troublesome times, including warnings about the hazardous consequences of not looking after oneself. 'How to care for yourself in times of crisis', published in the *Huffington Post* in 2009 – and republished in 2011 – is one of the most obvious examples of the hundreds of similar pieces of writing that have flourished in the years since the global financial crisis. In this article, a career coach and executive recruiting leader wrote the following.

> It would be a disservice to avoid the fact that so many of us are in the midst of what appears to be profound chaos, uncertainty and fear. We are hearing daily about the state of our economic environment and unemployment [. . .] Allowing stress to hijack

your ability to care for yourself has negative ramifications for your health, which inhibits the ability to successfully manage challenging circumstances [. . .] With this in mind, I'd like to offer some essential self-care tips. Maintain self-worth [. . .] Laugh and smile [. . .] Take care of the little things [. . .] [And] stay present [. . .] While it can be easy to allow things like layoffs, financial distress to elicit a diminished sense of self-worth and even self-neglect, it is more critical than ever to remain conscious of engaging in very simple practices to support you in caring for yourself and moving gracefully through global chaos that can become personal challenges. With this in mind, ask yourself this: What are some of the things that you do to care for yourself?[55]

The global financial crisis in 2008 led to a dramatic worsening of the economic situation worldwide, inaugurating a moment marked by diminishing opportunities, high levels of poverty and inequality, increasing precarious employment, great institutional instability and political distrust. A decade later, the consequences of this crisis still endure and many of them seem to have since become institutionalized and chronic, thus sparking a serious debate on whether we are currently living in a period of great social, political and economic regression.[56] Further, whereas the crisis has brought growing public awareness of the situation of instability and precariousness, the structural forces that shape people's lives remain rather invisible and incomprehensible to many. As a main consequence, feelings of uncertainty, insecurity, powerlessness and anxiety about the future have taken root, and discourses calling on us to withdraw into ourselves have found the perfect breeding ground to proliferate and sink into people's minds, especially among those who suffer the consequences most severely.

Some decades ago, Christopher Lasch argued that in times of trouble everyday life tends to become an exercise of 'psychic survival' – one in which people, confronted with an unstable, risky and unpredictable environment, resort to a sort of emotional retreat from any commitment other than their psychic self-improvement and personal well-being.[57] Likewise, Isaiah Berlin had previously noted that the retreat to our 'inner citadel', an individualistic doctrine that prompts us to escape into the fortress of our true self, 'seems to arise when the external world has proved to be exceptionally arid, cruel, or unjust'.[58] Jack Barbalet made similar observations, pointing out that in times 'when opportunities meaningfully to influence economic, political, and other processes are low, then persons are likely to experience themselves as centers of emotion'.[59] Thus, whereas not entirely new or specific to our time, the call to withdraw into ourselves seems to have been rekindled in the last few years, especially in the aftermath of the series of economic and social changes triggered in 2008.[60] As sociologist Michèle Lamont has recently argued, individuals of post-crash neoliberal societies have turned to the belief 'that they have to look inward for the willpower needed to pull themselves up by their britches and to resist the tide of economic decline'.[61] This belief has important social consequences: not only does it entail the danger of emptying the self from its communal and political content by replacing this content with a narcissistic self-concern,[62] but insofar as it convinces people that the way out of their problems is chiefly a matter of personal effort and resilience, the possibilities for a collective construction of socio-political change will remain limited, as well.

Mindfulness, Inc.

The growing offer of and demand for happiness therapies, services and products in the last few years should indeed be interpreted as both symptoms and causes of the rising cultural trend to look inwards in the search for the psychological keys and willpower to cope with uncertainty, deal with feelings of powerlessness, and find solutions to people's insecure situations.[63] Mindfulness is a good case in point. Mindfulness conveys the message that turning our priorities inwards does not entail any kind of defeat or hopelessness, but rather is the best way to thrive and empower ourselves in a frantic and tumultuous reality. Be it clothed in a spiritual aura or in a more scientific and secular language, mindfulness encourages people to trust that things will work out in life if they believe in themselves, if they are patient, are non-judgemental and learn how to let go. In this regard, mindfulness training instructs clients on how to focus on their inner and authentic landscape, embrace the present moment and authentic feelings, savour the small things in life, prioritize interests, and achieve positive, worriless and resilient attitudes irrespective of their surroundings. For instance, a special *TIME* magazine edition in 2016 titled *The Science of Happiness: New Discoveries for a More Joyful Life*, extensively devoted to issues related to mindfulness, spirituality and neuroscience, recommends in several of its articles that one should 'remain present' as the path to being 'more productive and happier',[64] should protect the time to enjoy oneself 'from people who need your time, like family',[65] and should 'find pleasure' even in the most mundane activities, like 'cutting the vegetables evenly, for example'.[66] One article, titled 'The Art of Being Present', tells us the story of Tim Ryan, Democratic congressman from Ohio, who was so fascinated by his mindfulness experience that he decided to push for the use of federal funds for mindfulness research:

> Stressed and exhausted, Ryan attended a mindfulness retreat led by Kabat-Zinn in 2008 shortly after the election. Ryan turned over his two phones and ended the experience with a 36–hour period of silence. 'My mind got so quiet, and I had the experience of my mind and body actually being synchronized', says Ryan. 'I went up to Jon

and said, "Oh, man, we need to study this – get it into our schools, our health-care system."'[67]

In the last few years, mindfulness has indeed been established as a main theme in public policies, schools, health institutions, prisons and the military – even reaching psychological programmes aimed at providing low-cost, effective treatment for depression for poor people (ranging from socially excluded African-American women in Chicago[68] to homeless people in shelters in Madrid[69]). It has also grown as a topic for scholars. Introduced in the late 1980s and popularized by positive psychologists during the early 2000s, interest in the concept mushroomed after 2008. To give but one example, whereas a search in PubMed from 2000 to 2008 yields around 300 publications bearing 'mindfulness' in the title or abstract, this same search from 2008 to 2017 yields more than 3,000 publications, which now include the fields of economics, business management and neuroscience.[70] At the same time, mindfulness has itself become a lucrative, global industry raking in more than $1 billion a year. Countless products labelled 'mindfulness', such as courses, online sessions, group retreats and even smartphone apps, are exponentially booming in popularity and reaping great profits. Take for example Headspace, the top mindfulness app among more than a thousand now available on the market, which has been downloaded more than six million times, and alone raked in more than $30 million in 2015.[71] In the sphere of labour, progressively more multinational corporations such as General Mills, Intel, Ford, American Express and Google – which recently opened the 'Search Inside Yourself' programme – are also implementing mindfulness techniques to teach workers how to better handle stress, cope with insecurity, and turn emotional management into more productive and flexible behaviour. Mindfulness has even hit the well-established coaching industry: 'mindful coaching' is now the trend in vogue.

Today mindfulness is treasured by all the happiness experts that plague the social spectrum, with positive psychologists at the forefront. Undoubtedly, mindfulness sits well with a science and a professional practice of happiness that reify interiority, insource responsibility, and turn the obsessive concern with our inner selves, bodies and psychic self-improvement into a moral imperative, a personal need and an economic asset. It also sits well with the individualistic assumptions and narrow sense of the social that characterize these happiness scholars and professionals, as well as the neoliberal view of the world at large. Like many other concepts and techniques endorsed by happiness scientists and experts, mindfulness thrives on the promise of acting as a panacea for many of the endemic problems that plague today's neoliberal societies. It also thrives on the belief that the root of these problems is to be found in individuals themselves, rather than in a socio-economic reality. Allegedly, it is not society that needs reform, but individuals who need to adapt, change and improve. Like many of its semantic relatives, mindfulness also supplies people with a sense of peace, normality and opportunity in an insecure market economy. What their followers find, though, is nothing but techniques that make them direct their attention to themselves instead of the surrounding world – and not always with the expected beneficial effects that mindfulness promises. As Miguel Farias and Catherine Wikholm indicate in their book *The Buddah Pill*, mindfulness often deepens feelings of depression and anxiety, as well as creates some sense of dissociation and detachment from reality as a consequence of excessive self-centredness.[72]

And the same message of obsessive self-concern and self-scrutiny applies to happiness in all of its not-so-different varieties, whether it comes from the nagging insistence of a self-help book; the teachings of a mindfulness guru in an $800 dollar course; the self-monitoring exercises of a smartphone application; or the sacred quarters of objective, scientific knowledge: what happiness advocates pledge as solutions to human problems is little more than 'flee inwards'. Indeed, what mindfulness and many other happiness-related concepts and techniques offered by experts and industry ultimately share is their underlying individualism and narrow sense of the social.

Happiness: the return of individualism with a vengeance
We should then ask whether or not positive psychological interventions and their individualistic conception of human happiness contribute to sustaining and creating some of the dissatisfaction that they actually promise to remedy. If more individualism equals more happiness and vice versa, then enhancing one's well-being through positive psychological advice and interventions might well carry the same hazardous sociological and psychological consequences that have been commonly associated with individualism.[73]

Positive psychologists and other happiness scientists pledge that, generally speaking, 'we now live longer and happier than ever before in human history'.[74] This claim is made on the alleged basis that individualist, modern societies provide people with increased self-understanding, greater freedom, more opportunity to choose, a natural-fit environment for self-realization, and more opportunities to pursue their goals and improve themselves at will.[75] Nevertheless, statements like that contrast with the fact that millions of people in these societies each year resort to happiness therapies, services and products such as coaching services, mindfulness courses, positive psychological advice, mood-boosting medication, self-improvement smartphone applications or self-help books, apparently because they do not feel happy, or at least happy enough, with their lives.

These statements also contrast with important work and studies that link the striking rates of depression, anxiety, mental illness, mood disorders, medication use and social detachment to the 'narcissist culture', 'me culture', 'I love me generation' and the many other labels applied to the egocentric, possessive individualism that predominates in capitalist and modern societies,[76] and which has weakened collective tissues of mutual care in these societies.[77] As a recent case in point, in early 2018 UK prime minister Theresa May decreed loneliness a matter of state importance[78] after the Jo Cox Commission on Loneliness report raised awareness of the 'shocking crisis' and 'devastating impact' of loneliness in people's lives as a result of increasing social isolation.[79] Following Schiller and Weber, Charles Taylor has also argued about the link between individualism and the progressive sense of 'disenchantment with the world' that comes with the flattening and narrowing of lives experienced by individuals in these same societies. According to Taylor, individualism has progressively displaced, dissipated and problematized all those traditional frameworks that connected people's lives to a higher social sense of order and purpose by turning the self and its inner life into the only legitimate horizon able to provide meaning and direction. Consequently, the vast array of sources of meaning and purpose have been severely contracted, with anything else that could be placed outside the sphere of the self (morality, society, culture, tradition, etc.) losing its power and legitimacy to drive people's lives – together with its charm, mystery and 'magic'.[80]

Further, positive psychologists' claims contrast with the results of sociological studies that relate increasing individualism to higher rates of depression and even suicide in developed as well as in developing countries. In this latter regard, social theorists such as Ashis Nandy analyse the shortcomings related to the rapid turn to happiness that India has undergone in the past decade. According to Nandy, a 'clenched-teeth pursuit of happiness' and a powerful belief in 'human self-engineering' have quickly become major cultural features in India, prompting many to believe firmly 'that it is up to them, individually, to do something about their own happiness, that happiness cannot happen or occur, nor can it be given: It has to be earned or acquired.'[81] Nandy sees the Indian turn to happiness as a 'byproduct of individualism', a cultural 'disease' and a 'regime of narcissism' coming from the West and spread through globalization. One of the main associated problems mentioned by the author is that happiness and its underlying individualism bring about a profound sense of loneliness and despair among citizens, which was previously absent and which would partly explain the rising suicide rate in India.

This analysis matches other relevant studies that understand happiness science as one of the main bearers of the individualist mantra of personal responsibilization.[82] These studies have indeed emphasized that happiness should not be viewed as the opposite of suffering. Rather, they point out that happiness does not only reproduce many of the hazards commonly associated with individualism – e.g., detachment, selfishness, narcissism, egocentrism – but also creates its own forms of suffering[83] (we will further develop this idea in chapters 4 and 5). Regarding the former, authors such as Mauss and colleagues have pointed out that since happiness is defined in terms of positive feelings and personal gains, striving for happiness might damage people's connections and increase both their sense of loneliness and detachment from others.[84] Similarly, many other authors have reported that happiness positively correlates with narcissism, which lies at the core of self-aggrandizement, selfishness, egocentrism, hubristic pride and self-absorption,[85] all of them aspects underlying a vast array of mental disorders.[86]

Further, happiness is also closely associated with self-blame insofar as the excessive insourcing of responsibility that it promotes has diffuse sources. In this sense, happiness scientists evoke a rhetoric of vulnerability in which the helpless suffer from a harm for which the responsibility is unclear, so there can be condemnation without offence.[87] As individuals themselves are made entirely accountable for their choices in life and for their sense of purpose and well-being, feeling bad as well as not being able to feel better and happier increasingly become experienced as sources of personal discontent, as signs of a flawed will and dysfunctional psyches, and even as marks of failed biographies. As Lipovetsky points out, reporting not being happy or not happy enough with our lives is today lived as a source of shame and guilt, an indication of a wasted life and an offence to personal worth, to the extent that people prefer to see and present themselves as happy or moderately happy rather than as unhappy, even in the face of unfavourable circumstances.[88] This excessive blame of individuals for their failure to lead happier lives would actually explain in part why individuals of individualist societies tend to rank themselves as above 7 out of 10 points in happiness questionnaires. According to some studies, a cognitive positive bias would account for the strong and systematic tendency amongst individuals of these societies to protect their self-esteem by inhibiting negative evaluations of their lives.[89]

Some positive psychologists indeed acknowledge that individualist societies might be partly responsible for the rise of stress, anxiety, depression, emptiness, narcissism, hopelessness and a large set of mental and physical disorders that characterize these same societies.[90] Nevertheless, the majority of these scholars claim that personal features better explain all these ailments, thus insisting on ruling out the idea that cultural, social or structural conditions have a significant effect on them, and reaffirming the idea that more happiness is hence the antidote to these ailments.[91] As mentioned, though, there is reasonable doubt in this respect, particularly when there are many arguments to support the criticism that happiness might actually convey just the same hazards that are commonly associated with individualism – plus carrying some new hazards of their own. Thereupon, looking inwards for remedies to many of today's social illnesses, including instability, uncertainty, anxiety, depression, hopelessness, solitude, frustration and sometimes even meaninglessness and disenchantment, might well be more part of the problem than the solution.

Be that as it may, positive psychologists and many other happiness scientists have successfully convinced many that virtually every social and individual achievement or problem can be traced back to a surplus or lack of happiness, respectively. And the idea, although not new, has sunk in deeply, making it into our most important institutions. The field of education, as seen in the next section, and organizations, in the next chapter, are indeed two of the most striking examples of this.

Educating for happiness

In 2008, Seligman and Layard had the following conversation regarding the application of positive psychological interventions to the field of education. The conversation was apparently so revealing to Seligman that in his habitual tone full of pathos he called it 'a conversion experience'.

> Richard and I were strolling through a seedy section of Glasgow in between sessions of the inaugural event of Scotland's Centre for Confidence and Well-Being, a quasi-governmental institution intended to counter the 'c'nnot do' attitude said to be endemic to Scottish education and commerce. We were the keynote speakers.
>
> 'Marty', Richard said in his mellifluous Etonian accent, 'I've read your work on positive education, and I want to take it to the schools of the United Kingdom.'

'Thanks, Richard', I said, appreciative that our work was being considered in high Labor [*sic*] Party circles. 'I think I am just about ready to try a pilot study in a Liverpool school.'

'You don't get it, do you, Marty?' said Richard, a mildly scathing tone in his voice. 'You, like most academic types, have a superstition about the relation of public policy to evidence. You probably think that Parliament adopts a program when the scientific evidence mounts and mounts, up to a point that it is compelling, irresistible. In my whole political life, I have never seen a single example of this. Science makes it into public policy when the evidence is sufficient and the political will is present. I'm telling you that your positive education evidence is sufficient – "satisficing", as we economists call it – and the political will is now present in Whitehall. So I'm going to take positive education to the schools of the United Kingdom.'[92]

Leaving aside the fact that implementing positive education programmes in schools when evidence in favour is just 'satisficing' instead of sound and compelling does not seem like the most responsible thing to do, it is worth noting that by the time Seligman and Layard were having this conversation, they were not talking about any novelty. Since the foundation of both fields, and drawing upon previous therapeutic trends and interventions in the educational realm, positive psychologists and happiness economists have been advising the national educational systems of many different countries to introduce happiness into their curricula, mainly on the basis that happiness would explain and predict learning, students' performance, school achievement, future success and lower depression rates in adulthood better than any other variable.

In this regard, Seligman and Layard's conversation revealed two main issues worth noting. First, it showed the powerful influence of these scholars in political and educational issues.

Schools are primary places where values, aspirations and models of selfhood are instilled into young people, so the increasing presence of these scholars in the educational realm is also very informative about the incidence that happiness has in current societies, especially in younger generations. Second, as we consequently show, this conversation advanced the extent to which a positive education, built upon the firm belief that emotional and individual factors are more fundamental facilitators of and barriers to learning than sociological ones, would gain a much stronger grip in educational culture in the years to follow. Even Seligman himself seems surprised by this fact today: as he has recently claimed, perhaps a bit ironically, 'we cannot help being impressed by the rapid growth and widespread dissemination of positive education worldwide'.[93]

The rise of the happy student

Certainly, in the years from 2008 to 2017 positive education progressively established itself as a top educational priority, with a large array of happiness-based programmes addressed to primary and secondary schools, colleges and universities, widely disseminated and generously funded in countries such as the United States, United Kingdom and Canada. All these programmes were very much welcomed by a neoliberal, educational culture in which developing emotional literacy, learning managerial and entrepreneurial skills, and engaging in the pursuit of happiness have gained increasing prominence over developing critical thinking, learning reasoning abilities and craft skills, or pursuing knowledge as defining features of students.[94] In this regard, the British Columbia Ministry of Education clearly stated in 2008 that the ideal students of today were those who possess 'management and organizational skills, show initiative, responsibility, flexibility and adaptability, self-esteem and confidence, believe actions and choices affect what happens in life, make efforts to reach personal potential by pursuing what [they] enjoy doing, and market [their] skills and abilities in the same way as [they] would a business'.[95] As a result, an increasing number of private and public associations, think tanks, consultants, advising policy makers and global networks have emerged in the last decade with the purpose of '[bringing] together teachers, students, parents, higher education, charities, companies and governments to promote positive education' and '[persuading] policymakers to change their policy frameworks so that practitioners are encouraged to educate for character and wellbeing'[96] – such are some of the aims of the International Positive Education Network, created in 2014 and soon partnered with several private foundations to accelerate the spread and deployment of positive education worldwide. Indeed, it was not long before positive education reached thousands of schools, colleges and universities in more than seventeen countries, including China, the United Arab Emirates and India.[97]

Both academic and institutional realms dedicated to spreading positive education have worked hand in hand in the last decade with positive psychologists and happiness economists, actively backing up and legitimizing these kinds of institutional and state initiatives. These initiatives echo and claim support from the scientific work provided by these scholars. Layard, for instance, defended the fact that these initiatives entail a huge, necessary change in the way students should be educated. The rationale put forward is that happiness-focused education proves to be not only good education, but also good economics. In this regard, Layard claims that reorienting educational institutions towards positive education by changing the attitudes of teachers, students and parents would provide cheaper changes to reduce the prevalence of mental illness in children, whose consequences in adulthood cost over 5 per cent of GDP in developed countries.[98] For their part, Seligman and colleagues also claimed that happiness should be taught in educational institutions 'as an antidote to depression', as well as 'a vehicle for increasing life satisfaction, and as an aid to better learning and more creative thinking'.[99] However, neither Seligman nor Layard nor any of the many pressure groups and lobbying organizations advocating for more happiness in educational settings seem to seriously entertain the idea that educational systems need to address many pressing, fundamental issues in the present other than the psychological. Again, structural and social aspects such as multicultural and social exclusion issues at schools, the growing education gap between rich and poor, the increasing economic difficulties of the population in accessing higher education, the declining investment in study grants and in quality state schools, colleagues and universities, and the increasingly competitive and precarious environment of universities, to name a few, do not usually receive much credit as pressing challenges. Presumably this is because, in line with Layard's rationale, addressing the root of all these problems would no longer make education such good economics.

An entrenched ideology

Under positive education's umbrella, happiness scientists have developed and implemented numerous happiness-based programmes and initiatives. For instance, the Social and Emotional Aspects of Learning (SEAL) programme, founded with more than £41.3 million and introduced to 90 per cent of British primary schools and 70 per cent of secondary schools, aims to teach students how to 'manage their emotions', 'feel optimistic about themselves and their ability to learn', 'reflect on longer-term goals' and 'learn to feel good about themselves', with happiness scientists arguing that these and other techniques should be incorporated into the curriculum.[100] For its part, the Penn Resiliency Program (PRP) addresses North American late-elementary and middle-school students with the aim of teaching them tools such as how 'to detect inaccurate thoughts', 'to challenge negative beliefs by considering alternative interpretations' and to 'cope with difficult situations and emotions', with happiness scientists arguing that the programme's application should not be circumscribed to schools but also applied to the domestic sphere.[101] In a similar vein, the PERMA (Positive Emotion, Engagement, Relationships, Meaning, and Achievement) programme, applied both in the US Army and in schools, distinguishes itself from programmes seeking to enhance well-being through the removal or reduction of negative factors (e.g., anti-bullying, 'quit smoking' and depression-reduction programmes) by aiming at the cultivation of positive emotions, positive behaviours and positive cognitions.[102] Further, the Pinnacle Program and GRIT studies address college students with the aim of assessing individual differences in talent, emotional mastery and self-motivational abilities in order to foster genius, teach perseverance towards ambitious goals and prevent discouragement.[103] The MoodGYM programme, a self-directed intervention aimed at increasing resilience and reducing depression among adolescents,[104] and the Breathe programme, aimed at instructing students about the perks of meditation, relaxation and emotional regulation,[105] are also good examples.[106]

Yet, whereas these and similar intervention programmes have been praised in the happiness literature, an increasing number of opponents who are also experts in education have not been as enthusiastic, critically analysing some of their most pernicious consequences and testing their alleged efficacy. Regarding some of the consequences, Katherine Ecclestone and Dennis Hayes' work on what they have called 'the therapeutic turn to education' is noteworthy.[107] In addition to the underlying individualistic and neoliberal biases to positive education, Ecclestone and Hayes point out that these educational programmes and interventions sell a false rhetoric of empowerment. This rhetoric, they continue, conceals the dangerous promotion of a vulnerable, fragile and 'diminished self' that infantilizes students, privileges emotional self-concern over intellectual thinking, and sets up learning to become completely dependent on therapeutic experts and psychological assessments. Ecclestone and Hayes emphasize that these techniques instil in students an obsessive concern with their inner emotional life that undermines students' autonomy and drags many into a vicious cycle of anxiety and therapeutic dependence: 'The majority of children and young people are not damaged, but the training will damage them. It is no accident that children reporting anxiety in unprecedented numbers have experienced [these kinds of] interventions [. . .]: therapeutic education inserts vulnerability and anxiety, children express it and then get more therapeutic interventions.'[108]

Regarding effectiveness, positive education interventions have not proven to be as effective as the happiness literature commonly claims, either. In this regard, it is worth pointing out that the promises and hopes that such interventions would work are not new. Rather the contrary: they sustained numerous and ambitious educational programmes over the course of the second half of the last century, despite several disappointments, some of them severe. One of the most prominent (and failed) attempts stems from the Self-Esteem Movement in the 1980s and 1990s, at which time an apparent epidemic of low self-esteem had caused the term to take root in popular jargon. This movement claimed that virtually every social and individual problem could be traced back to a lack of self-esteem: 'many, if not most, of the major problems plaguing society have roots in the low self-esteem of many of the people who make up society'.[109] Nathaniel Branden, one the leading figures of this movement, stated that there was not 'a single psychological problem – from anxiety and depression, to fear of intimacy or of success, to spousal battery or child molestation – that is not traceable to the problem of low self-esteem'; beyond a doubt, therefore, 'self-esteem has profound consequences for every aspect of our existence'.[110] For instance, the governor of California funded a 1986 Task Force on Self-Esteem and Personal and Social Responsibility for several years, with an annual budget of $245,000, to help solve problems such as crime, teen pregnancy, drug abuse and school underachievement. Although this and similar attempts were subsequently proven unsuccessful, in the 1990s the National Association for Self-Esteem (NASE) took over these previous attempts and launched a new programme of intervention, this time deploying scholars as well as popular North American self-help writers, such as Jack Canfield and Anthony Robbins. The results proved no better than previous attempts in the 1980s, encountering numerous theoretical and methodological problems on the way.

The Self-Esteem Movement, along with the theoretical and methodological aspects and implications of the notion of self-esteem in psychology, has been extensively analysed by Roy Baumeister and colleagues.[111] These authors conclude that 'we have not found evidence that boosting self-esteem (by therapeutic interventions or school programs) causes benefits', to which they wittily add that 'perhaps psychologists should reduce their own self-esteem a bit and humbly resolve that next time they will wait for a more thorough and solid empirical basis before making policy recommendations to the American public'.[112] Indeed, highly reminiscent of many of the assumptions and aims of the current interventions of positive psychologists in the educational sphere, the Self-Esteem Movement is a good example of how cultural and ideological artefacts often play a leading role not only in sustaining certain psychological premises and social interventions despite strong evidence against them, but also in motivating certain kinds of psychological research and interventions in the first place. Actually, the first reports on some of the most popular and promising happiness programmes have not been precisely flattering, as mentioned. For instance, a

2010 report on the effectiveness of the SEAL programme stated that it failed to have a positive impact in every goal it had set: 'our analysis of pupil-level outcome data indicated that SEAL (as implemented by schools in our sample) failed to impact significantly upon pupils' social and emotional skills, general mental health difficulties, pro-social behavior or behavior problems'.[113] Other reports remarked that there seems not to be any intervention programme on single emotional factors such as resilience, self-efficacy, self-control or grit that has causal effects on academic attainment; that is transferable across domains; or that allows predicting future behaviour in young people – e.g., 'While there is overwhelming evidence of a positive relationship between self-concept and related outcomes, there is little empirical evidence of a causal one.'[114] At best, claims Kathryn Ecclestone, the concepts and evidence that serve as the basis of these interventions are inconclusive and fragmented; 'at worst, [they are] prey to "advocacy science" or, in [their] worst manifestations, to simple entrepreneurship that competes for publicly funded interventions'.[115]

In conclusion, some have argued that movements such as positive psychology would improve scientifically if they actually acknowledged their historical and cultural background, as well as their ideological and individualist biases and preferences.[116] We would concur with this argument, but we do not think that this will happen. The main reason is that the strength of positive psychology lies, precisely, in the denial of these backgrounds and biases: it is by being presented as apolitical that it is truly effective as an ideological tool. As Sugarman points out,

[P]sychologists have been unwilling to admit their complicity with specific sociopolitical arrangements, for to do so would undermine a credibility forged on value neutrality presumed to be ensured by scientific objectivity and moral indifference to its subject matter. Consequently, as the historical record attests, in the main, psychologists have served primarily as 'architects of adjustment' in preserving the status quo and not as agents of sociopolitical change.[117]

This statement is well applied to positive psychology as well as to happiness economics, which draw much of their cultural power, scientific authority and social influence from supporting and practising as valid and universal what the individualistic, utilitarian and therapeutic worldview of neoliberalism has already presumed to be true and desirable for individuals and societies alike.

3
Positivity at work

I was starting to feel irresponsible, like the only way I could keep doing this was to forget about all the people my one-size-fits-all platitudes couldn't help. But with coachology comes great responsibility [. . .] Responsibility to rise above bullshit artistry. Responsibility to not try to solve people's problems you are in no way equipped to fix. Advising others on how to steer their professional lives and livelihood was a job I no longer wanted. This wasn't just a crisis of skills or cash flow; it was a crisis of conscience.

Michelle Goodman, *Confessions of a Failed Self-Help Guru*

The movie *Up in the Air* takes place in the aftermath of the global economic crisis of 2008. It was one of the worst times in recorded history for many American companies, which laid off thousands of workers, with devastating effects on their lives and families. Yet the conjuncture is exactly right for people like the character Ryan, a downsizing expert employed by a human resources outsourcing firm and who spends most of his time flying around the country and firing people. Ryan loves his job and his lonely life; he loves airports, affairs with no strings attached, and, especially, the feeling of independence and non-responsibility that his life brings him. He also gives motivational speeches to other businesspeople, in which he uses the metaphor of the empty backpack to convey his philosophy of life: success is about travelling light in life, free from the weight of our past and from any commitment to others. 'The slower we move the faster we die', says Ryan. 'We are not swans who live symbiotically with others. We are sharks.' An important aspect of the movie is the way he performs his job. Firing people is not just about communicating to workers from other companies that their jobs 'are no longer available'. He has a more essential task: to neutralize the anger and sense of hopelessness that comes with downsizing by replacing these feelings with a false sense of opportunity and optimism. He actually has a recurrent line to this effect: 'Anyone who ever built an empire or changed the world sat where you are now. And it is because they sat there that they were able to do it.' Ryan is charming and cynical; he knows his job is a dirty business, but he loves it and does it very well. His position, though, is threatened when Natalie, a young, promising psychologist recently hired by his company, devises a new, cost-effective system for firing people online, thus making expensive people like Ryan eventually expendable. She is supposed to take over Ryan's job, so he is forced to instruct her on the art of downsizing.

Indeed, Ryan sees his job as a sort of *techne*, which contrasts with the rigid psychological repertoires displayed by Natalie, the amateur. As he says to her in a conversation on a plane heading towards their first task together:

Ryan: What is it you think we do here?
Natalie: We prepare the newly unemployed for the emotional and physical hurdles of job hunting, while minimizing legal blowback.
R: That is what we are selling. It's not what we're doing.
N: Okay . . . What we are doing?
R: We are here to make limbo tolerable, to ferry wounded souls across the river of dread until the point where hope is dimly

visible. And then stop the boat, shove them into the water, and make them swim.

Ryan knows that in order to manipulate others' feelings, some sort of emotional dexterity or intelligence is required. The sense of frustration, anxiety and depression that comes with downsizing can only be neutralized by replacing them with motivation, optimism and a sense of hope and purpose towards the future, no matter how deceitful or patronizing this might be. Ryan's expertise in the art of emotional manipulation is well exemplified in Natalie's first performance, when she struggles to fire Bob, a worker who fights back against the news of being unfairly fired from a company he has been loyal to for decades.

Natalie: Perhaps you're underestimating the positive effect that your career transition can have on your children.

Bob: The positive effect? I make about 90 grand a year now. Unemployment is what, 250 buck a week? Is that one of your positive effects? [. . .] And I guess without benefits, I'll be able to hold my daughter as she . . . you know, suffers from her asthma that I won't be able to afford the medication for.

N: Well, tests have shown that children under moderate trauma have a tendency to apply themselves academically as a method of coping.

B: . . . Go fuck yourself . . . That what my kids will think.

In the face of Natalie's failure to neutralize Bob, Ryan takes over the task:

Ryan: Your children's admiration is important to you?

Bob: Yeah. Yeah, it was.

R: Well, I doubt they ever admired you, Bob.

B: Hey, asshole, aren't you supposed to be consoling me?

R: I'm not a shrink, Bob. I'm a wakeup call. You know why kids love athletes?

B: I don't know . . . Because they screw lingerie models?

R: No. That's why we love athletes. Kids love athletes because they follow their dreams.

B: . . . Well, I can't dunk.

R: No, but you can cook [. . .] Your resume says that you minored in French culinary arts [. . .] And yet you decided not to follow your dreams to work here, instead. How much did they pay you to give up on your dreams, Bob?

B: . . . Twenty-seven grand a year.

R: And when were you going to stop and come back and do what makes you happy?

B: Good question . . .

R: You have an opportunity here, Bob. This is a rebirth.

Ryan's intercession is a good example of the extent to which positive emotional techniques have become useful in today's organizational realm to insource responsibility and manage workers in terms of their happiness. Ryan touches on Bob's pride and delves into his anger and resentment to turn these feelings into a matter of Bob's own choice and responsibility. Neither managers, nor the company, nor the economic situation – all of which Ryan takes care to never mention – are guilty. Then a way out of the situation is presented to Bob as entirely dependent on his change of attitude as well as being in his best interest. Downsizing is now given an entirely different and positive meaning. It presents job loss as a wonderful opportunity for Bob's personal transformation, that is, as a sort of 'rebirth' in which new opportunities to achieve happiness unfold for him. Everything is up to Bob now.

Up in the Air portrays a small but good example of one of the ways in which happiness operates today within the sphere of organizations. As Barbara Ehrenreich argued, it has not only become a useful ideological tool to make apologies for some of the crueller aspects of the market economy, excusing its excesses and masking its follies.[1] Happiness has also become useful in introducing new repertoires and techniques that reshape the notions of work and worker in a way that conforms to the emerging needs and demands of the organizational setting, as we will subsequently develop. Indeed, had it been not as useful, neither happiness nor its advocates would enjoy the widespread influence they have in organizations today.

The anteroom of happy organizations

From the early twentieth century, but especially from the 1950s onwards, few scholars have contributed to institutionalizing certain insights into human behaviour as much as economists and psychologists. The economic and psychological spheres have intertwined at least from the time of Elton Mayo's Hawthorne Studies in the 1930s, an intertwinement that was strengthened over the second half of the twentieth century with the progressive appearance of hybrid disciplines and movements such as Economic Psychology, Human Resources Management, Consumer Research, Marketing and Coaching, to name just a few. Crucial concepts defining economic behaviour have been increasingly impregnated with psychological language at the same time that transformations within the market economy have had a great influence on mainstream psychological understandings of human behaviour. Happiness and personal needs are among the most representative examples of shared concepts that both economists and psychologists have dealt with during the past half century.[2]

The psychological theorization of these concepts was the hallmark of humanist psychology, which played a decisive role in connecting the spheres of economy and psychology within the industrial milieu. As Roger Smith and Kurt Danziger have claimed, humanist psychology shared a great deal of responsibility not only for the fact that Western post-war societies became 'psychological societies'[3] – as Abraham Maslow himself stated, 'we must psychologize human nature'[4] – but also for the fact that psychological repertoires and techniques of human needs and happiness have been modelling organizational needs ever since. Abraham Maslow's theory of motivation and his world-famous 'Pyramid of Needs' played an outstanding role in both aspects. Certainly, the humanistic third force psychology promoted by Carl Rogers, Rollo May, Gardner Murphy, James Bugental, René Dubos, Charlotte Buhler, etc. was not as successful in academia as it was in the cultural world in general and in the industrial sphere in particular.[5]

Within the industrial sphere, the theoretical contributions of the discipline proved to be essential in the transition from a 'job-minded' managerial period, mainly focused on the optimum adjustment of workers to the job's specifications and requirements – characteristic of the Taylorist age – to a 'people-minded' managerial period vastly concerned with the idea that it was the job that should fit and satisfy certain motivational, emotional, affective and social needs of individuals as the most effective way to raise productivity and task performance.[6] From the works of Elton Mayo, Henri Fayol, Gordon Allport, Henry Murray, Douglas McGregor and David McClelland up to the present, passing through what William Scott named 'industrial humanism'[7] – a widespread movement consolidated in the 1960s and in which a vast number of business schools, behavioural scientists, intellectuals and self-help writers took part – the study of human needs and happiness, as well as their relation to job performance and organizational productivity, has been a chief concern of managerial theories. On this matter, Maslow's theory of human motivation offered a suggestive and apologetic background. By elevating human needs and happiness to the status of first-order psychological constructs, Maslow not only helped consolidate the post-Taylorist idea that management of workers' emotional and motivational factors was of great economic utility for organizations, but also supported the managerial claim that the organization was one of the most privileged scenarios to which individuals must be committed in order to achieve what came to be their most important need: self-realization.

The success of Maslow's theory was closely related to the fact that it provided a model of human behaviour that legitimized a great number of organizational demands that were characteristic of post-war capitalism. As Luc Boltanski and Eve Chiapello pointed out, security formed an essential part of the implicit and distinctive definition of the work contract within this period,[8] and Maslow's 'Pyramid of Needs' imparted psychological evidence to the spread of the belief that the need for security was of crucial importance, thus resting at the base of his hierarchy. According to Maslow, certain needs of security and stability (that ranged from the mere physiological to more emotional and interpersonal ones) must be satisfied before the individual could consider developing higher personal tasks such as self-fulfilment. In other words, it was assumed that the individual required a secured economic basis from which to start 'growing as a person'.[9] Within the industrial sphere of post-war capitalism, the postulated path that went from economic security to individual self-realization was implicit in the notion of 'career', a long-term working itinerary that involved not only the promise of regular salary and promotion opportunities, but also the guarantee that the most valid and efficient workers would be eventually hired under permanent contracts.

Nevertheless, the market economy has changed remarkably in the last fifty years, and both the corporate setting and the notions of 'job' and 'security' have been transformed accordingly. Neoliberalism brought with it a highly fluid, risky, deregulated, individualized and consumption-centred economic setting[10] within which a new regime of 'flexible capitalism', as Sennett calls it,[11] or a 'new spirit of capitalism', as named by Boltasnski and Chiapello,[12] has arisen. This new spirit has been followed by the appearance of a new working ethics as a consequence of the continuous change in the nature of organizational life and the progressive dissolution over the past decades of the ideas of job security and stability. Thus, the previous work contract between employers and employees has vanished, and the previous dominant expectations of the workforce have become no longer tenable within current economic and organizational life.

> Organizations nowadays have to assimilate a new reality and treat each employee as if s/he were a firm. This change means that some of the suppositions that had dominated industrial society have to be abandoned, first and foremost, the idea that people are looking for job security. This is a 1950s concept born out of Abraham Maslow's famous 'pyramid of needs', with its postulate that fundamental needs must be satisfied before we can even begin to consider other types of fulfillment [. . .] [and that] the firm's first responsibility was to create a secure environment, with fulfillment only coming at a later stage.[13]

One of the most characteristic changes brought by the new working ethics is the exceptional stress on personal responsibility. Indeed, the progressive transition from external control to self-control may be regarded as one of the most significant features of the evolution of organizations and managerial theories within the last forty years. This transition is well exemplified in the replacement of the idea of 'career' with the idea of a succession of working 'projects'.[14] While careers were defined as specific paths in which individuals needed to learn a definite set of skills in order to perform efficiently and climb the organizational ladder, projects are defined very differently. They are conceived of as unstructured arrays of paths, objectives and risk-filled enterprises that demand individuals 'learn to learn', that is, be flexible, autonomous and creative – demands that apply to both individuals and corporations alike – so they can decide for themselves which skills, means and choices are the best for allowing them to adapt to a highly uncertain market, perform efficiently, grow as workers, and increase the odds of enrolling in more promising and challenging projects. The emergence of 'projects', which promised to replace the 'false autonomy' of 1960s careers with a 'genuine autonomy' based on self-knowledge, individual free choice and personal development, ended up proving useful to delegate to workers many of the contingencies and contradictions derived from the work context, thus displacing a great deal of the burden of market uncertainty and competition onto individuals themselves.

As a consequence of these transformations, the expected 'career itinerary' that went from job security to personal self-realization has vanished, and Maslow's model of the 'Pyramid of Needs' – relied on in the last few decades not only by managerial theory, but also by a multitude of clinical psychologists, counsellors, educators, etc. – has become more and more unable to provide satisfying answers to the rising demands and necessities of the emerging economic and corporate setting. Adding to this, an increasing number of academic studies challenging the scientific validity of Maslow's motivational theory, especially throughout the 1990s,[15] finally undermined its usefulness for managerial theory as an explanatory model for workers' subjectivity. Thus, new managerial approaches have been forced to look for new psychological models that rethink the notions of human needs and happiness and their relationship to task performance, organizational behaviour and job commitment. Alternative professional movements and academic disciplines addressing the nature of human needs and happiness have made their appearance in recent decades with the promise of filling this gap.

In this regard, positive psychology was an ideal candidate for the job. Strongly influenced by several insights into human and economic behaviour already present in humanist psychology, self-help literature and coaching,[16] positive psychology further offered a renewed discourse on human needs and happiness that fully met the emerging economic and organizational demands characteristic of neoliberal capitalism. Indeed, it could be said that, had it not already existed, corporations might have invented positive psychology themselves.

Inverting the 'Pyramid of Needs', or how happiness is now required to succeed

The ubiquitous use of the modern notion of happiness in the labour sphere should be regarded as one step forward in the process of managing workers' behaviour in terms of their psyche.[17] From the 1960s onwards, the psychological language of emotions, creativity, cognitive flexibility, self-control, etc. has progressively functioned as an effective way to palliate the structural deficits in recognition as well as the inherent paradoxes and contradictions that are characteristic of modern workplaces. Psychology has gradually made illegitimate the evaluation of workers' performance in terms of moral categories, providing instead a more neutral and scientific framework to reconceptualize workers' failures or successes in terms of their own 'deficient' or 'optimal' selves, and teaching people to cope with the burden of the risk of uncertain and competitive workplaces in terms of their personal autonomy and flexibility. In other words, the psychological language has made the devolution to workers of individual responsibility for the structural deficits of the workplace more and more possible. The modern notion of happiness takes this trend even further in encouraging the widespread assumption that if individuals work hard on themselves, they will overcome performance problems and find their way in the world of labour. One of the most distinctive contributions of positive psychology to this matter has been not the dismissal of Maslow's 'Pyramid of Needs', but its inversion.[18]

So far, managers, economists and psychologists have generated a vast scientific literature in which they relate workplace success to personal satisfaction, assuming the broadly accepted idea that a worker is happy because she or he is successful. Accordingly, successful outcomes produced happiness and satisfaction, and the claimed high correlation between both variables allowed taking the former as a reliable criterion to assess the latter. Both managers and human resources personnel were mainly concerned with the study of those working conditions – e.g., cooperative vs competitive work, communicative patterns, leadership and supervision, reward/punishment systems, job enlargement, systems of participation and recognition, etc. – and with the identification of those individual traits – e.g., extroverted vs introverted personality, high vs low IQ, achievement vs affiliative motivation, etc. – that were related to the enhancement of job performance and, as a consequence, that provided personal satisfaction. Although in the 1990s managers and psychologists started to suggest that the relationship between happiness and performance could be bidirectional, in most cases organizational studies still understood happiness as something derivate from optimum working conditions and/or high job performance.[19] Over the last decade, however, positive psychologists have contested this assumption, asserting that the relationship between happiness and success at work should be better understood in the reverse direction. Happiness scientists claim that 'past research', which 'demonstrated a relationship between happiness and workplace success', nevertheless failed to grasp the 'correct' causality between success and happiness, namely, 'that happiness is not only correlated with workplace success but that happiness [. . .] is an important precursor and determinant of career success'.[20]

Allegedly, happy workers are higher-performing and more productive. They purportedly show greater 'organizational citizenship behaviour'; they are more committed to their jobs; cope better with organizational changes and multitasking demands; show less burnout, emotional exhaustion and job withdrawal; and are more employable.[21] Happy workers supposedly show more autonomy and flexibility; engage in more risky behaviours by entering novel situations and pursuing newer and more challenging goals; make more creative and efficient decisions; easily recognize promising opportunities; and build richer and more extensive social networks. All of these are valuable personal features that are said to increase the odds of achieving more secure and better jobs and attaining higher incomes in the future.[22] Happiness scientists claim that this is so because happiness would trigger a sort of a 'Matthew Effect', according to which higher happiness levels lead to a series of short-term achievements and emotional advantages that would set the tone for long-term ones. According to happiness scientists this explains why some people end up better off than others, both in their lives in general and in their working projects in particular.[23] In his latest review on happiness and well-being studies, Ed Diener concludes that all 'these findings are compelling because they rule out reverse causality from good performance to job satisfaction'.[24] And many other authors, such as Shaw Achor in his book *The Happiness Advantage*, have supported and spread this idea.

> More than a decade of groundbreaking research in the fields of positive psychology and neuroscience has proven in no uncertain terms that the relationship between success and happiness works the other way around. Thanks to this cutting-edge science, we now know that happiness is the precursor to success, not merely the

---

result. And that happiness and optimism actually fuel performance and achievement [. . .] Waiting to be happy limits our brain's potential for success, whereas cultivating positive brains makes us more motivated, efficient, resilient, creative, and productive, which drives performance upward. This discovery has been confirmed by thousands of scientific studies [. . .] and dozens of Fortune 500 companies worldwide.[25]

On this premise, happiness scientists articulate a renewed discourse for the construction of a worker identity that is tightly attached to the workplace, to the new work ethic of capitalism, and to the new power distribution within the labour sphere. According to this discourse, happiness stands as a *conditio sine qua non* for adapting to economic changes, achieving work stability, fuelling performance, and increasing the odds of success in highly competitive and uncertain environments. Happiness, indeed, becomes not only a prerequisite for work – more and more managers claim to select workers according to their levels of happiness and positivity – but also the very content of the work itself, with positive emotions, attitudes and motivations rising as essential psychological features, even more important or essential than skills or technical qualifications.

The psychological capital of happiness

A good example of this renewed discourse provided by happiness scientists is the emerging notion of 'positive psychological capital'. This notion suggests moving beyond the idea of 'human capital' – a term popularized by the economist Gary Becker in the 1960s and which has gained increasing importance over the last few decades[26] – and focusing instead on the development of happiness-related aspects such as personal strengths, autonomy, self-efficacy, optimism, hope and resilience to increase workers' odds of success in challenging tasks, achieve a competitive advantage, make positive attributions about their outcomes, persevere toward goals, and 'bounce back and even beyond' when they are beset by problems and adversity.[27] In her book *Happiness at Work: Maximizing Your Psychological Capital for Success*, Jessica Pryce-Jones claims that 'the fundamental point of being happy at work is to enable you to achieve your full potential and to make the most of the highs and manage the lows on the way'.[28] The book is fully oriented to the individual, with little regard to structural working conditions or questioning corporations' goals and values. Indeed, workers who question these values are deemed obstructive and negative – e.g., some happiness gurus, like the multibillionaire Tony Hsieh, advise corporations to hire employees based on happiness and to lay off those who are less enthusiastic and more cynical about building a corporate culture of positive attitude.[29] Apparently, it is not working conditions that bring happiness and productivity to workers, but it is happiness that makes corporations productive and builds positive and productive working environments:

> Employees in the top happiness group have 180 percent more energy than those who are most unhappy at work. Everyone wants to be around people with energy because it's enthusing and motivating [. . .] The happiest employees report that they are 108 percent more engaged than their least happy colleagues [. . .] People in the top happiness category feel that they achieve their potential 40 percent more than unhappy employees. That's probably because they embrace goals 30 percent more and they're up for 27 percent more in terms of challenges too [. . .] Your working environment doesn't contribute to how happy you feel in your job. Shiny new offices, beautiful carpets, and high-tech offices, just like pay raises, cause a temporary hike in happiness, after which people will return to their usual level.[30]

Being interested in the job, committed to corporate values, managing emotions efficiently and, above all, using inner strengths at work to achieve your full potential are claimed to be the key ingredients in developing a high positive psychological capital. Allegedly, not only do workers with high positive psychological capital produce more, feel more energized and think more creatively, but they are also found to be less cynical about changes in their organizations, more resistant to stress and anxiety, and more engaged with the corporate culture.[31] To this effect, positive psychologists devise interventions for workers to 'readily lend themselves to the pace of change, limited time, and scarce financial resources that characterize today's workplace'.[32] These interventions promise employees they will increase their psychological capital at the same time as promising organizations they will turn this psychological capital into a highly productive asset.

Making 'happy workers' – not merely making workers happy – has become a first-order concern for many corporations, which increasingly turn to happiness experts in order to cheer up their employees, restore their enthusiasm for work, help them to cope emotionally with layoffs, and, especially, instruct employees in how to become more psychologically autonomous and more cognitively and emotionally flexible.[33] In this regard, it is especially interesting to find the emerging figure of the Chief Happiness Officer (CHO) cropping up in the last three years in more and more organizations from the US and Europe (including Zappos, Google, Lego and IKEA), and described as an HR Manager with a special qualification: the CHO believes that happy employees make better employees, so his or her principal function is to spearhead initiatives that increase the happiness of the workers to ensure that they bring out their best, stay motivated, find pleasure in what they do and improve their productivity. These experts, in turn, claim to use specific and science-based techniques in order to equip all kinds of workers with high self-regulation skills, learn-to-learn abilities and resilient strategies that would make them capable of making their own decisions, manage working relationships, cope with uncertainty, adapt to unexpected changes, and reframe adversity in a positive and productive way. Autonomy and flexibility are indeed among the most valuable skills that individuals must deploy to thrive in the unstable, liquid and competitive logic of neoliberal corporations.

Autonomy and flexibility are paradoxical properties, though. Whereas happiness scientists promise self-fulfilment at work and emancipation from organizational control, positive psychological techniques are nevertheless effective in doing the opposite. Indeed, a closer look at the organizational reality shows that far from fulfilling this promise, these techniques have proved rather useful for organizations to compel workers to internalize corporate control, to sideline the importance of objective working conditions when it comes to job satisfaction, and to make work contradictions, and self-exploitation more tolerable and even acceptable for employees.

Positive organizational behaviour

The increasing transference from external control to self-control in the last thirty years has been mainly channelled through the notion of 'corporate culture'. This idea understands the relationship between the worker and the organization as no longer being mediated by a working contract but instead by a moral bond of mutual trust and commitment. This new contract frames the interests of the corporation and its workers not as complementary, but as identical. In this regard, trust and commitment become the other face of self-control. Although neoliberal organizations no longer apply control through explicit and external mechanisms or promises of job security and career development, controlling mechanisms have not disappeared within the organizational sphere. Rather, organizations opt for internal forms to make workers identify with the organization. Instead of top-down control, organizations aim to shape workers as active units for the internalization, exemplification and reproduction of their corporate culture – i.e., the corporation's general principles, values and goals.

Corporate culture takes the shape of a semi-democratic environment that helps workers create an affective and moral bond of commitment and trust with the corporation itself and with their co-workers. On the one hand, corporate culture increases the workers' sense of belonging to the firm by making the working environment more 'home-like', thus blurring distinctions between the workers' public and private spheres.[34] On the other hand, corporate culture aims at inspiring employees to develop their professional projects, become absorbed by their tasks, go the extra mile, and persist in the face of difficulties by focusing on the positive aspects that are supposed to turn work into a win–win situation for both organizations and employees. In this regard, positive psychologists have developed the fields of 'Positive Organizational Behaviour'[35] and 'Integral Health Management'[36] to examine the role that positive states such as self-efficacy, optimism, hope, compassion and resilience play in turning happiness into engagement and motivation for employees and into investment – higher productivity and less cost – for corporations. Corporations such as Google, Inc., are usually set as paradigmatic examples of positive corporate culture:

> Employees can show up to work anytime they want, can bring their dog, wear pajamas, eat gourmet food for free, enjoy a free fitness center and trainer, see the onsite doctor if sick, wash their clothes, and partake in free espresso at each corner of their 'office'. This relaxed, fun environment has worked well for Google, Inc. because it provides a psychological benefit to encourage employees to be more committed, more creative, and more productive. Google Inc.'s method of job design is staying away from monolithic hierar-

chies that stifle and distract creative ideas. When highly motivated and highly capable people have a common vision, they do not need to be micromanaged [. . .] Google, Inc. thrives in a 'I think I can' culture, not the traditional 'no you can't' bureaucracy.[37]

Corporate culture encourages employees to consider the workplace as a privileged site in which to 'flourish', and positive psychology's repertoires and techniques are useful in shaping subjectivity in this direction. In this regard, the notion of psychological capital emphasizes that workers should view their jobs as not a necessity or a duty so much as an opportunity. For instance, in their book *Positive Psychology Coaching: Putting the Science of Happiness to Work for your Clients*, Biswas-Diener and Dean claim that 'so important is our work to our identity that we proudly claim our occupation as synonymous with who we are'.[38] Individuals are most fulfilled, they argue, when they have a 'calling-orientation' approach to work, meaning they work because they love to do it and because it makes them flourish, not because they 'have to':

People with a calling orientation typically love and value what they do in and of itself. They may be paid well for what they do but typically espouse the idea that they would 'do this for free' . . . ; these people like to think about their work, even when they are off the clock, and would be likely to take their work with them on vacation. It is important to note that these are not simply workaholics (although some may be) who are absorbed only with their jobs but are people who believe they are creating a better world [. . .] There's the shocker: it does not matter if people deliver pizza for a living or are highly specialized surgeons, it only matters how they perceive their work.[39]

The authors conveniently leave unaddressed the question of just exactly how someone can develop a calling when working as a pizza deliverer, a McDonald's cashier or an office cleaner, but forcefully marshal the working and lower-middle classes to the ideal of the upper-middle classes.

As Micki McGee has critically pointed out, this notion of calling – reminiscent of Protestantism, widespread in self-help literature, and secularized as the pursuit and realization of one's true self – is now extensively offered as an antidote to the anxiety-provoking uncertainties of the new economic social order.[40] But it is also offered as an opportunity for individuals to grow as persons and develop their full potential as workers. Drawing upon Peterson and Seligman's classification of positive strengths and virtues – as seen in the previous chapter – positive psychologists defend the idea that individuals who apply their authentic capabilities and talents achieve their highest levels of performance and the greatest outcomes in life, as well as an extraordinary sense of motivation, excitement and fulfilment as a result of doing what they are most fitted for.[41] The workplace, they claim, will provide people with one of the most privileged scenarios in which these authentic capabilities are to be flexibly and autonomously deployed, tested and improved.

Permanent flexibility

Besides engagement, another important feature that defines neoliberal organization is, paradoxically, 'permanent flexibility'. Described as 'the organization's ability to meet an increasing variety of consumer expectations while keeping costs, delays, organizational disruptions, and performance losses at or near zero',[42] flexibility depends much more on workers than on any technical factor. In this sense, an individual's ability to flexibly perform his or her tasks becomes a main source of corporate productivity, so psychological techniques aiming to enhance this kind of ability are highly valued and in demand.

Flexibility applies both to corporations (to their organizational structure) and individuals (to their cognitive and emotional structure) alike. The flexibilization of the organizational setting has produced low-cost and tangible benefits for corporations,[43] but the risks and insecurities associated with employment and production have exponentially increased. A new employment regime based upon less secure jobs, more fragmented and varied tasks and more precarious conditions has been established. The number of casual, flexitime, part-time and self-employed workers has dramatically increased in the last few years, and corporations have more legal protection than ever to change the level of employment through hiring and firing, to make changes in working time by introducing flexible working hours and making them coincide with highly productive periods, to increase job rotation, to require multitasking for the same wage, and so on.[44] As Uchitelle and Kleinfield pointed out, 'what companies do to make themselves secure is precisely what makes their workers feel insecure'.[45]

In this vein, Crespo and Serrano-Pascual have analysed the discourse of flexibility in European social policies promoted by the European Union. According to these authors, on the premise that more flexibility in working conditions would bring more security to the labour market – whose rigidity is seen as the cause of economic instability, decreased productivity and higher unemployment – these policies emphasize the deregulation of contractual guarantees and the need for work flexibility to further industrial adaptation and facilitate the dynamics of work creation.[46] As work security can no longer be guaranteed by the market, flexibility therefore becomes the only way for organizations and workers to navigate fast and unpredictable economic changes:

Flexibility, on the one hand, is about successful moves ('transitions') during one's life course [. . .] It is about progress of workers into better jobs, 'upward mobility' and optimal development of talent. Flexibility is also about flexible work organisations, capable of quickly and effectively mastering new productive needs and skills, and about facilitating the combination of work and private responsibilities. Security, on the other hand, is more than just the security to maintain one's job: it is about equipping people with the skills that enable them to progress in their working lives.[47]

Crespo and Serrano-Pascual claim that these policies are emblematic of a new work culture whose fundamental pillar is to weaken state regulation of the labour market and to normalize a work model that promotes individuals' responsibility for their working lives – including success, unemployment and adaptation – at the expense of collective responsibility and solidarity. Political and economic fragility are hence turned into personal vulnerability, and the sphere of labour into a depoliticized and psychologized realm in which workers, instead of organizations, become the principal object of managerial intervention.

Flexibility makes legitimate the transfer of the burden of organizational uncertainty onto workers,[48] with positive psychological techniques playing an important role in helping individuals work on their emotional and cognitive adaptability. Flexibility, in positive psychological terms, equals resilience. Allegedly, resilient workers do not let themselves be beset by problems and adversity, but sustain effort and manage to attain success by turning setbacks into opportunities for self-improvement and personal development. According to positive psychologists, these kinds of individuals are much more cognitively and behaviourally flexible; they cope better with multitasking demands, role restructuring and job redesign; they are better able to improvise in changing situations; and they are more capable of using adverse experiences in their favour to increase performance on subsequent tasks than non-resilient employees.[49] Resilient workers are also less prone to suffer from psychological problems such as depression, stress, 'burnout' or emotional exhaustion. As a profession involving distressful environments, interpersonal difficulties, devaluing feelings, witnessing tragedy, excessive workload and low-paid jobs, nursing is set as a glaring example of how resilience is essential at work – police officers, firemen and soldiers are also recurrent in positive literature. Resilient nurses are used to illustrate how despite adverse circumstances, anyone can adapt to, cope with and even grow from negative life experiences and hostile working conditions.[50] With resilience at the forefront, though, it seems that issues such as increasing financial resources, raising wages, offering more vacations, fighting for more recognition at work, or other ethical concerns become less essential issues when it comes to happiness and productivity.

Indeed, it is no wonder that organizations are so interested in selecting for resilience and in building resilient workers: invulnerable, self-responsible and adaptive, they seem like the perfect lid for the pot. Resilience has proven a useful concept to sustain implicit hierarchies, legitimate dominant ideologies and demands in the field of labour, and make individuals themselves deal with the psychological costs of their problematic, unstable and poor working situations. Today, the average worker moves several times in her or his lifetime, holds a number of limited duration contracts, performs more than one job at a time, and devotes more time and energy in moving from one job to another – a trend that applies to the United States as well as to Europe, according to the US Bureau of Labor Statistics[51] and *Eurostat*,[52] respectively. According to a recent LinkedIn study, a new breed of 'job-hoppers' has appeared, holding nearly three times more jobs in their lifetimes than those of decades before.[53] Today's average worker also spends considerably more time and personal resources in developing networking relations and adjusting to continuously changing market trends,[54] and an increasing number of the economically active population struggle to make ends meet even when two or more jobs are combined – a trend that affects both blue- and white-collar workers. All of this happens at the same time that workers face demands to perform at their highest possible levels as well as to go the extra mile to reconcile work with their private lives and other responsibilities, such as family – something especially difficult for women, who suffer from even lower salaries and higher levels of precariousness and unemployment than men.

Yet, instead of 'resilience' being acknowledged as a psychological euphemism for demanding individuals make a virtue of necessity given the hard conditions of today's working environments, it is instead presented as a fantastic ability that workers should capitalize on to develop their selves and their psychological capital, as the best way to flexibly navigate in the contemporary labour market.[55] Amongst many other examples, this idea is well expressed in the book *Resilience at Work: How to Succeed No Matter What Life Throws at You*. Here, the authors claim resilience is the most valuable psychological capability for workers to capitalize on the alleged opportunities that come with such working challenges, and to take advantage of any stressful state of affairs to flourish and keep growing as individuals.

> As a people, we want to believe that we can learn, change, and master whatever comes our way. The ability to 'pull ourselves up by our bootstraps' has long been one of our most treasured work-place traits. We have continually wanted to reinvent ourselves at the organizational and employee levels, which speaks to our long-standing ability to adapt to stressful changes [. . .] Contemporary social and economic pressures on an unusually massive scale make it harder for us to adapt in the highly developed ways we expect. Although we still want to believe in our ability to learn, change, and master stressful

situations, today's tumultuous changes can be undermining, if we lack the capabilities that lead to resilience. Resilience under stress is more important than ever before. This book is about how to be resilient, to succeed no matter what life throws at you.[56]

The concept of resilience has also had an enormous impact within so-called 'entrepreneurial culture', with entrepreneurship establishing itself as an important field of study in many universities, business research institutes and companies in the past decade. Conceived of as resilient, persistent, self-directed, optimistic and self-motivated people, entrepreneurs are presented as the engine of social change and economic progress, as individuals who truly innovate and apply imaginative ideas to create economic activity by aiming at fulfilling their personal goals, dreams and life projects at their own risk. Entrepreneurs are allegedly among those who flourish most because they have a clear purpose in life, are determined to achieve the goals they set for themselves and adapt to adverse circumstances with optimism. Entrepreneurs also know how to take advantage of the opportunities presented to them, learn from their own mistakes, and capitalize on these failures for their own benefit.

Moreover, the entrepreneur can be anyone. Rich or poor, old or young, male or female, anyone who undertakes entrepreneurship will be rewarded for it, whether with greater well-being, self-confidence, autonomy or sense of direction in life. That is what Peter Greer and Christ Horst, economists and directors of the pro-capitalist and Christian international association HOPE, say in their book *Entrepreneurship for Human Flourishing*;[57] it is also the message that many self-help writers, coaches, inspirational leaders and consultants spread and vouch for. All of them share the same immanent ideological conviction that the public should be made more aware that entrepreneurship is, first and foremost, a self-shaping journey worth taking.

What they do not frequently mention, though, is that contrary to this shared assumption, sociological data reveals that whereas the discourse of entrepreneurship has an origin in wealthy and developed countries, this discourse is more extended and pervasive where *levels of unemployment are high and economy is weak*. Therefore individuals see themselves forced to find their own ways in the scarce labour market. Indeed, according to the Approved Index,[58] countries such as Uganda, Thailand, Brazil, Cameroon and Vietnam lead the ranking of the most entrepreneurial countries in the world.

Autonomy, another paradox

Together with commitment and resilience, autonomy is also a key outcome that positive organizational behaviour seeks to study and enhance. Autonomy is highly valuable in neoliberal organizations because responsibility is no longer vertically distributed but horizontally spread and diffused. This means that individuals must assume a great proportion of the contingencies of work, being completely responsible for their performance and having to autonomously manage their personal abilities, material means and time to accomplish their objectives.[59] Autonomy accompanies the expectation that workers adopt an active and creative, self-organizing and self-directed role in the performance of their tasks. Sales agents are a good example of this: they have to develop their client portfolios, secure client loyalty, keep clients satisfied, and come up with innovative ideas to increase productivity or to make their work more efficient. The assumption is that the outcomes they obtain – whether successful or not – are exclusively dependent on their own effort.

Autonomy, which includes closely associated psychological concepts such as self-control, self-regulation and self-efficacy, is the target of many positive psychological techniques, ranging from those consisting in changing emotional styles (defined as the way individuals rationalize the causes of their successes and failures) to those focused on making frequent positive self-affirmations, training hope (defined as goal-directed thinking in which people perceive that they can produce routes to desired goals), practising gratitude and forgiveness, and cultivating optimism.[60] According to happiness scientists, the development and deployment of autonomy are not only beneficial for the organization (e.g., insourcing of responsibility and less expenditure in external control and surveillance) but also fundamental for individual flourishing, productivity and work success.[61] Thus, taking the notion of autonomy as one of the primary variables explaining individual happiness and well-being, positive psychologists, as well as a multitude of self-help writers, counsellors, motivational speakers and coaches, provide a multitude of happiness-based techniques for emotional and cognitive self-regulation. These techniques all promise workers that they will succeed in expanding their self-governing abilities in order to increase performance, build positive and profitable relationships, manage anger, develop healthy habits, cope with risk and uncertainty, rationalize everyday failures in a positive and productive manner, and so on.

The concept of autonomy, as praised by corporations and happiness scientists alike, is riddled with shadows and paradoxes, though. The notion of autonomy, indeed, affirms with one hand what it denies with the other. On the one hand, corporations want their workers to be self-directed, but also to conform to the corporate culture, which implies not to be independent at all, but rather to obediently comply with the corporation's principles, values and goals. Corporations also emphasize independence and initiative, yet they do so in a working context in which the majority of workers lack real control over their decisions, tasks and purposes. Time is also something out of workers' control. Employees are assessed by their availability at any moment, with technologies and the internet further dragging private and public spheres closer together. Moreover, corporations demand self-control, yet workers increasingly undergo sophisticated evaluation processes and incentive schemes, which are often obscure and hard to understand. Autonomy, hence, seems to be just simple rhetoric to make workers do what otherwise they would not if not so compelled, that is, if their job did not depend on it. To be sure, there is nothing wrong with corporations demanding workers be productive, but it is wrong to manipulate and twist language to make them believe that everything corporations do is for their own good, not for the corporations' own profit. It is also dubious to make workers believe that their interests are just the same as those of the corporation, starting from the fact that most workers have no real say in corporations' significant decisions.

On the other hand, the presentation of autonomy as tightly related to happiness and self-development too often conceals its real purpose: insourcing of responsibility for organizations' failures. The burden of risk derived from the adaptations of corporations to market changes and fluctuation has increasingly migrated to workers themselves. Workers are held fully accountable not only for their own failures, but for the failures of corporations, as well. This puts such a pressure on workers that it is too challenging for many to bear, given the high levels of competition, multitasking, stressful demands and constant downsizing threats that characterize neoliberal organizations as a whole. Michela Marzano, for instance, comments on the case of a French technician at Renault who committed suicide in 2006. The report on the suicide indicates that workers at the corporation were victims of a fierce management regime which blamed workers for the success and failures of the company. The report also emphasizes that whereas the national average suicide risk among the population was 10 per cent, the average among the workers at the Renault technological centre in Guyancourt,

Yvelines, reached more than 30 per cent.[62] Marzano makes the point that this was not an isolated case at all: no corporation is free from promoting a corporate culture that increasingly destroys a social fabric based on solidarity and mutual support. This culture emphasizes individuality, independence and personal responsibility. Indeed, this was precisely the case for the 2016 National Labor Relations Board in the United States, who issued a ruling against T-Mobile for including a mandatory provision in its employee handbook requiring workers to maintain a positive work environment. According to the board, the notion of a 'positive work environment' was 'ambiguous and vague' and had a dissuasive effect on workers from speaking freely and organizing – the ruling was just the culmination of a series of charges brought against the company for promoting policies that hampered union organization.[63]

In this sense, autonomy and independence at work might not be as useful to enhance workers' happiness as they are to build a positive environment that is only beneficial for those who impose it – as well as for those who claim to know how to scientifically build it. Thus, no matter how fictitious real autonomy might be, it not only serves to exercise real control over workers, but it also feels very real for many who end up believing, either from conviction or of necessity, that their happiness and worth as workers and as individuals depend almost entirely on their performance.

Conditio sine qua non

The reverse causality between work success and happiness entails a significant transformation within the working sphere. What we have called 'the inversion of the Pyramid of Needs' advances an entirely new logic in the construction of workers' selfhood,[64] which is not limited to complementing previously existing models of subjectivity in the labour sphere. Instead, it aims to progressively replace them. Positive psychologists have channelled an organizational cultural process in which happiness has been progressively established as the *conditio sine qua non* for thriving in the current working sphere. By stating that the causal relationship between happiness and work success is one of the most striking 'findings' of the last decades, positive psychologists claim to have proven that the achievement of high levels of happiness stands out as the precondition not only for increasing work performance and job satisfaction, but also for increasing people's chances of fulfilling a wide range of personal and working needs such as getting a job, securing income, thriving in work projects, building profitable social networks, having satisfying and profitable working relationships, and dealing with the psychological impact of stressful organizational demands and conditions.

Yet the logic of this inversion is not circumscribed by the sphere of labour. The claim that happiness is a precondition for fulfilment and success applies as well to virtually any other sphere of everyday life. Ultimately, the main idea that lies behind happiness repertoires and techniques is that happier people are not only more productive and efficient workers but, most importantly, better citizens. In twenty-first-century capitalism, a powerful happiness industry has indeed emerged and expanded with the simple but alluring promise that by transforming into happier selves through the vast myriad of happiness products and services available, individuals will increase their value as social, political and economic subjects. The following chapter develops this issue and examines the main psychological features underpinning the ideal of the happy citizen.

4
Happy selves on the market's shelves

Advertising is based on one thing and one thing only: happiness [. . .] But, what is happiness? Happiness is a moment before you need more happiness.

Don Draper, *Mad Men*

On the website possibilitychange.com, thousands of people exchange inspiring stories of personal change and achievement in the face of adversity, and tips on how to take control of one's life. Some coaches, personal counsellors and self-help writers also take advantage and advertise their self-made psychological expertise as a service that anyone who wants to improve their lives and discover the secrets of happiness can acquire at a moderate price. Amy Clover, now a professional online coach, is a good example of this. She shares her own experience about how she turned from a depressive, obsessive person into a happy one by realizing that everything depended on pulling herself up by her own bootstraps, taking control of her thoughts and feelings, and refocusing her situation in a more positive way:

I always thought happy people were fakers [. . .] I was so used to struggling that I couldn't imagine a life in which every day was easy. I couldn't grasp the idea that other people's happiness could be real. Or maybe I just didn't want to [. . .] I drank heavily and took diet pills to make myself more attractive so that people would concentrate on my outsides (heaven forbid they find out how much was actually wrong with me). I felt trapped by my disorders, by everything I thought was wrong with me. It got to the point of holding so much in, I didn't think I could handle it anymore [. . .] I made the choice then and there, to change my life. Over the next few years, I took steps to overcome my depression, as impossible as that might sound. I decided not to give up and refused to give over to my disorders. I failed a lot, but every time I fell down, I got right back up again. 7 years later, I am a bubbly personal trainer and online coach, determined to empower you to overcome your setbacks and discover your happiness. No matter where you are in life, if you are not happy, something needs to change. Life is too short to be lived in a haze of hopelessness [. . .] There are indeed some diseases, disorders, and situations that you will have no control over, that cannot be changed. But you always have the choice of how you react to them and what to do when they threaten to take over your life [. . .] I am the biggest proponent for therapy because it was so crucial to my journey. Even if you haven't been diagnosed with anything in particular, therapy can help sort out confusing thoughts and issues that you may be carrying with you which could be keeping you from full-fledged happiness [. . .] THE MOST IMPORTANT THING TO DO IS TO MAKE THE CHOICE TO FIGHT FOR HAPPINESS. Why can't you be the one living the life you've always dreamed of? Why can't you be the success story you read about in magazines? Why can't you be the one to change the world?[1]

This and many similar stories put forward a few main and interrelated points that we will address in this chapter. First, this story and others like it reveal the extent to which happiness has become the yardstick of a life well lived, both morally and psychologically. Achieving happiness is now seen as the culmination of a story of personal improvement through struggle and self-help, where setbacks are opportunities for growth. These stories assume that personal effort will always and amply pay off – 'I failed a lot, but every time I fell down, I got right back up again. 7 years later, I am a bubbly personal trainer and online coach, determined to empower you to overcome your setbacks and discover your happiness.' These happy, positive moments of personal triumph are indeed the side of life that people are supposed to present to themselves and to others, whereas moments of weakness, failure and suffering should be dealt with personally and kept concealed as if they are shameful signs of an ill-domesticated psyche – 'I drank heavily and took diet pills to make myself more attractive so that people would concentrate on my outsides (heaven forbid they find out how much was actually wrong with me).' However, it is worth noting the fact that Amy publicly shares her problems. This entails no contradictions with what has already been mentioned; on the one hand, because it further reinforces the idea of happiness as a 'fight', both with oneself and with one's circumstances; and, on the other hand, because these problems are only shared retrospectively, that is, once Amy feels she is on the right path to happiness and once she can use herself as an example of self-improvement.

Second, these stories underline the extent to which happiness builds upon a generic narrative of self-betterment. Happiness aims at potentially accommodating anyone in any situation through the same, all-encompassing therapeutic scheme: acknowledgement of the problem; adoption of a firm resolution to take control of oneself; seeking expert technical aid if needed; and reframing thoughts and emotions through a more positive prism, as shown in Amy's self-portrait. No specific path to amelioration is provided. It is up to individuals themselves to translate and discover how this one-size-fits-all scheme might suit their particular lives and problems (whether it be an addiction or a difficult relationship). For instance, whereas happiness scientists and professionals claim that finding meaning and purpose in life is essential for leading happier lives, they never specifically say what exactly gives someone purpose: this is something that only individuals can tell. In this regard, the narrative of happiness lacks specific content so it can be highly plastic and mobile, that is, adaptable to a wide variety of situations, capable of being shared by many others, and able to acknowledge individual particularity but without being sensitive to it. This allows happiness to become an easily commodified narrative able to potentially accommodate anyone regardless of particular circumstances.

Third, these stories take for granted that virtually anyone, regardless of how content or how dissatisfied they might be, is always in need of more happiness in his or her life. Happiness is depicted as the continuous improvement of the positive, not as the mere absence of the negative. Happiness is first and foremost made out to be a continuum, that is, not as a special or final stage in life but as an ongoing, never-ending process of personal amelioration in which individuals should always aim for higher levels of happiness, irrespective of how they feel about themselves. It is assumed that people can always improve. In this sense, as we will see later on in the chapter, the pursuit of happiness engages individuals in an endless process of self-making, based on an ambivalent narrative that combines the promise of a better version of themselves with the assumption of a fundamental incompleteness of the self that places individuals in a position where they always lack something, if only because full happiness and full personal development, inasmuch as they are ideal horizons, will always be unattainable. This ambivalent narrative allows happiness to be turned into an ideal commodity for a market that closely ties happiness insatiability with constant consumption – a link wittily summarized in this chapter's epigraph from Don Draper, the famous lead character of the American period drama television series *Mad Men*.

All these aspects are essential to understanding why happiness has turned out to be so central in today's marketplace, acquiring its own, distinct entity as a commodity. Today, happiness is no longer just a side objective or a catchy word for other commodities to use to lure people with vacuous promises and ephemeral states of pleasure. On the contrary, happiness has become itself *the* product, developing into the core economic dynamo of a market that promises individuals a continuous increase in their happiness, on the premise that their highest personal, economic and political value equals the highest development of their own selves – with happiness constituting the supreme measuring rod of such development.

Twenty-first-century capitalism has indeed given birth to a huge and powerful economy of happiness. This is not a figurative expression. Happiness has itself become the fetish commodity of a global and multibillion industry that emerged and continues to expand around the offer of and demand for a prolific myriad of happiness 'emodities'. These are services, therapies and commodities produced and consumed qua scientific techniques and psychological management aids to effect some sort of personal transformation.[2] They are sold and purchased following the shared belief that happiness is undeniably the worthiest personal investment to make, as happier individuals are not only rendered healthier, more adaptive, self-motivated and productive people, but also, and most fundamentally, better citizens.

The strong insertion of happiness into the market is of great sociological importance. The fact that the market has turned happiness into one of its central commodities becomes itself a parsimonious, albeit powerful explanation for why the pervasiveness and influence of happiness have both intensified and consolidated over the last few decades. This goes both ways: the fact that happiness has become such a central concept in defining an individual's personal, economic and political value has given consumer capitalism an invaluable and legitimate (apparently objective and measurable) concept to commodify.

On that basis, in this chapter we lay down the argument that one of the main reasons why happiness has come to be such a central and effective commodity in today's consumer capitalism is because all of these happiness 'emodities' do not limit themselves to offering fleeting moments of joy, evasion, hope, reassurance and so on. On the contrary, more or less explicitly, all these happiness 'emodities' successfully recast the pursuit of happiness into a lifestyle, a habit of mind and soul, and ultimately, a model of selfhood that turns citizens of neoliberal societies into *psytizens*. We might define the notion of *psytizen* as an individualistic and consumerist subjectivity that renders citizens of neoliberal societies as clients for whom the pursuit of happiness has become second nature, upon the conviction that their full functionality and value as individuals are strongly tied to their continuous self-optimization through psychological means. As argued elsewhere,[3] this model of selfhood is not only consistent with the economic dictums of emotional self-management, authenticity and constant self-improvement characteristic of capitalist economy; it also provides legitimacy to these core economic demands by reformulating and reproducing them in the form of personality through psychological and emotional language. Thus, we understand happiness not as an emotion so much as a specific and normative model of selfhood defined primarily in psychological and emotional terms and strongly imbricated in and shaped by the market.

The argument laid out here resonates with critical sociological accounts of therapeutic culture.[4] It also resonates with previous critical analyses of the relationship between happiness and the market. In this latter regard, for instance, authors such as Sam

Binkley have pointed out that the contemporary psychological discourse of happiness

> facilitates the conversion of a logic of economic policy into one of personal, emotional and corporeal practice. The vitality, optimism, and 'positive emotion' that happiness inspires in us is none other than the refraction of enterprise as enshrined in neoliberal discourse, brought to bear against the vestiges of social government that we carry within ourselves. The disposition to opportunistically pursue the happy life is a reflection of neoliberalism's invocation to self-interested, competitive conduct.[5]

In what follows, we address the tight interconnection between the commodification of happiness in its many varieties and the main psychological features that all these commodities, in close association with scientific and expert knowledge, simultaneously presuppose and target as the prototypical personality of the optimally functioning, happy citizen (or *psytizen*). We propose that *emotional self-management*, *authenticity* and *flourishing* are the three psychological features that best define this personality and its articulation with the happiness industry. Although these three features are tightly interlocked, we address each of them separately.

Manage your emotions!

Self-management stands out as one of the key features that define the happy individual. Happy individuals are first and foremost those who know how to rationally and strategically manage their thoughts and feelings to motivate themselves, persist in the achievement of their goals even in the face of adverse circumstances, and act efficiently to maximize their chances of success. Self-help writers, coaches, positive psychologists and many other happiness experts all concur that the acquisition and development of self-steering abilities is of the utmost importance for attaining significant and desirable outcomes in virtually every sphere of their everyday lives[6] – e.g., as Peterson and Seligman wrote in their manual of the sanities, 'children, adolescents, and adults who consistently exercise the muscle of self-control are happier, more productive, and more successful individuals'.[7]

This assumption has been one of the main critical matters for many authors who, following Foucault's works, argue that the insistence on self-management contributes to the erroneous yet ideologically aligned claim that individuals can control their lives at will, thus making them more vulnerable to the belief that they are responsible for anything that happens to them.[8] This belief is further intensified by a positivist, scientific discourse that makes self-management an individual skill as well as a psychological trait, thus morphing an ideological demand into a natural, universal attribute. Happiness scientists indeed assume that individuals are equipped with a psychological mechanism or inner muscle which presumably allows the self to be completely governed by the self, especially when exercised and developed through the right psychological techniques.

Turn happiness into habit

This assumption provides fertile ground for a market that promises to expand people's self-governing capacities to improve their mental and physical health, prevent illnesses, cope with stress, deal with feelings of powerlessness, and rationalize failures in a more positive and productive manner. Individuals have a whole range of 'science-based' techniques available to them for exercising their self-control. These claim to be suitable to anyone's needs or situation. Such techniques include those aiming to change cognitive styles – defined as the way individuals rationalize the causes of their successes and failures[9] – and those focused on making frequent positive self-affirmations.[10] Others involve hope training – defined as 'goal-directed thinking in which people perceive that they can produce routes to desired goals (pathways thinking) and the requisite motivation to use those routes (agency thinking)'[11] – practising gratitude and forgiveness, or cultivating optimism – defined as 'an individual difference variable that reflects the extent to which people hold generalized favorable expectancies for their future'.[12]

All of these techniques share some features that are worth pointing out. On the one hand, these techniques are specially tailored for quick consumption. None of them aims at deeply or structurally changing the psyche. On the contrary, they are depicted as services focused solely on practical aspects which can be easily understood, controlled, managed and changed by individuals themselves. On the other hand, all of these techniques claim to offer fast and measurable returns on little investment and effort. Thus, instead of entailing thorough and complex psychological analyses, these techniques concentrate on providing easy, time-saving and theoretically affordable guidelines to problem-solving and effectively turning everyday drawbacks into productive stimuli.

To enable a more efficient commodification, these techniques obliterate any reference to the unconscious, in the first place. The unconscious, which by definition implies a lack of agency by assuming that certain aspects of the psyche are out of the reach of the individual, is instead replaced by the idea that the psyche in its totality is fully knowable, amenable to mathematical scrutiny, and wide open to manipulation by the individual herself or himself. Second, these techniques provide individuals with a non-technical and more colloquial language about the 'psyche' – e.g., optimism, hope, self-affirmations, gratitude, satisfaction, etc. – thus facilitating their use and understanding. This is especially relevant when individuals are depicted as 'self-therapists', that is, possessing the inner capacity to heal on their own, and the most complete knowledge and understanding about their particular needs, goals, problems, fears, etc. Third, these techniques depict self-control as a gentle process in which individuals should avoid any negative emotion, memory or self-valuation to instead focus on their achievements, strengths, positive feelings and memories, dreams, expectations, etc.

Ultimately, all of these techniques aim to turn happiness into a habit, that is, into a fully interiorized and automatized behaviour, an integral part of people's everyday chores. This goal is indeed a recurrent theme for positive psychology, coaching, and a whole genre of self-help literature that, from Samuel Smiles and Horatio Alger to Norman Vincent Peale, from Nicholas Hill up to Daniel Carnegie or Anthony Robbins, has insisted that the most efficient way of achieving happiness is to adopt its pursuit as a habit. For instance, positive psychologist Sonja Lyubomirsky has bluntly defended this same idea. In her famous book she concludes the following:

> Clearly, everyone's goal should be to turn positive thinking and behavior strategies into habits [. . .] Your aim should be to create the habit of instigating a happiness activity: Go ahead and forgive, savor, thrive, look on the bright side, and count your blessings. Aim to do it unconsciously and automatically. This kind of habit helps you get over the hump of implementing a happiness activity on a regular basis [. . .] This book's message can be understood as the exhortation to establish new, healthy habits. Because such activities as looking on the bright side, savoring the moment, practicing forgiveness, and striving for important life goals make a difference in your happiness, it is certainly a good idea to make a habit of doing them.[13]

In this line of thinking, concepts which combine the capacity for self-control with the effective management of the emotional life, such as 'emotional intelligence', have become of particular importance to defining the happy individual. Defined as 'the ability to perceive and accurately express emotion, to use emotion to facilitate thought, to understand emotions, and to manage emotions for emotional growth',[14] emotional intelligence has ceased to be considered an oxymoronic expression, to instead become one of the most important competencies that individuals must attain to successfully navigate in almost any sphere of life, acquiring special prominence in the world of labour in particular and in the market economy at large. Notions such as emotional intelligence are indeed expressions of a much wider social demand for emotional rationality, with emotions falling heavily into the private sphere of individual responsibility. Emotions are today at the centre of the self-care therapeutic ethos of neoliberal societies: they are considered one of the principal sources of mental and physical health and social adaptation, but also the source of suffering, maladjustment and mental and physical disorders, so it is demanded that individuals strive for their correct regulation and management. Accordingly, the demand for emotional self-management stands out as one of the key elements to incentivize consumption. This is so to the extent that what drives consumers today is not the desire for higher status so much as the desire to efficiently govern and control their own emotional life,[15] something that has been both shaped and channelled by a happiness industry that expands to the analogic as well as to the virtual market. We illustrate this point below.

Put the 'app' in your happiness
Consider the following example. With more than three million users in the English-language version, Happify is today amongst the most popular smartphone applications in a virtual market of happiness commodities that is growing exponentially. Like an increasing number of similar applications commonly sold under the labels 'Health & Fitness', 'Well-being', 'Self-help',

'Self-development' or simply 'Happiness' (e.g., Track Your Happiness, Happy Life, Happy Habits: Choose Happiness, Happier, The H(app)athon app), Happify allows monitoring in real time of the emotional state of individuals in order to provide them with examples of how to work on their positive emotions and thoughts, to instruct them in how to achieve higher goals in different spheres of their lives, or how to increase their levels of happiness. Full access to the application costs $14.95 a month (as of late 2018).

To use the application Happify, users first have to sign in specifying their personal goals, assess their initial levels of happiness, and fill in a reduced version of the VIA (Values in Action) Survey, the questionnaire developed by Seligman and Peterson's 'manual of sanities' in 2004 to spot the inner, authentic strengths in people. The application offers several tracks to follow. 'Cope better with stress', 'Feel less overwhelmed as a working parent', 'Motivate yourself to succeed', 'Find your calling' and 'Build a stronger marriage' are just some of them. The application also recommends some 'basic' tracks for users, such as 'Conquer negative thoughts'. This track is presented as a scientifically based activity created by Derrick Carpenter, a positive psychologist coach who holds a Master of Applied Positive Psychology from the University of Pennsylvania, and who 'coaches everyone from Fortune 500 executives to US Army officers and stay-at-home moms on positive psychology and emotional resilience'. The first two activities proposed in this track are 'uplift' and 'today's victories'. In both activities users are instructed in the power of positivity, encouraged to reflect on what they do, and coached to focus on what they have recently achieved for themselves. It is promised that if users get past their possible scepticism and follow instructions to the letter, they will be able to double their happiness scores within a few days.

When a track is completed, new tracks are featured for users to follow next. The application continuously rewards users with happiness points when tasks are performed well; monitors their emotional improvement as they go; and provides them with daily stats on their 'emotional fitness'. It also includes the possibility of cross-referring these emotional stats with physiological information, such as heart rate, sleep patterns and other physical activity captured through the supplementary use of smartwatches or the accelerometers included in many smartphones. Further, the application recommends users to share this real-time emotional and physical data with other users and friends in the 'community' section, to exchange tips and advice with other users, and to enter online challenges for 'who is happier'. Besides offers for regular users, Happify also offers specific packages for premium users under categories such as 'Family and kids', 'Love and intimacy' and 'Work and money'. One of the most remarkable packages is 'Business solutions', a specific modality addressed to training employees in positive emotions to become more productive, focused and engaged in the workplace. It promises workers 'a substantial return on a modest investment' through simple mind-changing exercises. A user testimonial included on the website says the following about this modality:

> The skills that I have learned on Happify have helped me deal with challenges in a different way. I also feel more motivated and productive at my job – I used to be a procrastinator, but I am a doer now. I no longer pile up my work, and I am thinking in a more positive way, which has increased my confidence and happiness about life.[16]

One of the most appealing aspects of these apps is that they all proudly claim to provide 'effective, evidence-based solutions for better emotional health and well-being in the 21st century'.[17] Science is used here to increase the app's added value. A quick look at the website soon leads the user to the section 'the experts behind Happify', where renowned positive psychologists such as Barbara Fredrickson or Sonja Lyubomirsky head a long list of psychologists, coaches and social scientists who vouch for the application. In this regard, the website announces that 'Happify's tracks were created with some of the best and brightest minds – experts, research scientists, and practitioners – who believe in what we are doing and are passionate about improving people's lives.' Benefits are actually mutual. Many happiness researchers see these kinds of smartphone applications as highly accessible, versatile and cost-effective technologies that would shape the future of happiness research and send it to new heights.[18] In 2016, the platform 'Happify Labs' was launched, aiming to 'collaborate with scientific researchers from around the world to accelerate the science in positive psychology and positive neuroscience'. The platform, which in 2017 had already raised $9 million, is able to access large-scale data on people's behavioural patterns, comments, feedbacks and personal records that could be used for scientific research. In this regard, one of the goals of the initiative is

> to enable the company to team up with academic researchers to conduct clinical trials on behavioral health interventions involving positive psychology and neuroscience. Researchers would gain access to data from Happify users. The unit works with commercial partners to improve access to affordable and readily available emotional health and well-being solutions. Ambitions for the new unit include addressing resilience, mindfulness, depression, anxiety, chronic pain and mood disorders on-demand.[19]

The success of Happify and similar happiness emodities hinges on the tight-knit and reciprocal relationship between the quantification and the commercialization of happiness. Whether happiness is a self-evident good – as positive psychologists and happiness economists claim – or not, the truth is that had it remained just as a quality or abstract value, happiness could not have been inscribed so strongly either in the political accounting systems of nations, or in mass-scale decision-making processes, or in the sphere of the market. For a certain domain to be governable and marketable, not only concepts and repertoires to speak and think about it are necessary, but also methods to quantify, assess, commensurate and calculate its efficiency as a value.[20] Measurement allows the calculation of the specific return that individuals and corporations can get in different realms of life through the consumption and application of happiness. It also adds a halo of credibility and legitimacy over commodities. Happify, in this sense, is sold to users not with the idea that it is simply fun or entertaining, but with the promise that its efficiency is scientifically sound – e.g., Happify claims that 86 per cent of its users show a significant increase of happiness after eight weeks of regular use.

The alleged positive balance between investment and benefits is indeed another of the main charms with which happiness science and industry have introduced and institutionalized happiness so powerfully within the spheres of politics, consumption and organizations. Happiness commodities are usually offered as cheap, win–win resources that bring straight benefits to consumers and third parties alike, be it in the form of more efficient coping abilities and prevention strategies – and hence monetary savings for individuals in psychological treatments – or higher and more durable mental and physical health – and hence monetary savings for health institutions and insurance companies – or better labour performance, greater motivation, higher task commitment and less absenteeism at work – and thus monetary savings for corporations with management and human resources issues.

Most importantly, the success of these kind of self-tracking applications highlights not only the extent to which it is demanded that individuals take responsibility for their own health status and sense of well-being, but also how willingly individuals agree to (and enjoy) monitoring and managing themselves daily. It is not surprising that these kind of applications are actually instruments for massive surveillance in which emotions, thoughts and body signals are used within mass-scale statistics to profile, research, predict and shape people's behaviour behind the promise of increasing their happiness. The most surprising issue here is the great extent to which individuals have come to engage in their own self-surveillance, for the profitability of big business. This is indicative of the fact that individuals of neoliberal societies, especially new generations, have strongly internalized the mantra that an examined and self-managed life is the life most worth living and spending. This mantra, as present in neoliberal ethics as it is in the scientific and popular discourse of happiness today, is further spread and channelled through these kinds of applications, which not only take this ideological demand for granted (and take for granted that users already take it for granted), but turn self-surveillance into a supposedly innocuous game.

Although these self-tracking applications might provide users with the feeling of being in full control of their psychic and emotional life, that is, of doing what is supposed to be best for their health and well-being, we argue that the applications tend to obscure some important issues. For instance, these applications obscure the fact that they encourage individuals to be extremely self-absorbed with their inner lives and make them constantly worried about how to achieve higher levels of control over their thoughts, emotions and bodies. The dark side of these applications is that they advance new forms of discontent related to the daily checking, monitoring and correcting of our inner states. In this sense, the alluring promise of complete self-management easily turns into a threat: not engaging in constant self-surveillance entails the danger of becoming unhappy and unruly beings that do not care much about themselves.

Furthermore, these applications obscure the fact that they reify interiority. As if these applications captured and quantified users' psyche with surgical precision, they give the appearance of turning interiority inside out, depicting it in an objective way through colourful images, numbers, charts and graphs. But instead of accurately monitoring and managing themselves, individuals rather perform their subjectivities and identities through these applications. In this sense, individuals would not be discovering and managing who they really are as much as shaping their selves according to certain assumptions about and demands on how they should think, act and feel. This also applies to the second feature explored here: authenticity.

Be yourself!

Authenticity is another core component in defining the happy personality. In his famous book *On Becoming a Person: A Therapist's View of Psychotherapy*, humanist psychologist Carl Rogers defined authenticity in a rather Kierkegaardian and existentialist fashion: 'to be that self that one truly is'.[21] According to Rogers, authenticity was about expressing one's own real feelings and thoughts without fear, 'rather than presenting an outward façade of one attitude while actually holding another attitude at a deeper or unconscious level'.[22] The process of becoming a person, thus, implied two main aspects. First, it entails realizing that the source of psychological problems lies within, and they are mainly a matter of personal perspective: 'Behavior is not directly influenced or determined by organic or cultural factors, but primarily (and perhaps only), by the perception of these elements. In other words the crucial element in the determination of behavior is the perceptual field of the individual.'[23] Second, the process of becoming a person entails discovering those competencies and skills which feel more authentic to the individual. This latter aspect was subsequently developed by Abraham Maslow. In his book *Motivation and Personality*, Maslow stated that self-realization resulted from finding and putting into practice what individuals are fitted for: 'A musician must make music, an artist must paint, a poet must write, if he is to be ultimately at peace with himself'.[24] Maslow claimed that individuals grow as persons by doing what they do best: practising their inner abilities and interests would lead individuals to a psychologically healthy and fulfilling life.

Positive psychologists draw heavily upon this humanistic approach to authenticity. According to them, authenticity is also about 'presenting oneself in a genuine way and acting in a sincere way', 'being without pretense' and 'taking responsibility for one's feelings and actions'.[25] Similarly, positive psychologists claim that individuals who act authentically achieve great and positive outcomes 'as a result of their focus on what they do best'.[26] Yet, contrary to humanist psychology and other similar cultural approaches before it – e.g., the Romantic movements in the second half of the nineteenth century,[27] some positive liberal approaches to liberty and individualism at the end of it,[28] and many religious and New Age movements during the twentieth century, especially in the United States[29] – positive psychologists take this notion of authenticity one step further and conceptualize it as a psychological personality trait by reframing it within an evolutionist and positivist perspective, thus portraying it as a stable characteristic of individuals rooted in biology and capable of being measured, classified and objectively described.

Authenticity as a trait

Peterson and Seligman's famous 'manual of sanities' is a good example of positive psychology's approach to authenticity. The authors argue that there exists a set of six universal 'virtues' and twenty-four 'strengths', all of which they claim to be universal and deeply 'grounded in biology through an evolutionary process that selected for these aspects of excellence as means of solving the important tasks necessary for survival of the species'.[30] Some of the virtues and strengths include 'creativity', 'persistence', 'self-control', 'emotional intelligence', 'good citizenship', 'leadership', 'hope' and 'spirituality'. According to these authors, the particular and quantitative combination of these virtues and strengths delineates the psychological features that would define what constitutes authenticity in each individual. According to Peterson and Seligman, all of these virtues and strengths are characterized by at least the following three features. First, they have to fulfil the individual, that is, to give him or her a sense of authenticity, invigoration and excitement. Second, they tend to produce desirable outcomes for those individuals who put them into practice. Third, as psychological traits, they are stable across different times and situations. Drawing upon these features, positive psychologists have spread the idea that individuals are naturally equipped with a certain set of inner psychological features which entail 'a particular way of behaving, thinking, or feeling that is authentic and energizing to the user'.[31]

From this perspective, authenticity is therefore presented as a critical feature for individuals to develop, and display across every public and private realm of their everyday lives. Positive psychologists assume that the more authentic individuals are, the more happiness they will get from their environments, relationships, choices and any endeavour that they undertake.[32] For instance, in the personal realm, an authentic life is presented as synonymous with a mentally healthy life. In this sense, authenticity would provide individuals with a high level of self-acceptance insofar as they do not act against their true nature, as well as with a great deal of self-esteem and a strong sense of self-efficacy. Both self-esteem and self-efficacy are characterized as fundamental, acting as psychological buffers against potential mental vulnerabilities and setbacks in life. In the social realm, authenticity is made synonymous with autonomy and independence. It is seen as characteristic of self-confident individuals, unafraid to express their true identities and lifestyles. Authentic individuals are also depicted as more reliable because they are presumably more 'congruent' and 'spontaneous', since they do not hide behind a facade. In the realm of labour, authenticity is deemed synonymous with high performance and work success, since authentic individuals presumably tend to choose the tasks for which they are naturally suited and prepared, and so on.

Most importantly here, authenticity becomes essential in an economic realm for which it is synonymous with utility. In this sense, individuals' authenticity appears as fundamental for a market that simultaneously presumes and spreads the idea that individuals shape their selves according to their tastes and preferences. The idea behind this is that every choice, made by any person, at any moment, reflects who they really are and what they really want. This does not mean that consumers are presumed to prefer authentic commodities over counterfeit products or staged experiences,[33] but does mean that any form of consumption is liable to both express and reaffirm at the same time an authentic choice that conforms to self-image.[34] The market and happiness science plainly overlap here. The difference is just a matter of emphasis: whereas the market defines authenticity as the act of choosing among a plurality of options that feel more or less suitable to oneself, positive psychologists and other happiness scientists define authenticity as the impulse to do what feels more natural and pleasurable. 'If something makes you feel good, embrace it' is a phrase that can be found in a commercial as well as in a positive psychology paper, a self-help book, or a coach's expensive training course.

Commodify your authenticity: people as brands

As authenticity stands out as a first-order social demand as well as a vital, scientific concept to define the happy person, it also becomes essential to a happiness industry offering advice on how to unveil and develop what is psychologically genuine in all of us. This advice comes from multiple fronts and takes many shapes. From the academic field, for instance, positive psychologists offer a wide range of methodologies enabling individuals to spot their inner and authentic skills and to guide them through the path of putting those capabilities into practice. In this regard, clients have a whole variety of tools at their disposal, such as the ISA (Individual Strengths Assessment) and the VIA (Values in Action) questionnaire, also implemented in smartphone applications such as Happify, mentioned earlier. From our point of view, these tools are all good examples of therapeutic services in which therapists and clients engage in a relationship of mutual exchange, and in which authenticity is to be understood as something that is negotiated and co-produced, rather than discovered.

Like self-management techniques, authenticity methodologies aiming to spot the authentic selves of individuals do not address deep psychological problems, traumas or negative aspects; rather, they offer clients a gentle, painless and quick process of self-discovery which only focuses on positive experiences, memories and perspectives. On the one hand, positive psychologists Linley and Burns emphasize that 'the questions that make up the ISA are all designed to encourage people to talk about their great experiences, their enjoyment, their best successes, who they are at their core, and when they are at their best',[35] since clients who focus on negative aspects tend to narrow their attentional focus, disengage and withdraw. On the other hand, methodologies such as the ISA promise that, within a few therapeutic sessions and follow-ups, clients are able to interiorize the self-discovery process and work on themselves on their own, turning this gentle sort of self-reflection into a habit – 'Assist your clients to develop habits of doing things they want to focus on and let that habit create a natural focus for them.'[36]

From professional and popular fields such as coaching, self-help literature, employment consultation or popular management, advice on authenticity is usually more focused on instructing individuals in how to turn the symbolic value of their genuine capacities into a powerful emotional and economic asset. In this sense, these professional development workers draw upon the repertoires and tools developed by positive psychologists but channel authenticity as an efficacious form of 'personal branding', a notion that has yielded a multitude of books, magazines, websites and training programmes, especially in the last few years. Authors such as Lair, Sullivan and Cheney have extensively and critically analysed the historical evolution and social consequences of this phenomenon. According to them, personal branding should be seen as much more than a simple and necessary strategy for individuals to make their way in a context of economic turmoil and work competition. These authors suggest personal branding as a remarkable symptom of the increasing process of responsibilization, as well as a useful concept to legitimize a highly individualized professional world that strongly resonates with the by-your-own-bootstraps mythos characteristic of neoliberal ideology.[37]

Personal branding is the example *par excellence* of the commodification of authenticity, that is, of self-commodification. Defined as the art of investing in oneself in order to improve one's chances of success, satisfaction and employability, this concept merges the principles of product development and promotion with the idea of authenticity to aim at the explicit self-packaging of individuals. Personal branding depicts individuals as trademarks who must define what makes them different, authentic and indispensable to others, what strengths and virtues they can offer

Happy selves on the market's shelves

that are distinguishable and profitable to others, what personal values they inspire in other people – self-improvement, ambition, grit, social abilities, creativity, etc. – and which strategies they can undertake in order to trade themselves most productively as a brand and hence improve their chances of work and business success. Once one's idiosyncrasy has been defined, the individual also has to learn the arts of self-expression and persuasion, acquiring social skills which allow him or her to influence people and manage relationships efficiently. To this effect, across hundreds of business magazines, internet sites and virtual platforms, innumerable coaches, consultants and personal advisors advertise their services in how to build a competitive personal brand on the basis of efficiently marketing and exploiting one's authentic capacities, especially on social media.

Authenticity 2.0

In her book *The Happiness Effect: How Social Media Is Driving a Generation to Appear Perfect at Any Cost*, Donna Freitas extensively analyses the impact that the pervasive discourse of happiness has had on the social networks, especially in younger generations. Among other issues, Freitas documents the extent to which teenagers have interiorized the idea that they must appear happy at any cost. This idea, she claims, goes beyond cultural, social and racial boundaries, permeating new generations indiscriminately.

The colleges and universities I visited were incredibly diverse – geographically, ethnically, socioeconomically, and in terms of their religious affiliation or lack of one and their level of prestige. Yet across them all, one unifying and central theme emerged as the most pressing social media issue students face: the importance of *appearing* happy. And not just happy but, as a number of students informed me, blissful, enraptured, even inspiring. I heard this at one of the most elite private institutions in the United States and

133

at a school that doesn't even appear high enough on the rankings for people to care where it ranks. The imperative transcends every demographic category [. . .] Students have learned that signs of sadness or vulnerability are often greeted with silence, rejection, or worst of all, bullying. The importance of appearing happy on social media – the duty to appear happy – even if you are severely depressed and lonely is so paramount that nearly everyone I spoke to mentioned it at some point. And some students spoke of virtually nothing else.[38]

The happiness imperative, already documented by authors such as Barbara Ehrenreich almost a decade ago,[39] seems to have found on social media today further cultural spread and dissemination, especially amongst the so-called digital natives. There is an ingrained, oppressive demand made on younger generations to curate, craft and communicate via social media an authentic yet only positive version of themselves. Indeed, failing to conform to a positive presentation of oneself to the rest of the world, including showing any trace of negativity, defeat, failure or even political signification, is overtly stigmatized and sanctioned by others, as well as being threatening to the sense of self-worth and social fitness of the youngest. The interviews conducted by Freitas in her study show that the concern with appearing happy among youth is 'so extreme that it can eventually sound almost pathological'.[40] In an additional survey she conducted on a wider sample of 884 students, 73 per cent actually responded affirmatively to the statement 'I try always to appear positive/happy with anything attached to my real name.' Furthermore, according to Freitas the youngest have deeply internalized the idea that an authentic albeit positive curation of self-image is actually necessary, since one's own image is very much understood as a brand that can be commodified. To this regard, 79 per cent of the students responded affirmatively to the statement 'I'm aware that my name is a brand and I need to cultivate it carefully.' In line with these results, one of the interviewees responded: 'I think [social media] is a good way to market. I think you can market yourself though it [. . .] I try to show myself in a positive light.'[41]

This idea manifests most vividly in the rising movement of 'YouTubers'. Also known as vloggers, the most successful, popular YouTubers have become leading examples of how to capitalize on identifying, defining and crafting their own identities and talents in order to sell their image and skills to millions. Regardless of the topic they talk about, from their own lives to how to use a lipstick or play certain videogames, what these YouTubers sell through low-budget videos made in their bedrooms is their personal brands. They sell who they are, their own voice, their private persona. That is what the YouTubers' business is about: reaping huge benefits from advertisement by exposing and thus commercializing their everyday lives. They do this by cultivating an authentic, unique and inspiring image. The positive therapeutic culture is now a part of this worldwide business, as well. A new 'vlogging cure movement' is emerging and expanding, attracting thousands of followers every day. More and more YouTubers have started to make a profitable business out of sharing their personal experiences of how to overcome troubles and personal disorders by positing themselves as living, lay examples of how it is possible to build a more authentic and positive viewpoint even in the face of adverse circumstances.

Interestingly, though, even the very idea of not being authentic can be lucratively commodified as a mark of authenticity. Consider in this regard the case of PewDiePie, the pseudonym for Felix Kjellberg, a 29-year-old Swedish gamer and comedian with more than 50 million followers, who rakes in 9 billion views all around the world and an annual revenue of $15 million. Today, he has his own production company. One of PewDiePie's most famous phrases is 'Don't be yourself. Be a pizza. Everybody loves pizza', which mocks this demand for authenticity. The phrase not only became extremely popular, but it made it into the publication of his own book collection of inspirational, funny quotes under the title *This Book Loves You*, which soon became a best-seller. The book was described as 'beautifully illustrated inspirational sayings by which you should live your life'. Undoubtedly, what PewDiePie sells is his own personal brand, that is, his own authentic and unique personality and worldview. Also undoubtedly, authenticity sells better, even if being authentic means mocking authenticity as a way of defining one's own personal brand.

Yet, as happiness researchers and experts including Seligman himself argue, while authenticity is crucial for the definition of the happy individual, perhaps no feature stands out more as a defining characteristic of the happy self than 'flourishing' and the closely related term 'self-development'. Next, we analyse this notion of flourishing.

And flourish!

In 2005 Seligman had another 'eureka' moment. This time, it did not happen in his garden, but while teaching in the Master of Applied Positive Psychology programme at the University of Pennsylvania, the headquarters of the positive psychology movement. According to his own account, a conversation with a brilliant student made Seligman suddenly realize that the theory of human happiness that he had sketched in his famous book *Authentic Happiness: Using the New Positive Psychology to Realize Your Potential for Lasting Fulfillment*, in 2002, neglected to emphasize the importance of a very crucial component: personal flourishing. This idea had started growing on him in 2003, when he wrote the preface of *Flourishing: Positive Psychology and the Life Well-Lived*, the first manual entirely devoted to the concept, edited by the important positive psychologists Corey Keyes and Jonathan Haidt and published by the American Psychological Association.[42] According to Seligman, flourishing is essential because it is the concept that best captures the close relationship between happiness and personal success.[43] For him, some successes in life might bring joy and contentment to people, but true happiness is only achieved when that success is well earned and only due to the development of one's own authentic capabilities, thus bringing individuals a genuine sense of personal growth. Otherwise, said Seligman, individuals could easily confuse happiness with pleasure.[44]

In this sense, the concept of flourishing helped positive psychologists distinguish their own academic niche from that of happiness economists, usually more focused on addressing happiness from a utilitarian, hedonic perspective. It also aimed to overcome some of the critiques raised against the ideological and tautological definition of happiness as a self-evident good. Thus, while happiness economists kept claiming to have no further external reason to justify why happiness was the most legitimate and universal goal for human beings – as Layard has repeatedly argued – Seligman's second revelation allowed positive psychologists to now claim to have a reason of their own: because pursuing happiness helps individuals thrive and develop their selves to their fullest potential and optimal functioning levels, this in turn explains why some people become healthier and more successful in life than others[45] – yet it might be well argued that this is no less an ideological and tautological reason than that of happiness economists. Happiness therefore would be good because it is not mainly about seeking pleasure, but about searching for personal betterment.

Following Seligman's lead, positive psychologists soon started to claim that flourishing was the most fundamental aspect of the definition of human happiness: 'I now think', said Seligman, 'that the gold standard for measuring well-being is flourishing, and that the goal of positive psychology is to increase flourishing.'[46] A whole array of new scientific evidence seemed to prove that flourishing was the most likely reason why some people end up better in life than others, with people in a permanent state of flourishing showing higher mental and physical health, more productivity, higher-quality marriages and friendships, more efficient coping with adversity, and fewer symptoms of depression when compared to those who do not flourish or who languish.[47] The underlying rationale is that people are not happier because they do better in life, but are happier and do better in life because they flourish. The rationale continues as follows: the more people flourish, the better they will perform and feel about themselves. Flourishing, therefore, would also explain why certain societies are more advanced and better developed than others. Seligman himself, for instance, illustrated this idea by claiming that if countries like Denmark lead the ranking of the happiest countries in the world, it is because 33 per cent of their citizens experience happiness as personal growth, whereas countries like Russia would be among the lowest-ranking countries because only 6 per cent of Russians experience flourishing.[48] In other words, societies would grow as their citizens flourish, instead of the other way around.

The key point here is actually the idea of a 'permanent state of flourishing'. The personal and social benefits that personal flourishing allegedly carries are actually and primarily associated with its suffix '-ing'. To flourish is a never-ending process: an end in view, not an end stage. It is in this regard that flourishing becomes a central concept (if not the most central) in the definition of the happy individual: it not only encompasses and articulates other central concepts such as self-management (of emotion and thoughts) and authenticity (strengths and virtues), but it best expresses happiness as a pursuit based on the constant improvement of the self. This idea, as we subsequently comment, fits squarely with the core demands of insatiability and constant self-improvement characteristic of advanced capitalist societies.

A new breed of 'happychondriacs': self-made individuals in constant self-making

As mentioned at the beginning of this chapter, the pursuit of happiness builds upon an ambivalent narrative of the self that is constructed upon two main pillars, which are to be seen as two faces of the same coin. First, there is a projective narrative in which the self psychologically unfolds and develops as it strives to catch up with the best version of itself; and second, a narrative of a fundamental incompleteness of the self or permanent state of 'un-self-realization' in which individuals always lack something, be it more efficient self-management skills, more accurate knowledge of ourselves, or more meaning, commitment, resilience and positive attitudes in our lives. In this sense, people are rendered as self-made individuals, albeit self-made individuals whose 'selves' are never completely or fully 'made' because it is presupposed that they can always be fuller and better.

This presents an important paradox: happiness, the primary vocation of which is claimed to be building fulfilling and more highly developed selves, must nevertheless generate a narrative in which non-fulfilment and permanent incompleteness are what actually define the self. Incessant incompleteness is one of the central 'knots' of the flourishing narrative, that is, what initiates and motivates it, helps it unfold and makes it work. No matter how successful the lives people might lead, the happy self must be constantly in the making, and thus in need of expert advice that helps individuals to carry out the ongoing project of pursuing the best part of themselves.

As previously mentioned, this paradox is fundamental to turning happiness into a perfect, invaluable commodity, in particular for a market economy that links the neoliberal ideal of limitless self-improvement to the principle of incessant consumption.[49] Not surprisingly, flourishing or self-development accounts for the biggest portion of a happiness industry that hinges on this incompleteness to market its commodities. From products and advice on beauty, fashion, fitness, nutrition, sex, marriage, friendship, business or work relationships to techniques and self-assessment methods for mastering and improving assertiveness, public speaking, stress and anger management, relaxation, resilience, cognitive flexibility or emotional skills, the underlying idea is that nobody is attractive enough, athletic enough, intimate enough, assertive enough, engaged enough, healthy enough, good enough or happy enough. There is always a new diet to follow, a vice to quit, a healthier habit to acquire, a treatment to try, a flaw to fix, a goal to accomplish, an experience to live, a need to meet, or time to optimize. As Carl Cederström and André Spicer point out:

> The only reasonable explanation for why self-improvement continues to grow year after year is that people restlessly keep trying new advice, irrespective of whether their previous attempts have worked [. . .] In a consumerist society, we are not meant to buy one pair of jeans and then be satisfied. The same goes for self-improvement. We are not expected to improve only one area of our lives. We are encouraged to upgrade all parts of our life, all at once. We should be fitter, happier, healthier, wealthier, smarter, calmer, and more productive – all at once, all today. And we are under pressure to show that we know how to lead the perfect life.[50]

Yet, while we concur with the bulk of Cederström and Spicer's argument, we argue that it is not personal perfection so much as normalizing the obsession with one's own self-improvement that the market seeks to induce in consumers. Certainly, the happiness industry thrives on producing a new breed of 'happychondriacs',[51] that is, by instilling in consumers the sense that the normal and most functional way of living is to be fixated on their inner selves, to be continuously preoccupied in correcting their psychological flaws, and to be permanently concerned with their own personal transformation and betterment.

Since we will further develop the relationship between happiness, normality and functionality in chapter 5, we will now illustrate the point made here by means of one example.

Become your best possible self

The Best Possible Self (BPS), developed in 2006 by the positive psychologists Kennon Sheldon and Sonja Lyubomirsky, is a popular exercise available in many self-help books, coaching courses and virtual platforms such as Happify. It can also be found in the Positive Psychology Toolkit, a compilation of scripts, exercises, activities, interventions, advice, and 'action cards' with 'detailed suggestions of how to build new positive habits into your life'[52] that positive psychologists have designed for happiness professionals to use with their clients, and sell for a monthly subscription (in late 2018) of $24. BPS consists of a series of fifteen-minute sessions where individuals are encouraged to picture what their future, most developed selves, look like – '"Think about your best possible self" means that you imagine yourself in the future, after everything has gone as well as it possibly could [. . .] Think of this as the realization of your life dreams, and of your own best potentials.'[53] According to Sheldon and Lyubomirsky, BPS advances higher levels of happiness because 'it allows an opportunity to learn about oneself, to illuminate and restructure one's priorities, and to gain better insight into one's motives and emotions'.[54] Picturing their best possible self helps individuals not only to improve a goal-focused attitude and gain a sense of future projection, but also to gain awareness of what they lack in the present so they can change it according to their ideal image. References to one's own past, though, should be avoided, so people do not get stuck in negative self-valuations and critical judgements. Alongside the experimental data used to prove that BPS is a 'potent intervention' to 'reap long-term emotional benefits',[55] Lyubomirsky adds the testimonial of a woman named Molly who privately shared her excitement about the exercise, which had helped her 'realize' that she 'could be doing more' to reach her goals, and that 'with a little effort' and persistence she would be able to 'achieve this best possible life' for herself. According to Lyubomirsky,

> Molly demonstrates several benefits of the Best Possible Self strategy. She gained insight into her goals and needs, recognized what might make her happy, and became more confident in how to get what she wants. She is now more likely to strive effortfully to achieve her dreams and, I hope, to be a happier person.[56]

The exercise puts forwards some points worth commenting on. The first one is the usual simplicity characteristic of this and many similar positive psychological exercises. The huge gap that lies between the great importance placed on flourishing and self-improvement by positive psychologists and the simple and almost naive kinds of exercises they propose to that effect is surprising. How can a fifteen-minute writing exercise yield any actual improvement in people's lives? All too often, these exercises give the impression of being little more than a solemnization of common sense (e.g., thinking about one's goals is expected to make anyone think about how to best achieve them), rather than scientific techniques. Undoubtedly, simplicity is a key ingredient with which to turn these self-improvement exercises into ideal commodities, promising substantial psychological and emotional returns while demanding little if any investment from suppliers and consumers alike. This and many similar techniques can indeed be understood as eclectic and uncomplicated 'technologies of the self[57] that draw upon a mixture of New Age teachings, talking cure schemes, stoicism, and a marked humanist background where the very commodity produced is nothing more than a performative process of narration in which individuals reorganize their experience as they tell it.

The simplicity of BPS and other similar techniques also opens up the question of whether these kinds of simple exercises actually work, and why. Positive psychologists maintain that their techniques and exercises yield demonstrable positive effects on people, despite the criticisms raised against their effectivity. Mongrain and Anselmo-Matthews, for instance, replicated two landmark positive psychological exercises. The authors compared the experimental situation (original exercises) with a control group (early memory exercise) and a 'positive placebo' group (positive memory exercise) created 'to assess whether there was anything "special" about the PPEs [positive psychological exercises] other than the access of positive self-representations'.[58] The conclusion was that the experimental situation yielded no significantly different results from the placebo situation. One suggested explanation after the study was that if some positive psychological exercises work it is mainly because people who usually engage with such exercises are already familiar with their logic. These people also tend to be highly motivated and interested in becoming happier. In this regard, these authors suggest that positive psychological exercises do not work for everyone; rather they work mainly for all those 'happiness seekers' who already believe in these activities.

Another possible explanation might lie in the fact that these kinds of exercises are remarkably inductive. In this sense, as these exercises already take for granted the claim that individuals are never as good as they could be, those who perform the exercises, whether they previously believed in them or not, are prompted to take on this very same assumption as true. The instructions for the BPS exercise as presented by Sheldon and Lyubomirsky, indeed, are already strongly biased in favour of their own hypothesis, hence inducing individuals to consider that (just as positive psychologists presume) they are not as developed as they could be and that the mere act of picturing or writing about better versions of themselves already yields strong positive benefits.

> You have been randomly assigned to think about your best possible self now, and during the next few weeks. 'Think about your best possible self' means that you imagine yourself in the future, *after everything has gone as well as it possibly could*. You have worked hard and succeeded at accomplishing all of your life goals. Think of this as the realization of your life dreams, and of your own best potentials. In all of these cases you are identifying the best possible way that things might turn out in your life, in order to help guide your decisions now. *You may not have thought about yourself in this way before, but research suggests that doing so can have a strong positive effect on your mood and life satisfaction*. So, we'd like to ask you to continue thinking in this way over the next few weeks, following up on the initial writing that you're about to do.[59]

The counterproductive consequences that these assumptions and beliefs might produce are also worth noting. Flourishing is indeed a good example of how happiness generates its own forms of suffering, as we have analysed elsewhere.[60] On the one hand, this is so because whereas flourishing posits the goal of self-development at the core of the definition of healthy, normal and effective functioning selves, what is *de facto* produced is a wide variety of permanently unhealthy, abnormal and dysfunctional selves.[61] Self-development is like a mirage on the horizon, a moving target with no given end in sight. Likewise, the injunction to continuously strive for higher levels of self-improvement breeds a paradoxical effect. Individuals might feel overburdened by this imperative, obsessively interpreting and evaluating everything they do, think and feel as only worthwhile insofar as it contributes to their own flourishing. In this regard, the pursuit of happiness might not be an antidote to suffering, nor flourishing the opposite of un-self-realization, because the same narratives that promote happiness and self-improvement engender the narratives of suffering and constant incompleteness on which they are built.

Thus, from this point of view, it seems that turning the pursuit of happiness into a *modus vivendi* might not always bring the positive effects that are promised and that many people expect to get. On the contrary, engaging with an incessant quest for personal advancement and betterment might easily turn into something exhausting, obsessive and, ultimately, disappointing. How many generations have already been told that the solution to their problems was to develop their true self but have unsuccessfully struggled to find it?

5

Happy is the new normal

The method of averting one's attention from evil and living simply in the light of good is splendid as long as it will work [. . .] But it breaks down impotently as soon as melancholy comes; and even though one be quite free from melancholy one's self, there is no doubt that healthy-mindedness is inadequate as a philosophical doctrine, because the evil facts which it refuses positively to account for are a genuine portion of reality; and they may after all be the best key to life's significance, and possibly the only openers of our eyes to the deepest levels of truth.

The Varieties of Religious Experience, William James

'I don't really get it', Jamie said as he lay on the floor to do his daily back and knee exercises. 'You're already pretty happy, aren't you? If you were really unhappy, this would make more sense, but you're not.' He paused. 'You're *not* unhappy, are you?'

'I *am* happy', I reassured him. 'Actually', I added, pleased to have an opportunity to show off my new expertise, 'most people are pretty happy – in a 2006 study, eighty-four percent of Americans ranked themselves as "very happy" or "pretty happy", and in a survey of forty-five countries, on average, people put themselves at 7 on a 1 to 10 scale and at 75 on a 1 to 100 scale. I just took the

Authentic Happiness Inventory Questionnaire myself, and on a range of 1 to 5, I scored a 3.92.'

'So if you're pretty happy, why do a happiness project?'

'I *am* happy – but I'm not as happy as I should be. I have such a good life, I want to appreciate it more – and live up to it better.' I had a hard time explaining it. 'I complain too much, I get annoyed more than I should. I should be more grateful. I think if I felt happier, I'd behave better.'

'Do you really think any of *this* is going to make a difference?' he asked, pointing to the printout of my first blank Resolutions Chart.

'Well, I'll find out.'

'Huh', he snorted. 'I guess so.'

I ran into even more skepticism soon after, at a cocktail party. The usual polite chitchat devolved into a conversation more closely resembling a Ph.D. dissertation defense when a longtime acquaintance openly scoffed at the idea of my happiness project.

'Your project is to see if you can make yourself happier? And you're not even depressed?' he asked.

'That's right', I answered, trying to look intelligent as I juggled a glass of wine, a napkin, and a fancy version of a pig in a blanket.

'No offense, but what's the point? I don't think examining how an ordinary person can become happier is very interesting.'

I wasn't sure how to answer. [. . .] 'I'll do my best', I answered. Then I walked away to find someone else to talk to.

This guy, discouraging as he'd been, hadn't actually hit on my real worry about my project: Was it supremely self-centered to spend so much effort on my own happiness?

I gave this question a lot of thought. In the end, I sided with the ancient philosophers and modern scientists who argue that working to be happier is a worthy goal.[1]

The above extract belongs to Gretchen Rubin's *The Happiness Project: Or, Why I Spent a Year Trying to Sing in the Morning,*

Clean My Closets, Fight Right, Read Aristotle, and Generally Have More Fun. The book remained on the *New York Times* best-seller list for 99 weeks following its release in 2009, even holding the number 1 spot several times. The fragment starts with a recreation of a conversation between Rubin and her husband Jamie and then moves to a conversation with someone she met at a party, neither of whom understand the point of trying to be happier when she is already happy enough.

Rubin's replies illustrate well the core assumptions underlying the scientific discourse of happiness, already addressed in this book. These include the depiction of happiness as a scientific, measurable state; happiness as a self-centred, self-dependent and individualistic endeavour; as an ongoing, never-ending project; as the worthiest goal in life to pursue; as, in short, the yardstick by which we should measure the worth of our biographies, the size of our successes and failures, and the magnitude of our personal and emotional development. The passage is certainly interesting because it also underlines the extent to which scientific and popular discourses on happiness come together around these same assumptions. This is rather explicit here. In this regard, Rubin not only justifies her 'happiness project' on the basis of allegedly well-informed, scientific knowledge on the topic; she also echoes line by line the script provided by happiness scientists. Indeed, the following piece written by positive psychologist Sonja Lyubomirsky – whom Rubin quotes in the book, by the way – could have been the final line in Rubin's passage:

All of us want to be happy, even if we don't admit it openly or choose to cloak our desire in different words. Whether our dreams are about professional success, spiritual fulfillment, a sense of connection, a purpose in life, or love and sex, we covet those things because ultimately we believe that they will make us happier. Yet few of us truly appreciate just how much we can improve our happiness or know precisely how to go about doing it. To step back and consider your deep-seated assumptions about how to become a happier person and whether it's even possible for you – what I hope this book will spur you to do – is to understand that becoming happier is realizable, that it's in your power, and that it's one of the most vital and momentous things that you can do for yourself and for those around you.[2]

More interesting for this chapter are some underlying assumptions featured in both the scientific and popular discourse of happiness and which Rubin's book clearly introduces. First, it is worth noting the extent to which Rubin connects happiness with goodness. Rubin justifies her search for more happiness not only on psychological grounds, that is, in the sense of higher personal development, but also on moral grounds: the happier a person is, the better a person becomes – e.g., 'I have such a good life, I want to appreciate it more – and live up to it better [. . .] I complain too much, I get annoyed more than I should. I should be more grateful. I think if I felt happier, I'd behave better.' The identification of happiness with goodness is by no means particular to Rubin's book, but a widely spread assumption tightly related to the contemporary notion of happiness, as well. As Alenka Zupančič argues, the maxim that a happy person is a good person is characteristic of a pervasive discourse that spreads a perverse kind of morality according to which 'a person who feels good (and is happy) is a good person; a person who feels bad is a bad person'. As Zupančič rightly points out, 'It is this short circuit between the immediate feelings/sensations and the moral value that gives its specific color to the contemporary ideological rhetoric of happiness.'[3]

Relatedly, and most interesting here, Rubin's book is a good example of the extent to which happiness has wormed itself into the very fabric of the ordinary. In this sense, Rubin's book should not only be read as one of the many apologetic examples instructing people on how they should organize their everyday experience and make it gravitate towards the pursuit of happiness. Her book should also be read as a symptom of the extent to which the psychological continuum 'happiness–unhappiness' has taken over the continuum 'functional–dysfunctional' – and with it, the continuums 'healthy–unhealthy', 'positive–negative', 'good–bad', 'normal–abnormal'. As argued hereafter, there is indeed a new zeitgeist according to which unhappiness has been made synonymous with malfunctioning, whereas happiness has come to outline the psychological standard of healthy, normal and functional lives. In this regard, it might be said that the language of happiness has progressively hijacked the language of functionality: today, happy has become the new normal, and positive psychologists, together with happiness economists and other happiness experts, professionals and popular writers, have widely contributed to shape, spread and legitimate this idea.

Revisiting the average person

Positive psychology's endeavour to expand the reach of psychology by shifting towards a more positive viewpoint on the study of health and human potential required not only presenting new notions to study scientifically. The offer made already in 2000 was indeed much more ambitious. Positive psychology aimed at turning happiness into a positive theory of personality through which to problematize the very concept of functionality, that is, a theory that challenged the psychological definition of what it is to perform, act and feel within standards and expectations of emotional and social fitness. As positive psychologists Sheldon and King bluntly put it in their 2001 paper 'Why Positive Psychology Is Necessary', the new science of happiness aimed at 'revisiting the average person' by interrogating 'what is the nature of the effectively functioning human being'.[4] Such interrogation suggested that the cut-off point that defined good, adaptive psychological and social functioning should be elevated.

Although a similar suggestion could actually be traced back to at least the 1950s works of Marie Jahoda – who defended the view that is was improper to talk about sick societies, since positive mental health was solely an individual and personal matter or, more precisely, a matter of the human mind[5] – positive psychologists pushed this idea further and with committed resolution. The field insisted on the idea that people should not be content to just do and feel fine, but should ask themselves how could they do and feel healthier and better. Otherwise they would languish instead of flourish. Not doing and feeling well enough started to be seen as just as insufficient and dysfunctional as not doing and feeling well at all. Pages and pages were filled with the idea that well-being was not the mere absence of depression, as health was not the mere absence of illness or normality the mere balance between good and bad, positive and negative. On the contrary, positivity, both emotionally and cognitively, should overcome negativity on the path to achieving effective balance and well-functioning psyches.

The correspondence made between positivity and functionality is expressly evident in the way positive psychologists address emotions and relate them to issues of effective, optimal functioning. In this regard, positive psychologists draw a sharp divide between what they consider positive and negative emotions – a divide that extends to the classification of thoughts, attitudes, habits and personal strengths – stating that they are two separate psychological entities that play antagonistic roles, yield different outcomes in life, and predict functional and dysfunctional behaviours, respectively. Thus, whereas positive emotions are claimed to advertise better citizens, productive workers, loving partners and resilient, healthy and flourishing individuals, emotions such as envy, hatred, angst, anger, sadness, boredom and nostalgia are deemed to prevent individuals from building strong psyches, developing healthy habits and building fluent, solid and long-lasting identities and social relationships. According to this viewpoint, functionality is not a matter of psychological and emotional balance, but a matter of higher positivity over negativity. Allegedly, the frequent experience of positive emotions relative to negative ones stands as the leading *cause* explaining why some people are more psychologically and socially fit than others – e.g., cope better with uncertainty, display more flexible behaviour, show fewer physical and mental problems, develop abilities more effectively, capitalize better on opportunities, live longer, build higher-quality social relationships, etc.[6]

Positive psychologists, indeed, successfully institutionalized a new, positive 'emotional hierarchy',[7] that is, a new set of coordinates to structure the psyche and society, to relate them, classify them and make them legible in emotional terms. If 'traditional', clinical psychology had created a hierarchy that distinguished between mental health and illness, positive psychologists introduced a new axis to differentiate between complete and incomplete mental health. Accordingly, someone with low symptoms of mental illness but with a negative balance of positive versus negative emotionality would be in a state of incomplete mental health. Only those who showed high levels of positivity and low symptoms of mental illness would be in a state of complete mental health. Thus, in other words, positive psychologists split the notion of health into two types: negative and positive. Aspects such as optimism, hope, self-esteem and well-being would now fall into the category of complete mental health, whereas pessimism, insecurity and dissatisfaction with life would fall into the category of incomplete mental health. Positive psychologists hence would take on the mission of working to discover the psychological features that profile individuals' effective functioning, and would devise the right positive techniques that would help people go beyond their baseline to achieve the status of complete mental health.

Just after the onset of the movement, critics such as Barbara Held argued that positive psychology's approach to human behaviour was founded upon the polarizing assumption that 'positivity is good and good for you, and negativity is bad and bad for you'.[8] For positive psychologists, only those behaviours that contribute to increasing individuals' happiness are rendered as functional and adaptive, whereas those emotions, thoughts and attitudes that fail to contribute to happiness or diminish it tend to be depicted as maladaptive and unhealthy. Already in 2002, Seligman had stated that positive psychology proved that whereas positive emotional and cognitive states advance functional and adaptive behaviours, negative emotional and cognitive states are 'maladaptive in most endeavours', this presumably accounting for why 'pessimists are losers in many fronts'.[9] Seligman indeed insisted that, contrary to negativity, positivity is always beneficial for individuals, even if that meant being positive 'at a cost perhaps of less realism'.[10] Some positive psychologists were aware that founding the field on this polarizing division between the different nature and functionality of positive and negative emotions was misguided. They claimed that 'it would be a major mistake to assume that all that is positive is good',[11] and forewarned that the main 'pitfall of focusing on positive emotional experiences as definitive of the good life is the tendency to view any negative emotion as problematic'.[12] However, this major, polarizing viewpoint grew and strengthened as the movement gained in visibility, popularity and authority.

In this regard, the work of Barbara Fredrickson, already awarded the Templeton Prize in Positive Psychology in 2000 for her famous 'broaden-and-build theory' on positive emotions, is very illustrative of this latter approach.[13] According to Fredrickson, positive and negative emotions are psychologically different, play distinctive roles, and define more and less functional persons, respectively. As stated in her theory, unlike negative emotions, positive ones would increase awareness and cognitive processes in a way that widens individuals' outlook on the world and allows them to take in more information about their surroundings, hence creating a broadening effect. Relatedly, contrary to negative emotions, positive ones would enable individuals to 'produce' durable and 'effective personal resources' such as 'competence (e.g., environmental mastery), meaning (e.g., purpose in life), optimism (e.g., pathways thinking), resilience, self-acceptance, positive relationships, as well as physical health', hence creating a building effect 'upon which people draw to navigate life's journey with greater success'.[14] From Fredrickson's perspective, people who exploit the 'broaden-and-build effects' of positive emotions are considered people who 'flourish' – that is, individuals who are both 'completely mentally healthy' and 'live within an optimal range of human functioning'.[15] Thus, the key point of the theory was that happy individuals 'don't simply feel good and do good', but rather 'do good by feeling good'.[16]

Fredrickson further hypothesized a natural, inherent opposition between positive and negative emotions, claiming that whereas negative emotions would have evolved for survival, positive emotions have been naturally selected for their effects on personal growth.[17] Positive and negative emotions were hence claimed to hold an inherent and functional incompatibility and asymmetry, which manifested at evolutionary, physiological, psychological and social levels. Regarding incompatibility, Fredrickson's 'undoing hypothesis' stated that 'positive emotions are somehow incompatible with negative emotions'.[18] Apparently, positive emotions would work as both 'buffers' and 'efficient antidotes for the lingering effects of negative emotions'.[19] Although she pointed out that the 'precise mechanisms' of this undoing effect 'remain unknown', according to Fredrickson it seemed beyond doubt that positive emotions help individuals lessen and counterbalance the harmful physiological, psychological and social resonance of negative emotions, such as a higher probability of cardiovascular problems, depression, or an impoverished display of coping strategies and socioemotional skills, respectively.[20] Resilient individuals were given as representative examples of 'expert users of the undoing effects of positive emotions', as well as examples of the causative effects of positive emotions on adaptive behaviour – since positive emotions 'build psychological resilience, not just reflect it'.[21]

Regarding asymmetry, Fredrickson claimed that 'whereas negativity dominates positivity in intensity, positivity dominates negativity in frequency',[22] meaning that for positive emotions to yield their broadening, building and undoing effects, ratios of positive emotions to negative ones should be at least 2.9:1.[23] For instance, for Fredrickson 'successful marriages are characterized by positivity ratios of about 5:1, whereas marriages on cascades toward dissolution have ratios of about 1:1'.[24] The reason given is that higher ratios of positive emotions to negative ones trigger 'upward spirals' that counter the 'downward spirals' of negativity and augment individuals' functional resources, 'including their cognitive resources (e.g., trait mindfulness), psychological resources (e.g., environmental mastery), social resources (e.g., positive relations with others), and physical resources (e.g., reduced illness symptoms)'.[25] Although Fredrickson carefully points out that too many positive emotions – e.g., ratios of about 11:1, according to Fredrickson and Losada[26] – could be somehow detrimental, positive psychologists generally claim that no signs of dysfunction are found even at very high levels of happiness and positivity.[27]

The widespread enthusiasm generated by Fredrickson and Losada's 'positivity ratios' – which, according to Fredrickson, entailed a 'huge discovery' in psychological science[28] – waned significantly after the publication of Brown, Sokal and Friedman's devastating critique in 2013. In their paper, Brown and colleagues thoroughly examined the theoretical and methodological foundations of this ratio, especially the use of differential equations to justify its existence. Whereas Fredrickson stated that these equations provided solid mathematical evidence for the 'tipping point beyond which the full impact of positive emotions becomes unleashed',[29] Brown and colleagues convincingly argued the contrary, claiming that 'the existence of a critical minimum positivity ratio of 2.9013 is entirely unfounded' on the basis of this method.[30] Brown and colleagues, indeed, said they were 'surprised' that nobody had actually questioned the rationale behind the notion of positive ratios:

> Fredrickson and Losada (2005) in effect claimed – on the basis of an analysis of verbal statements made in a series of one-hour meetings held in a laboratory setting by business teams of exactly eight people, combined with some solemn invocations of the Lorenz equations – to have discovered a universal truth about human emotions, valid for individuals, couples, and groups of arbitrary size and capable of being expressed numerically to five significant digits [. . .] Purely on that basis we are surprised that, apparently, no researchers have critically questioned this claim, or the reasoning on which it was based.[31]

Fredrickson herself acknowledged this critique in her response to the paper, claiming that 'I've come to see sufficient reason to question the particular mathematical framework Losada and I adopted to represent and test the concept of a critical tipping point positivity ratio that bifurcates mental health into human flourishing and human languishing.'[32] In saying this, she nevertheless claimed that there was no reason to 'throw out the proverbial baby with the bath water', adding that the theoretical bases of the positivity ratios 'not only remain unchallenged but stand now on even firmer empirical footing'.[33] According to Fredrickson, although the mathematical foundation which the positivity ratio was founded on 'no longer seems to be a steady platform', it was still safe to claim that 'higher is better' when it comes to positive emotions compared to negative ones. She argues that this is the case for understanding and nurturing optimal human functioning: 'the claim that flourishing mental health is associated with higher positivity ratios than is non-flourishing remains unchallenged'.[34]

A fallacious divide

The mathematics behind the positivity ratios was entirely misleading, as was the theoretical and functional divide that positive psychology posited between positive and negative emotions. Far from remaining unchallenged, as suggested by Fredrickson, this distinction has various pitfalls, omissions and mistakes that are worth pointing out. On the one hand, the general framework for emotions provided by positive psychology is rather reductionist. Emotions are complex experiences that encompass a broad range of different and imperfectly related phenomena, such as feelings (bodily and sensory changes and perceptions), appraisals (awareness and subjective valuations), performances (communicative and expressive patterns), historical and cultural meanings (shared connotations, values and narratives), and social structures (embedded scripts, norms, rules, and social patterns of behaviour).[35] Positive psychology, by contrast, clings to a naturalistic approach to emotions, understanding 'emotions as inherent'[36] – i.e., emotions as a fixed set of universal states – which both asocial and ahistorical conceptualization neglects the very complexity and multifarious nature of emotions, as shown in several historical, psychological and sociological approaches to the concept.[37]

Relatedly, positive psychologists fail to grasp that emotions are as much properties of groups, communities and societies as they are of individuals. This is not only because emotions have an interpersonal functionality, such as communication, persuasion and identification, but because any emotion inheres in cultural and social meanings,[38] as well as in class, gender and racial issues.[39] Positive psychologists' approach to emotions also overlooks the extent to which the emotional life of individuals is intricately connected to changing patterns of choice and consumption,[40] as well as to social structures – i.e., social situations and power relations.[41] Positive psychologists also neglect the fact that emotions are ways of defining and negotiating social relations and personal views of the self within certain moral orders.[42] Indeed, despite the numerous studies stressing the morality of happiness,[43] positive psychologists opt instead for evolutionist and positivist perspectives that minimize, neutralize and even reject the deep moral content that saturates notions such as personal fulfilment, well-being and self-realization.

On the other hand, the sharp divide between positive and negative emotions drawn by positive psychology neglects the fact that when it comes to emotions, positive and negative cannot be separated if we are to make good sense,[44] either sociologically or psychologically. Ambivalent feelings colour any event in life. The news that a relative has just passed away after a long and painful disease might make an individual sad and relieved at the same time, just as shoplifting might cause blends of guilt and excitement, or watching a horror movie could incite both fear and enjoyment. It would therefore be inaccurate to understand emotions as separate entities with precise contours or as combinations of simpler or more basic feelings. As Jerome Kagan points out, although 'agents, observers, and scientists are often forced to select one term from a set of mutually exclusive categories, such as afraid, sad, happy, guilty, surprised, or angry, [what] individuals often experience [is] a combination of the states that these abstract concepts name'[45], that is, an emotional blend for which we have no name but which should itself be regarded as a coherent and irreducible emotional state, not as a mere addition of supposedly more basic and simpler emotions. In this regard, it might be said that there is neither a specific state or experience that can be unambiguously called 'happiness', nor a state or experience that is not at the same time good and bad, positive and negative, pleasant and unpleasant, functional and dysfunctional.

Similarly, the claim that positive emotions yield positive outcomes and negative emotions lead to negative results is oversimplistic. For instance, emotions such as hope always combine an energizing wish or belief that the desired outcome will occur with the anxiety or fear that it will not.[46] Joyfulness propels individuals to engage in challenging activities, but also to be less persistent in the face of difficult tasks, to make less accurate choices, to take higher risks, and to facilitate conformity and acquiescence.[47] Forgiveness might reduce hostility towards others, or might increase it in certain circumstances. For example, forgiveness might be beneficial for couples who seldom engage in arguments, but detrimental to those who frequently fight.[48] Emotions such as anger might lead to destructive behaviours and to inflicting humiliation, but also to challenging authority and to tightening interpersonal and communal bonds in the face of injustice or shared threats.[49] Nostalgia might drive individuals to sadness and longing for the past, but it can also repair that longing with a particular belonging, pushing people to engage in critical retrospective and prospective thinking, and to build or strengthen common identities.[50] Envy might lead towards resentment and hostility, but it is also associated with increased effort, attentional shift towards means to attain a desired goal, and admiration.[51] As for positivity, it is not always beneficial and advantageous either. Optimistic anticipations of future outcomes, for instance, might increase the risk of depression when faced with negative life events,[52] and positive moods might increase emotional disengagement and prevent care, empathy and solidarity with others under specific circumstances – e.g., Tan and Forgas showed that 'happy mood increased selfishness when allocating resources in the dictator game compared to sad individuals, both in a public setting and in the laboratory'.[53] In this latter regard, it has also been argued that whereas positive emotionality might increase subjective empathy, it is often associated with a decrease in empathic objective performance, as well as with increased stereotyping and judgement errors in explaining own and others' behaviour[54] – e.g., people in a positive mood tend to ignore situational factors and are more likely to succumb to inferential biases than people in a negative mood.[55]

Relatedly, the ingrained assumption in happiness science that, contrary to negative emotions, positive ones best build character and better hold society together[56] does not stand sociological and historical analysis. See, for example, Smail's analysis of hatred and virtuosity in late-medieval society,[57] Barbalet's analysis of shame and social order in the eighteenth century,[58] or Cahill's work on embarrassment and trust.[59] Emotions such as envy, humiliation, fear and anger are as favourable or unfavourable to building personality and social cohesion as are love or compassion. Although emotions such as frustration, resentment and hatred tend to be depicted as failures in the formation of the psyche, as well as detrimental and even inimical to social relations, these emotions stand out as the main driving factors in the formation of crucial everyday social dynamics, such as group cohesiveness or collective movements – for instance, Hochschild has pointed out that in the late 1960s the women's movement grew stronger and more effective by proclaiming a shared resentment towards husbands, fathers, employers and other men in their quest for liberation.[60] Hatred pushes individuals forward to take up social and individual action in the face of oppression, showing when resources are unfairly distributed or threatened, or when individuals experience a lack of recognition, that is, a form of social disrespect or annihilation of one's social being.[61] In this regard, emotions such as hatred are as essential to political action and reaction as they are to one's sense of worth and identity. Positive psychologists, by claiming to turn these emotions into positive ones in order to render them adaptive and valuable, do not just expunge these emotions from their personal and social functionality, but also strip them of their core political nature.

Positive psychologists, hence, should acknowledge the fact that when it comes to emotions there are no secondary characters or a priori functional or dysfunctional outcomes. On the contrary, any emotion provides essential information about how individuals construct their personal narratives, relate to others, navigate in their social environment, and cope with the hardships, pressures and opportunities of everyday life. Emotions also provide crucial insights into the social and political incentives that move and drive individuals and groups of individuals towards action, mobilization, cohesiveness and change. The main challenge, thus, is to fully grasp the functionality of every emotion and the role that each emotional response plays in shaping, maintaining or challenging certain individual, social and cultural dynamics in certain contexts – such as personal and social identities, joint action, collective humour, mutual recognition, political resistance, consumption or national memory – not to disregard some of them by claiming that they have natural or inherent negative and hence dysfunctional or maladaptive properties.

In the face of this sound criticism, some positive psychologists have very recently started to defend what they call a 'second wave positive psychology', that is, a more sensitive approach to human happiness that includes a more dialectic and integrative approach regarding its characteristic positive/negative divide.[62]

Nevertheless, whether this reforming suggestion would help move the field towards a more reflexive position or not, the fact that such kinds of claims have begun to emerge even from its own ranks evidences the extent to which the positive/negative divide is firmly established in the field – as well as in many other popular and professional discourses on human happiness which draw upon it.

Persuasive and numerous criticisms notwithstanding, this positive emotional discourse – that fetishizes happiness, reduces the notion of functionality to the exclusive realm of the psychological, and identifies health, success and self-improvement with high levels of positivity – enjoys widespread acceptance in happiness science today. Paradoxically, far from overcoming the alleged negative bias of traditional psychotherapy, the strong, polarizing division of positive and functional emotions versus negative and dysfunctional ones brought forward new ways of pathologization, that is, a new emotional stratification according to which negative people do not qualify for leading completely healthy, functional lives. Getting rid of undesirable memories, negative feelings and judgemental self-valuations to instead adopt an optimistic inclination towards life seems to have been established as an emotional requisite for preserving a subjective sense of well-being and self-worth.

Keep resilient and don't worry

Years before starting the business of positive psychology, Seligman had devoted most of his academic career to studying the concept of 'learned helplessness'. His paper 'Learned Helplessness', published in the *Annual Review of Medicine* in 1972, and his book *Helplessness: On Depression, Development, and Death*, published in 1975, generated enormous impact and attention. The concept of learned helplessness showed how, in objective conditions of induced impotence, individuals tended to accept their situation and normalize it, understanding that there was little they could do to effect any change over those situations. From our point of view, the concept is in itself very interesting, and could have contributed to the understanding of mechanisms of social reproduction and transformation in which feelings of powerlessness and vulnerability play a decisive role in the use and distribution of power; the display of coercive strategies in certain organizations; or the defusing of public outrage by replacing it with conformity and apathy. However, this is not the direction that Seligman and many other psychologists building upon the concept chose to explore. Instead, Seligman was interested only in a very specific issue, which we may dub a Darwinian one: within the experimental condition of helplessness, some subjects refused to remain passive and continued to look for ways to avoid the helplessness situation. Seligman (somewhat tautologically) attributed this fact to psychological individual traits such as optimism: people who did not resign themselves to an unfortunate circumstance were featured as optimists – at the same time that optimism was defined as the psychological innate capacity to not succumb to misfortunes. According to Seligman, some people just had that way of reframing adversities not only to overcome them but also to learn and to grow from them. This is today known as resilience.

In the prestigious *Harvard Business Review* Seligman published the article 'Building Resilience', where he offers a striking example of the view that if success is caused by resilience, then lack of success, unemployment and downward mobility are conversely and logically the result of a weak psychic make-up.

Douglas and Walter, two University of Pennsylvania MBA graduates, were laid off by their Wall Street companies 18 months ago. Both went into a tailspin: They were sad, listless, indecisive, and anxious about the future. For Douglas, the mood was transient. After two weeks he told himself, 'It's not you; it's the economy going through a bad patch. I'm good at what I do, and there will be a market for my skills.' He updated his résumé and sent it to a dozen New York firms, all of which rejected him. He then tried six companies in his Ohio hometown and eventually landed a position. Walter, by contrast, spiraled into hopelessness: 'I got fired because I can't perform under pressure', he thought. 'I'm not cut out for finance. The economy will take years to recover.' Even as the market improved, he didn't look for another job; he ended up moving back in with his parents.

Douglas and Walter (actually composites based on interviewees) stand at opposite ends of the continuum of reactions to failure. The Douglases of the world bounce back after a brief period of malaise; within a year they've grown because of the experience. The Walters go from sadness to depression to a paralyzing fear of the future. Yet failure is a nearly inevitable part of work; and along with dashed romance, it is one of life's most common traumas. People like Walter are almost certain to find their careers stymied, and companies full of such employees are doomed in hard times. It is people like Douglas who rise to the top, and whom organizations must recruit and retain in order to succeed. But how can you tell who is a Walter and who is a Douglas? And can Walters become Douglases?[63]

The answer to the first question was that Douglases are more resilient than Walters; that is, Douglases 'rise to the top' because they have the capacity to transform adversity into opportunity, suffering into personal victories, negativity into existential positivity. According to Seligman, the world smiles on those who try hard and smile back, no matter what, and the competitive, unstable and precarious world of labour is no exception. As for negativity, all is not lost. On the contrary, there is still a way in which negativity can be used to one's own advantage. Although for positive psychologists negativity is bad for almost any endeavour people undertake in life, these scientists also have the remedy for the disease they have helped to create. Insofar as negative thoughts and emotions are morphed into something positive, that is, insofar as they can be 'positivized' and turned into means for personal growth and flourishing, negativity can teach us a positive, powerful lesson.

Positive psychology asserts that resilient people thrive because they are psychologically buffered against potential feelings of defeat, 'bounce back and beyond' to sustain effort and attain success even in the face of misfortune or stressful circumstances, and capitalize well on their positive emotions after reframing negativity into positive coping resources:[64] 'Being able to move on despite negative stressors does not demonstrate luck on the part of those successful individuals but demonstrates a concept known as resilience.'[65] Following Seligman's story, resilience, as he mentioned, was one of the crucial aspects that distinguished Douglas from Walter – 'The Douglases of the world bounce back after a brief period of malaise; within a year they've grown because of the experience. The Walters go from sadness to depression to a paralyzing fear of the future.' Thus, inquiring into the personality and psychological dimensions that made people resist and grow through adversity would teach positive psychologists the ways in which they could make Walters become Douglases. According to Seligman, years of scientific study of the concept had finally helped positive psychologists find the psychological keys to scientifically ground and rigorously accomplish this task: 'We have learned not only how to distinguish those who will grow after failure from those who will collapse, but also how to build the skills of people in the latter category', continued Seligman.

However, positive psychology did not invent resilience. Quite the contrary: it had been present in both academic and non-academic contexts some decades before the foundation of the field. In the academic realm, for example, scholars such as Michael Rutter and Ann Masten in the late 1980s and 1990s had already talked about the psychological mechanisms that protected people from adversity and predicted successful adaptation despite challenging or threatening events.[66] In non-academic fields, the concept of resilience had been popularized by bestselling authors such as Dave Pelzer in 1995 in the United States, with the book *A Child Called 'It': One Child's Courage to Survive*, or Boris Cyrulnik in 1999 in France, with the book *Un merveilleux malheur* (*A Wonderful Misery*), all of them widely inspired by memoirs such as Viktor Frankl's 1946 *Man's Search for Meaning*. What all these stories had in common was that they related someone's traumatic experience and how they survived it. Also common is the narrative of self-improvement that they presented: people involved in those stories had not only survived tragedy, but most importantly, had been powerfully and positively transformed after going through it. For positive psychologists these stories proved that some people were not only more capable of bouncing back and beyond in the face of adversity, but also that a sort of 'adversarial growth' followed trauma. Positive psychologists coined a term for this: post-traumatic growth (PTG), a concept that began to draw attention in the early 2000s and was consolidated in 2006 with the publication of the *Handbook of Posttraumatic Growth: Research and Practice*,[67] a handbook devoted to delineating the framework and background of the concept.

PTG was presented as a more specific concept than resilience, which applied especially to traumatic events and the people who had not only adapted well afterwards, but also experienced a sense of increased appreciation for life, a richer existential and spiritual life, a positive sense of rebirth, or an increased sense of personal authenticity and betterment.[68] Unlike post-traumatic stress disorder (PTSD), allegedly more characteristic of negative therapy – and too closely associated with the social nightmares of the Vietnam War – PTG would instead focus on the more positive endeavour of studying and nurturing narratives and experiences of personal flourishing in the aftermath of traumatic events[69] like cancer, heart attack, accidents, sexual abuse, catastrophes, terminal illness and war. Positive psychologists started gathering the testimonials of people who claimed to have experienced growth after trauma, from novels, biographies and their own research subjects. Findings, though inconclusive, seemed to suggest that 'people who are optimistic, intrinsically religious, and experience more positive affect'[70] were generally more likely to experience PTG.

More critical examinations of the concept challenge the scientific validity of PTG, pointing out that the notion might be more illusory and less a real phenomenon.[71] In more prosaic terms, it seemed that PTG was just a scientific way of expressing the common saying 'what does not kill you makes you stronger'. More prosaic even, PTG was also, if not mainly, about saving lots of money. People diagnosed with PTSD cost institutions and governments a disability payment of $3,000 a month for the rest of their lives, lawsuits aside. In his chapter 'Turning Trauma into Growth', Seligman suggested that 'that kind of money can lead to exaggerated and prolonged symptoms'.[72] Although he said he believed people were not malingering, he nevertheless mentioned that these diagnoses could indeed rob people of their pride and preclude them from the necessary motivation to improve their personal conditions. PTG would therefore focus not only on preventing trauma, but mainly on promoting and nurturing personal growth after tragedy – and, incidentally, on saving taxpayers some money.

Nevertheless, resilience and PTG are not circumscribed to therapeutics. On the contrary, these concepts have been powerfully introduced into the world of labour and even the military.

With his article 'Building Resilience' Seligman seemed to kill two birds with one stone. On the one hand, he wanted to promote positive psychology's progress on resilience by putting it before the regular readers of the magazine, including businesspeople, managers, coaches, personal development workers, and many organizations interested in concepts such as hardiness, grit and emotional toughness, all of whom had been applying happiness, resilience and other positive psychological concepts and techniques to labour since the early 2000s – as seen in the previous chapter. On the other hand, he wanted to promote positive psychology's progress on resilience in the military, something which he and other positive psychologists had recently started working on. In this regard, Seligman's article explicitly connected (and even equated) the working and military spheres, emphasizing how much these spheres could learn from each other: 'We believe that businesspeople can draw lessons from [resilience], particularly in times of failure and stagnation. Working with both individual soldiers (employees) and drill sergeants (managers), we are helping to create an army of Douglases who can turn their most difficult experiences into catalysts for improved performance.'[73]

Training modules on resilience and PTG have actually been star applications of the $145 million initiative Comprehensive Soldier Fitness (CSF) conducted in the US Army in close collaboration with positive psychologists such as Martin Seligman and Barbara Fredrickson. According to the father of positive psychology, in a matter of a few years the initiative in general and resilience training in particular have been successfully proven to increase soldiers' ability to adaptively respond to stressful demands in combat, to recover faster from traumatic events and to positively engage with their tasks.[74] Seligman's involvement with and enthusiasm for the CSF (he was so excited about it that he claimed his participation in the initiative to be completely *pro bono*) were not only evident in the way he encouraged schools and organizations to take note of the progress that resilience training had achieved with soldiers (which schools and organizations did, as shown in chapters 2 and 3). The same qualities were also manifest in his book of 2011, where he devoted a large part to disseminating the many benefits of the project, as well as to praising the indispensable work of the US Army with a great deal of patriotism and spirituality.[75]

Yet, despite Seligman's and many other positive psychologists' advocacy for the big scientific and practical successes reaped by the project, many others find that the CSF initiative has been largely criticized.[76] One of the first and harshest criticisms came from the Coalition for an Ethical Psychology, which raised several ethical concerns about the involuntary enlistment of soldiers in the programme; the possibility of the programme distracting their attention from other serious, adverse effects derived from combat exposure; moral doubts regarding efforts to build indomitable soldiers; and concerns about spirituality training inappropriately promoting Christianity.[77] The commission also raised concerns regarding the scientific validity and effectiveness of the programme, highlighting that the 'CSF evaluation research appears to be deeply flawed and recent claims that the program "works" appear to be gross misrepresentation of the data'.[78] Similar ethical, methodological and technical issues were raised by many other scholars,[79] including design problems; lack of pilot testing and control groups; use of non-empirically validated resilience training on soldiers; and significant revisions of and improvisations on the modules due to their lack of impact:

> In summary, of the main components of CSF, the Master Resilience Trainers have had only a very small effect on (self-reported) resilience and in some cases are not even providing any training at all, and the Comprehensive Resilience Modules have performed even

worse [. . .] The combination of skewed data, very small effect sizes, and the various confounding factors described earlier, makes it difficult to assert that soldiers are becoming much more resilient, even as measured by their self-reports.[80]

Moreover, aside from scientific, technical issues questioning their validity and effectiveness, the social and moral consequences derived from the discourse and uses of resilience in the army and organizations raise important questions. Are resilient soldiers who recover fast and easily from the atrocities they are forced to commit more estimable than those who suffer the terrible consequences? Are resilient workers, immune to the cruelties, exploitation and coercive strategies deployed by organizations, more admirable than their victims? That is very doubtful, both theoretically and morally. Further, resilience raises important questions about the social understanding and treatment of suffering. What about those who suffer for not being able to be resilient or keep a positive attitude in the face of adverse circumstances? What about those who struggle with the idea of not being able to feel happy or happy enough with their living conditions? Does not this resilient, positive discourse promote conformism and justify implicit hierarchies and ideologies? Does not the insistence on keeping a positive attitude regardless of circumstances actually deprive negative feelings of legitimacy and turn suffering into something useless and even despicable? We think it does.

Useless suffering

Cunégonde, the aristocratic heroine of Voltaire's novel *Candide*; Pollyanna Whittier, the young orphan of Eleanor Porter's classic of children's literature *Polyyanna*; and Guido Orefice, the main character of Roberto Benigni's film *Life is Beautiful*, all have something in common. Despite going through atrocious misfortunes and tragedies, they remain convinced that all is for the best in this valley of tears. Although life hits them hard, it is beautiful after all. The world could strip them of their honour, their family or their freedom, but it could never keep them from resorting to playing 'the glad game', an activity consisting in finding the positive side to every situation, no matter how miserable it may be. The dark reverse in the stories of these inspirational, loving characters is that happiness is presented as being as much a personal choice as suffering, so those who choose not to play the glad game are suspected of wanting misfortune, and therefore, responsible for it.

Presented in a less fictional vein, this message lies at the core of the scientific discourse of happiness in general and concepts such as resilience in particular. The novels presented above, the many happiness biographies available on the market of self-help literature, and the scientific concept of resilience all convey two main morals: that suffering is useless if no positive lesson is derived from it, and that prolonged suffering is a choice since no matter how inevitable some tragedies are, individuals have the power to find their way out of it. Happiness scientists, indeed, convey and frequently repeat the message that a positive outlook is available for everyone to adopt, regardless of their particular circumstances. If the stressed, the depressed, the marginalized, the exploited, the poor, the bankrupt, the addicted, the grieving, the ill, the lonely, the unemployed, the nostalgic, the failed and so forth do not lead happier and more fulfilling lives, it is because they have not tried hard enough; because they have not tuned up their mood and attitudes into a positive mode, or because they have not made lemonade out of the lemons that life gives to them. Consider the following example. When asked if focusing on positive emotions could actually be just a luxury that very few can afford given certain awful and challenging conditions in their lives, Barbara Fredrickson replied

I think positive emotions are available to everybody. There's been research done with people in slums across the globe and with prostitutes, looking at their well-being and satisfaction with life. The data suggest that positive emotions have less to do with material resources than we might think; it's really about your attitude and approach to your circumstances. Hard lives often appear worse to the outside observer. If we see somebody living on the streets, we think that person's life must be awful every minute. We think that having certain illnesses or physical limitations must be terrible all the time. But if you study people who have these illnesses or live on the streets, you find that they still feel good when they are with their friends or families, and they feel excited when they encounter something new, and so forth.[81]

Certainly, reframing the negative into the positive, or displaying a positive self-concept that helps to resist the inevitable drawbacks of life, might be as beneficial and recommendable in some circumstances as it is level-headed (see the discussion of positive psychological advice and the solemnization of common sense in chapter 4). That is not problematic. The problem arises when positivity turns into a tyrannical attitude that holds people responsible for most of their misfortunes and factual powerlessness, regardless of how myopic, ungrounded or unfair this may be. Even more problematic still is when a science of happiness claims that this tyrannical positive attitude is grounded in empirical, objective evidence. In a world where everyone is held responsible for their own suffering, there is little place for pity or compassion.[82] In a world where everyone is said to be inherently equipped with the required mechanisms to turn adversity into advantage, there is little room for complaint, either.

Questioning the existing state of affairs, defamiliarizing the familiar, and inquiring into the processes, meanings and practices that shape our identities and everyday behaviour are fundamental endeavours of social critical thinking.[83] Envisioning alternative and more liberating ways to live, organize desire, gear expectations, and provide justice and gratification are also part of it, since some degree of utopian thought is not just inevitable in, but indispensable to, both critical and constructive social analyses. Unsurprisingly, though, the ideology of happiness disables all that. This ideology presents itself as the banner of reality, yet it is by no means less utopian than any other attempt to perfect human nature and society, no matter how much happiness advocates, scientists and professionals claim otherwise. Those in power will always claim that reality is on their side,[84] not because of the accuracy of their claims, but mainly because they have the power to make these claims seem true. Positive psychologists like Fredrickson can afford to openly state that positive emotions and the good life are available to everyone irrespective of their circumstances, including homeless people and prostitutes, because these scientists have not only the authority to make such an unfounded and conservative claim, but also the authority to impose it.

That happiness scientists have often been belligerent towards critical social thinking is no secret, calling it negative, deceptive and even dishonest. These scientists believe that we should get rid of this kind of negativity because it only fuels pointless and fruitless claims for social and political change. For example, Ruut Veenhoven stated that negativity only fuelled pointless, fruitless and overstated claims for social and political change,[85] because allegedly there is already enough scientific evidence to prove that life is generally and globally getting better.[86] Such negative claims, he said, were only part of 'a long tradition of social criticism and apocalyptic prophecies'[87] fuelled by social theorists and journalists who, 'following the works of Marx, Freud, Durkheim, Riesman, Ritzer, or Putnam [. . .] earn their living dealing with social problems and for that reason tend to emphasize evil'.[88]

These intellectuals, he argued, spread a 'negative view' of modern society that veiled our awareness of actual improvement. Seligman had already elaborated this idea in similar terms, claiming that 'these social sciences have been muckraking, discovering a good deal about the institutions that make life difficult and even insufferable', but telling us nothing about 'how to minimize these disabling conditions'.[89]

These sorts of claims are not only scientifically disappointing insofar as they are historically naive and intellectually misinformed; they are also politically dangerous because they prompt us to accept the Panglossian and over-simplistic viewpoint that we already live in the best of all possible worlds. As Thomas, one of the main characters in Thomas Mann's novel *Buddenbrooks*, said, the point is not to simply accept that we live in the best of all possible worlds, which we cannot know; the point is rather to interrogate whether we live in the best of the worlds imaginable. That is what critical social thinking invites us to reflect about. Nonetheless, the tyranny of positive thinking tends to make us accept the former while preventing us from imagining the latter.

But repressing negative emotions and thoughts does not only contribute to justifying implicit social hierarchies and supporting certain ideologies. It also delegitimizes and banalizes suffering. The pervasive insistence on turning the impractical negative into a productive positive, so as to keep an optimistic attitude towards ourselves and the world, turns emotions such as anguish, anger and sorrow not only into something disruptive and undesirable, but, worse, into something fruitless, useless or 'for nothing', as Levinas said.[90] The Cunégondes, the Pollyannas and the Guidos of the world turn suffering not only into something offensive for those who do not suffer, but also into a less bearable and more humiliating feeling for those who do. Satisfied individuals who attribute the 'merit' of feeling happy with their lives to themselves feel entitled to blame those who do not feel the same for their irresponsibility in not making the right choices, adapting to adverse circumstances, and being flexible enough to take failures as opportunities to flourish and lead better lives. Sufferers, hence, have to deal not only with the individual burden of their own feelings, but also with the sensation of guilt derived from not being able to overcome their own circumstances. The tyranny of the positive prompts us to see sadness, hopelessness or mourning just as minor setbacks or fleeting stages in life that would go away if we tried hard enough. This suggests that negativity can and should disappear without leaving any trace or mark on the psyche – even more so now that positive psychologists have allegedly found the scientific way to replace despair with optimism. But the insistence to always look on the bright side of life, despite its good intentions, tends to hide some deep misunderstandings of and indifference towards those who really suffer.

William James claimed that in life there will always be real losses and real losers. Tragedy, whether small or major, cannot be avoided, if only because answering important moral questions such as 'how should I live?' always entails a situation where a good conflicts with another good. Only the narrow-minded fail to see the many possible selves and paths that have been sacrificed to become what we are and to live as we live.[91] There is not a single, more authentic or supreme self to become, nor is there a single and unequivocally supreme goal in life to pursue. This extends to the very idea of happiness. With any moral choice, whether exercised or imposed, personal or collective, some good is always sacrificed – some self worth becoming, some values worth fighting for, or some social projects worth achieving. Therein lies the irreducible tragedy that comes with choice and which is rooted in the very nature of everyday personal, social and political experience. Not even the best of the sciences of happiness could spare us from the small or major pains and losses that inextricably come with the small and major sacrifices that we make in life.

Conclusion

In his 1962 piece 'Instructions On How to Wind a Watch', the Argentinian writer Julio Cortázar wonderfully expressed the extent to which we have become obsessed with time and how that obsession has turned time from being our servant into our master. The watch in Cortázar's piece works as a metaphor for time:

> Think of this: When they present you with a watch they are gifting you with a tiny flowering hell, a wreath of roses, a dungeon of air [. . .] They aren't just giving you this minute stonecutter which will bind you by the wrist and walk along with you [. . .] They are gifting you with a new, fragile, and precarious piece of yourself, something that's yours but not part of your body, that you have to strap to your body like your belt, like a tiny, furious bit of something hanging onto your wrist. They gift you with the job of having to wind it every day, and obligation to wind it, so that it goes on being a watch; they gift you with the obsession of looking into jewelry-shop windows to check the exact time, check the radio announcer, check the telephone service. They give you the gift of fear, someone will steal it from you, it'll fall on the street and get broken. They give you the gist of your trademark and the assurance

that it's a trademark better than the others, they gift you with the impulse to compare your watch with other watches. They aren't giving you a watch, you are the gift.[1]

Cortázar's piece also provides a useful metaphor for what happiness has come to be today: an obsession, of course, but also a false and deceptive gift. Happiness is not a precious human treasure discovered by some disinterested people in white coats who have resolved to just hand happiness to people in order to liberate them, like Prometheus handing fire from Olympus to mere mortals. If anything, like the recipient of Cortázar's watch, we ourselves are the gift to happiness. Most of what we do on behalf of our happiness, beneficial or not, disappointing or not, deceitful or not, is first and foremost favourable and beneficial to those who claim to hold its truths. Engaging in the pursuit of happiness does not necessarily imply working for our better selves or for a better society, yet it always entails working for the very legitimacy, pervasiveness and power of happiness itself as a concept, as a business, as an industry, and as a consumerist lifestyle. Happiness has become useful to control our lives because we have become servants of its obsessive pursuit; because it is not happiness that stretches and adapts to us: to the chiaroscuros of our feelings, the ambiguities of our thoughts or the complex texture of our lives. It is rather we who have to stretch and adapt to fit happiness's consumerist logic, to comply with its tyrannical and veiled ideological demands, and to accept its narrow, reductionist and psychologistic assumptions. Realizing this might indeed be a disappointing feeling, given the expectations that happiness advocates create for us. But to think otherwise, that is, to not think critically, would just maintain the happiness machinery that a handful of powerful and influential scholars, experts and professionals have set in motion for us.

We honestly believe that the science of happiness helps some individuals, that some of its advice and methods do make people feel better, and that happiness might be an important and interesting concept to study from a scientific perspective. But we do not think that happiness is the supreme, self-evident good that positive psychologists, happiness economists and other happiness scientists and experts often brag about having discovered. On the contrary, in its current form and usages, happiness is a powerful tool for organizations and institutions to build more obedient workers, soldiers and citizens. The figure of obedience in our times takes the form of a work on and maximization of the self. In the eighteenth and nineteenth centuries the claim to individual happiness had a transgressive flavour. But through an ironic detour of history, happiness is now smoothly woven into the fabric of contemporary power.

If happiness was self-evident, as happiness scientists have tirelessly claimed, then we would not actually need scientists and experts to tell us: we would just know. And if it finally turns out that happiness is self-evidently good but everyone except these experts has so far been so blind as to not see it, then we think that happiness would be too important to be left in the hands of a dubious, reductionist science marked with ideological biases, embedded in the market, conveniently recycled for technocratic policies, and utterly compliant with the corporate world, with the army and with neoliberal education. There is, indeed, every reason to distrust the experts who claim to hold the secrets of happiness. We have seen where these claims come from, how they have been put to use, who benefited the most from them and what interests lie behind them. Furthermore, we have heard similar promises and claims many times before. Most fundamentally, we should distrust happiness advocates because despite their tired, enduring promises to hand us the keys to the good life, those keys are still nowhere to be found. All we have is 'words, words, words', just words, as Hamlet said to Polonius. To this day, indeed, while the extent to which people have benefited from the emergence and consolidation of the science of happiness is not clear, there is no doubt that positive psychologists, happiness economists and a whole array of personal development workers have reaped tremendous gains.

We have every reason also to believe that those psychological secrets will never arrive. This is so first and foremost because if there is any secret to happiness, any magic key to open its golden box, that secret might well not be of a psychological order. That psychology has the scientific keys to unveil every important social phenomenon is something that we have heard many times before, as well. Positive psychologists themselves claimed that they were not business-as-usual psychologists, but they have ended up being as 'usual' and as 'business' as they can be. Positive psychologists are convinced that we can understand happiness by digging into the minds of happy people in the very same way that other psychologists assure us that we can understand abuse by entering the bully's mind, success by digging in the minds of the successful, murder by digging in the minds of killers, or love, religion and terrorism by digging in the heads of lovers, believers and terrorists, respectively. Psychologists have been working under this assumption for so long that there is no reason to think this will change. The positive branch of psychology is no exception. Actually, too often it seems that both psychologists and positive psychologists would be prepared to repeat history just to not acknowledge their own history – their past excesses, their cultural roots and their ideological debts.

When discussing concepts such as happiness, psychologists in general, but in particular positive psychologists and happiness scientists, do not simply describe it, but rather shape and prescribe it. It escapes no one how convenient it seems that the psychological profile of the happy person portrayed by happiness advocates, and further spread and channelled through the market, match almost perfectly the self-made, self-managed and self-determined neoliberal portrait of the ideal citizen – epitomized in the figure of Gardner, in both its real-life and fictional depictions (as commented on in the Introduction). Indeed, what would be the odds that a really new, independent and unbiased science of happiness came to the conclusion that the very same psychological features that define the happy individual match perfectly the very psychological features that the neoliberal worldview assumes as the most desirable features for citizens to develop? What are the odds that the very same needs and demands for autonomy, flexibility, resilience, persistence and self-management characteristic of the emerging, unstable and competitive organizational setting so perfectly mirror the psychological profile of the happy worker provided by these scientists? To be sure, social science is not impermeable to ideological and economic influences. Nonetheless, these influences may not be sharper and clearer anywhere than in the science of happiness, whose evident institutional alliances, political intercourse and market embedment too frequently speak for themselves.

Social science is not infallible either. Yet happiness scientists and experts often talk as if they were unerring, garnishing their studies with a long assortment of expressions such as 'breakthrough findings', 'solid evidence', 'empirical discoveries' or 'undisputed benefits'. They often talk as if they were gurus, oracles or even enlightened. The main problem here, though, is not that everything these scientists say is wrong. What they say is often just common sense reformulated in a solemn, psychological jargon. The main problem, rather, is that everything these scientists and experts say is very easily accepted by many people willing to believe in their claims, despite a massive corpus of evidence against the main assumptions and claims of these experts and scientists. And the more data and evidence is produced to support claims in favour, the more and more analyses from multiple fronts that come to weaken, dispute and even refute that evidence. If anything, what the concept of happiness and its main advocates have actually proved is their inveterate resilience to facts and arguments against, whether coming from outside or from within their own ranks. More research and funding keep coming, though, because many people are still prone to believe in the possibility that they will some day get to know the real secrets of happiness.

This is somewhat understandable. Despite all the criticism, happiness has proved to be highly resilient because, as simple as it may seem, it instils in people a certain sense of hope, power and consolation. To an increasing number of people, the promise that, regardless of their vulnerable and disadvantaged situations, the pursuit of happiness would provide them with a way out is indeed of crucial importance. But happiness does not equal hope, let alone real power – at least not the reductionist, psychologist and supremacist vision of happiness these scholars and experts espouse. We should not let ourselves be beset by the belief that this kind of happiness will provide the way out of all our problems. The cult of happiness is at best a numbing distraction, not a cure for the deepening sense of vulnerability, powerlessness and anxiety. We should hence find a way out of happiness itself, that is, we should first question all these dangerous assumptions that come with it and which might very well sustain many of the problems that affect us. We certainly need hope, but we need it without the numbing, tyrannical, conformist and almost religious optimism that comes with happiness, as Terry Eagleton points out.[2] We need a kind of hope based on critical analysis, social justice and collective action, that is not paternalistic, that does not decide what is good for us on our behalf, and that does not aim to spare us from the worst, but that places us in a better position to confront it. Not as isolated individuals but together, as a society.

Conclusion

Interiority is no place where we want to build and spend our lives. It is not the place where we will be able to achieve any significant social change, either. We do not want to be controlled by dubious promises of self-transformation or to live obsessed with our thoughts, feelings and expectations of self-improvement. The intention of all those who are convinced that pursuing our happiness is in our very best interests is appreciated. Yet we must want to reject the offering. Otherwise, we could end up trying to chase the long shadow of that promised best version of ourselves, which, as in Zeno's paradox, never stops moving without ever reaching its aim. This moving arrow may in fact not only never reach its aim, but more importantly, may also have successfully distracted us from building a sense of togetherness and collectivity by emphasizing individuality and by stigmatizing any kind of negativity.

At the end of this study we must emphasize one more time the crucial character of negative feelings. Popular protests and social change are made of the accumulation of many angry and resentful citizens. To hide such negative feelings under the rug of positive thinking is to *de facto* stigmatize and make shameful the emotional structure of social malaise and unrest. Some will undoubtedly retort that we prefer to deprive hard-working citizens of the benefits of the science of well-being by waving some vague idea of collective consciousness. Happiness, some dyed-in-the-wool empiricists will claim, is the only tangible good we can put our hands on, here and now. The answer to this argument and our final objection can be found in a famous refutation of utilitarianism by the anarchist Harvard philosopher Robert Nozick, in 1974.[3] Nozick asked his readers to engage in a thought experiment that consisted in imagining that we are hooked up to a machine that provides whatever pleasurable experience we may wish. Our brains would hence be stimulated in such a way that we would believe we were living the life we

Conclusion

wanted. So Nozick's question was: given the choice, would you prefer the pleasurable machine to your real life (presumably, more miserable)? An answer to this question seems today even more relevant than before, especially now that the science of happiness (and virtual technologies) has become so dominant. Our answer, like Nozick's, is that pleasure and the pursuit of happiness cannot trump reality and the pursuit of knowledge – critical thinking about ourselves and the surrounding world. An 'experience machine' of the type that Nozick imagined and Huxley novelized is today the equivalent of a happiness industry that aims at controlling us: it not only blurs and confuses our very capacity to know the conditions that shape our existence; it also makes them irrelevant. Knowledge and justice, rather than happiness, remain the revolutionary moral purpose of our lives.

Notes

Introduction

1 Edgar Cabanas, '"Psytizens", or the Construction of Happy Individuals in Neoliberal Societies', in *Emotions as Commodities: Capitalism, Consumption and Authenticity*, ed. by Eva Illouz (London and New York: Routledge, 2018), pp. 173–96.

2 Thomas Piketty, Emmanuel Saez and Gabriel Zucman, *Distributional National Accounts: Methods and Estimates for the United States*, NBER Working Paper No. 22945, December 2016 <https://doi.org/10.3386/w22945>.

3 Jonathan J. B. Mijs, 'Visualizing Belief in Meritocracy, 1930–2010', *Socius: Sociological Research for a Dynamic World*, 4 (2018) <https://doi.org/10.1177/2378023118811805>.

4 Eva Illouz, *Oprah Winfrey and the Glamour of Misery: An Essay on Popular Culture* (New York: Columbia University Press, 2003).

5 http://www.margaretthatcher.org/document/104475

6 Eva Illouz, ed., *Emotions as Commodities: Capitalism, Consumption and Authenticity* (London and New York: Routledge, 2018).

7 Eva Illouz, *Saving the Modern Soul: Therapy, Emotions, and the Culture of Self-Help* (Berkeley and Los Angeles: University of California Press, 2008); Eva Illouz, *Cold Intimacies: The Making of Emotional Capitalism* (Cambridge: Polity, 2007); Illouz, *Oprah Winfrey and the Glamour of Misery*; Edgar Cabanas and Eva Illouz, 'The Making of a "Happy Worker": Positive Psychology in Neoliberal Organizations', in *Beyond*

the Cubicle: Insecurity Culture and the Flexible Self, ed. by Allison Pugh (New York: Oxford University Press, 2017), pp. 25–50; Edgar Cabanas and Eva Illouz, 'Fit fürs Gluck: Positive Psychologie und ihr Einfluss auf die Identität von Arbeitskräften in Neoliberalen Organisationen', *Verhaltenstherapie & Psychosoziale Praxis*, 47.3 (2015), 563–78; Edgar Cabanas, 'Rekindling Individualism, Consuming Emotions: Constructing "Psytizens" in the Age of Happiness', *Culture & Psychology*, 22.3 (2016), 467–80 <https://doi.org/10.1177/1354067X16655459>; Edgar Cabanas and José Carlos Sánchez-González, 'Inverting the Pyramid of Needs: Positive Psychology's New Order for Labor Success', *Psicothema*, 28.2 (2016), 107–13 <https://doi.org/10.7334/psicothema2015.267>; Cabanas, '"Psytizens", or the Construction of Happy Individuals'; Edgar Cabanas, 'Positive Psychology and the Legitimation of Individualism', *Theory & Psychology*, 28.1 (2018), 3–19 <https://doi.org/10.1177/0959354317747988>; Illouz, *Emotions as Commodities*. The authors wish to acknowledge that some paragraphs and sentences from these sources have been partially reproduced in this book.

8 Barbara Ehrenreich, *Smile or Die: How Positive Thinking Fooled America and the World* (London: Granta Books, 2009).

9 Barbara S. Held, 'The Tyranny of the Positive Attitude in America: Observation and Speculation', *Journal of Clinical Psychology*, 58.9 (2002), 965–91 <https://doi.org/10.1002/jclp. 10093>.

10 Sam Binkley, *Happiness as Enterprise: An Essay on Neoliberal Life* (New York: SUNY Press, 2014).

11 William Davies, *The Happiness Industry: How the Government and Big Business Sold Us Well-Being* (London and New York: Verso, 2015).

12 Carl Cederström and André Spicer, *The Wellness Syndrome* (Cambridge: Polity, 2015).

Chapter 1 Experts on your well-being

1 Martin E. P. Seligman, *Authentic Happiness: Using the New Positive Psychology to Realize Your Potential for Lasting Fulfillment* (New York: Free Press, 2002), p. 25.

2 http://www.apa.org/about/apa/archives/apa-history.aspx

3 Seligman, *Authentic Happiness*.

4 Seligman, *Authentic Happiness*, p. 25.
5 Seligman, *Authentic Happiness*, p. 28.
6 Seligman, *Authentic Happiness*, p. 28.
7 Martin E. P. Seligman and Mihaly Csikszentmihalyi, 'Positive Psychology: An Introduction', *American Psychologist*, 55 (2000), 5–14 <https://doi.org/10.1177/0022167801411002>, p. 6.
8 Martin E. P. Seligman, *Flourish: A New Understanding of Happiness and Well-Being – and How to Achieve Them* (London: Nicholas Brealey, 2011), p. 75.
9 Seligman and Csikszentmihalyi, 'Positive Psychology: An Introduction', p. 8.
10 Kristján Kristjánsson, 'Positive Psychology and Positive Education: Old Wine in New Bottles?', *Educational Psychologist*, 47.2 (2012), 86–105 <https://doi.org/10.1080/00461520.2011.610678>; Roberto García, Edgar Cabanas and José Carlos Loredo, 'La Cura Mental de Phineas P. Quimby y el Origen de la Psicoterapia Moderna', *Revista de Historia de La Psicología*, 36.1 (2015), 135–54; Dana Becker and Jeanne Marecek, 'Positive Psychology: History in the Remaking?', *Theory & Psychology*, 18.5 (2008), 591–604 <https://doi.org/10.1177/0959354308093397>; Eugene Taylor, 'Positive Psychology and Humanistic Psychology: A Reply to Seligman', *Journal of Humanistic Psychology*, 41 (2001), 13–29 <https://doi.org/10.1177/0022167801411003>.
11 Seligman and Csikszentmihalyi, 'Positive Psychology: An Introduction', p. 13.
12 Martin E. P. Seligman and Mihaly Csikszentmihalyi, '"Positive Psychology: An Introduction": Reply', *American Psychologist*, 56 (2001), 89–90 <https://doi.org/10.1037/0003-066X.56.1.89>, p. 90.
13 Martin E. P. Seligman, *Learned Optimism: How to Change Your Mind and Your Life* (New York: Pocket Books, 1990), p. 291.
14 Seligman and Csikszentmihalyi, 'Positive Psychology: An Introduction', p. 6.
15 Seligman and Csikszentmihalyi, 'Positive Psychology: An Introduction', p. 13.
16 Seligman, *Flourish*, p. 7.
17 C. R. Snyder, Shane J. Lopez, Lisa Aspinwall, Barbara L. Fredrickson, Jon Haidt, Dacher Keltner and others, 'The Future of Positive Psychology: A Declaration of Independence', in *Handbook of Positive Psychology*, ed. by

C. R. Snyder and Shane J. Lopez (New York: Oxford University Press, 2002), pp. 751–67, p. 752, emphasis in the original.

18 Martin E. P. Seligman, 'Building Resilience', *Harvard Business Review*, April 2011 <https://hbr.org/2011/04/building-resilience>, para. 7.

19 Bruce E. Levine, 'Psychologists Profit on Unending U.S. Wars by Teaching Positive Thinking to Soldiers', *Huffpost*, 22 July 2010 <https://www.huffingtonpost.com/bruce-e-levine/psychologists-profit-on-u_b_655400.html?guccounter=1>.

20 Christopher Peterson and Martin E. P. Seligman, *Character Strengths and Virtues: A Handbook and Classification* (New York: Oxford University Press, 2004), p. 4.

21 Peterson and Seligman, *Character Strengths and Virtues*, p. 5.

22 Peterson and Seligman, *Character Strengths and Virtues*, p. 6.

23 Ryan M. Niemiec, 'VIA Character Strengths: Research and Practice (The First 10 Years)', in *Well-Being and Cultures: Perspectives from Positive Psychology*, ed. by Hans Henrik Knoop and Antonella Delle Fave (Dordrecht and Heidelberg: Springer Netherlands, 2013), pp. 11–29 <https://doi.org/10.1007/978-94-007-4611-4_2>.

24 Gabriel Schui and Günter Krampen, 'Bibliometric Analyses on the Emergence and Present Growth of Positive Psychology', *Applied Psychology: Health and Well-Being*, 2.1 (2010), 52–64 <https://doi.org/10.1111/j.1758-0854.2009.01022.x>; Reuben D. Rusk and Lea E. Waters, 'Tracing the Size, Reach, Impact, and Breadth of Positive Psychology', *The Journal of Positive Psychology*, 8.3 (2013), 207–21 <https://doi.org/10.1080/17439760.2013.777766>.

25 Pierre Bourdieu, *Distinction: A Social Critique of the Judgment of Taste* (London: Routledge, 1984).

26 Ehrenreich, *Smile or Die*.

27 Elaine Swan, *Worked Up Selves: Personal Development Workers, Self-Work and Therapeutic Cultures* (New York: Palgrave Macmillan, 2010), p. 4.

28 Seligman, *Flourish*, p. 1.

29 https://coachfederation.org/files/FileDownloads/2016ICFGlobalCoachingStudy_ExecutiveSummary.pdf

30 Martin E. P. Seligman, 'Coaching and Positive Psychology', *Australian Psychologist*, 42.4 (2007), 266–7, p. 266.

31 Seligman, *Flourish*, p. 70.

32 Seligman, *Flourish*, pp. 1–2.

33 George A. Miller, 'The Constitutive Problem of Psychology', in *A Century of Psychology as Science*, ed. by Sigmund Koch and David E. Leary (Washington, DC: American Psychological Association, 1985), pp. 40–59 <https://doi.org/10.1037/10117-021>.

34 Henry James, 'The Novels of George Eliot', *The Atlantic Monthly*, 18 (1866), 479–92 <http://www.unz.org/Pub/AtlanticMonthly-1866oct-00479>.

35 John Chambers Christopher, Frank C. Richardson and Brent D. Slife, 'Thinking through Positive Psychology', *Theory & Psychology*, 18.5 (2008), 555–61 <https://doi.org/10.1177/0959354308093395>; John Chambers Christopher and Sarah Hickinbottom, 'Positive Psychology, Ethnocentrism, and the Disguised Ideology of Individualism', *Theory & Psychology*, 18.5 (2008), 563–89 <https://doi.org/10.1177/0959354308093396>.

36 Brent D. Slife and Frank C. Richardson, 'Problematic Ontological Underpinnings of Positive Psychology: A Strong Relational Alternative', *Theory & Psychology*, 18.5 (2008), 699–723 <https://doi.org/10.1177/0959354308093403>; Alistair Miller, 'A Critique of Positive Psychology – or "the New Science of Happiness"', *Journal of Philosophy of Education*, 42 (2008), 591–608 <https://doi.org/10.1111/j.1467-9752.2008.00646.x>; Richard S. Lazarus, 'Author's Response: The Lazarus Manifesto for Positive Psychology and Psychology in General', *Psychological Inquiry*, 14.2 (2003), 173–89 <https://doi.org/10.1207/S15327965PLI1402_04>; Richard S. Lazarus, 'Does the Positive Psychology Movement Have Legs?', *Psychological Inquiry*, 14.2 (2003), 93–109 <https://doi.org/10.1207/S15327965PLI1402_02>.

37 James K. McNulty and Frank D. Fincham, 'Beyond Positive Psychology? Toward a Contextual View of Psychological Processes and Well-Being', *American Psychologist*, 67.2 (2012), 101–10 <https://doi.org/10.1037/a0024572>; Erik Angner, 'Is It Possible to Measure Happiness?', *European Journal for Philosophy of Science*, 3.2 (2013), 221–40.

38 Myriam Mongrain and Tracy Anselmo-Matthews, 'Do Positive Psychology Exercises Work? A Replication of Seligman et al.', *Journal of Clinical Psychology*, 68 (2012), 382–9 <https://doi.org/10.1002/jclp.21839>.

39 James C. Coyne and Howard Tennen, 'Positive Psychology in Cancer Care: Bad Science, Exaggerated Claims, and Unproven Medicine', *Annals*

of Behavioral Medicine, 39.1 (2010), 16–26 <https://doi.org/10.1007/s12160-009-9154-z>.

40 Marino Pérez-Álvarez, 'The Science of Happiness: As Felicitous as It Is Fallacious', *Journal of Theoretical and Philosophical Psychology*, 36.1 (2016), 1–19 <https://doi.org/10.1037/teo0000030>; Luis Fernández-Ríos and Mercedes Novo, 'Positive Psychology : Zeitgeist (or Spirit of the Times) or Ignorance (or Disinformation) of History?', *International Journal of Clinical and Health Psychology*, 12.2 (2012), 333–44.

41 Ruth Whippman, 'Why Governments Should Stay Out of the Happiness Business', *Huffington Post*, 24 March 2016 <http://www.huffingtonpost.com/ruth-whippman/why-governments-should-st_b_9534232.html>.

42 Richard Layard, 'Happiness: Has Social Science a Clue? Lecture 1: What Is Happiness? Are We Getting Happier?', *Lionel Robbins Memorial Lecture Series* (London: London School of Economics and Political Science, 2003) <http://eprints.lse.ac.uk/47425/>.

43 Richard Layard, 'Happiness and Public Policy: A Challenge to the Profession', *The Economic Journal*, 116.510 (2006), C24–33 <https://doi.org/10.1111/j.1468-0297.2006.01073.x>, p. C24.

44 Richard A. Easterlin, 'Does Economic Growth Improve the Human Lot? Some Empirical Evidence', in *Nations and Households in Economic Growth: Essays in Honor of Moses Abramovitz*, ed. by Paul A. David and Melvin V. Reder (New York: Academic Press, 1974), pp. 89–125, p. 118.

45 Amos Tversky and Daniel Kahneman, 'The Framing of Decisions and the Psychology of Choice', *Science*, 211.4481 (1981), 453–58 <https://doi.org/10.1126/science.7455683>; Amos Tversky and Daniel Kahneman, 'Judgment under Uncertainty: Heuristics and Biases', *Science*, 185.4157 (1974), 1124–31 <https://doi.org/10.1126/science.185.4157.1124>.

46 Ed Diener, Ed Sandvik and William Pavot, 'Happiness Is the Frequency, Not the Intensity, of Positive versus Negative Affect', in *Subjective Well-Being: An Inter-Disciplinary Perspective*, ed. by Fritz Strack, Michael Argyle and Norbert Schwarz (Oxford: Pergamon Press, 1991), pp. 119–39 <https://doi.org/10.1007/978-90-481-2354-4_10>, p. 119.

47 Daniel Kahneman, Ed Diener, and Norbert Schwarz, eds., *Well-Being: The Foundations of Hedonic Psychology* (New York: Russell Sage Foundation, 1999).

48 Richard Layard and David M. Clark, *Thrive: The Power of Psychological Therapy* (London: Penguin, 2015).

49 Binkley, *Happiness as Enterprise*.

50 Naomi Klein, *The Shock Doctrine: The Rise of Disaster Capitalism* (New York: Picador, 2008).

51 OECD, *OECD Guidelines on Measuring Subjective Well-Being* (Paris: OECD, 2013) <https://doi.org/10.1787/9789264191655-en>, p. 3.

52 Layard, 'Happiness: Has Social Science a Clue?'.

53 Richard Layard, *Happiness: Lessons from a New Science* (London: Allen, 2005), pp. 112–13, emphasis added.

54 Derek Bok, *The Politics of Happiness: What Government Can Learn from the New Research on Well-Being* (Princeton: Princeton University Press, 2010), p. 204.

55 Thomas H. Davenport and D. J. Patil, 'Data Scientist: The Sexiest Job of the 21st Century', *Harvard Business Review*, October 2012 <https://hbr.org/2012/10/data-scientist-the-sexiest-job-of-the-21st-century/>.

56 Adam D. I. Kramer, Jamie E. Guillory and Jeffrey T. Hancock, 'Experimental Evidence of Massive-Scale Emotional Contagion through Social Networks', *Proceedings of the National Academy of Sciences*, 111.24 (2014), 8788–90 <https://doi.org/10.1073/pnas.1320040111>.

57 Sydney Lupkin, 'You Consented to Facebook's Social Experiment', *ABCNews*, 30 June 2014 <http://abcnews.go.com/Health/consented-facebooks-social-experiment/story?id=24368579>.

58 Robert Booth, 'Facebook Reveals News Feed Experiment to Control Emotions', *The Guardian*, 30 June 2014 <https://www.theguardian.com/technology/2014/jun/29/facebook-users-emotions-news-feeds>.

59 Wendy Nelson Espeland and Mitchell L. Stevens, 'A Sociology of Quantification', *European Journal of Sociology*, 49.3 (2008), 401–36.

60 Richard Layard and Gus O'Donnell, 'How to Make Policy When Happiness Is the Goal', in *World Happiness Report*, ed. by John F Halliwell, Richard Layard and Jeffrey Sachs (New York: Sustainable Development Solutions Network, 2015), pp. 76–87, p. 77.

61 Kirstie McCrum, 'What Exactly Does Happiness Cost? A Mere £7.6 Million Say Britons', *Mirror*, 15 May 2015 <http://www.mirror.co.uk/news/uk-news/what-exactly-happiness-cost-mere-5702003>.

62 Gallup, *State of the American Workplace: Employee Engagement Insights for U.S. Business Leaders* (Washington, DC: Gallup, 2013).

63 Luigino Bruni and Pier Luigi Porta, 'Introduction', in *Handbook on the Economics of Happiness*, ed. by Luigino Bruni and Pier Luigi Porta

(Cheltenham: Edward Elgar, 2007), pp. xi–xxxvii; Bruno S. Frey and Alois Stutzer, *Happiness and Economics: How the Economy and Institutions Affect Human Well-Being* (Princeton: Princeton University Press, 2006).

64 Angner, 'Is it Possible to Measure Happiness?'

65 OECD, *Guidelines*, p. 23.

66 Norbert Schwarz, Bärbel Knäuper, Daphna Oyserman and Christine Stich, 'The Psychology of Asking Questions', in *International Handbook of Survey Methodology*, ed. by Edith D. de Leeuw, Joop J. Hox, and Don A. Dillman (New York: Taylor & Francis, 2008), pp. 18–36.

67 I. Ponocny, C. Weismayer, B. Stross and S. G. Dressler, '*Are* Most People Happy? Exploring the Meaning of Subjective Well-Being Ratings', *Journal of Happiness Studies*, 17.6 (2015), 2635–53 <https://doi.org/10.1007/s10902-015-9710-0>, p. 2651.

68 Alejandro Adler and Martin E. P. Seligman, 'Using Wellbeing for Public Policy: Theory, Measurement, and Recommendations', *International Journal of Wellbeing*, 6.1 (2016), 1–35 <https://doi.org/10.5502/ijw.v6i1.429>, p. 14.

69 Adler and Seligman, 'Using Wellbeing for Public Policy', p. 14.

70 Thomas Piketty, *Capital in the Twenty-First Century* (Cambridge, MA: Belknap Press, 2014); Joseph Stiglitz, *The Price of Inequality: How Today's Divided Society Endangers Our Future* (New York and London: W. W. Norton, 2013).

71 Jonathan Kelley and M. D. R. Evans, 'Societal Inequality and Individual Subjective Well-Being: Results from 68 Societies and over 200,000 Individuals, 1981–2008', *Social Science Research*, 62 (2017), 1–23 <https://doi.org/10.1016/j.ssresearch.2016.04.020>, p. 33.

72 Kelley and Evans, 'Societal Inequality and Individual Subjective Well-Being', p. 35, emphasis added.

73 Layard and O'Donnell, 'How to Make Policy', p. 79.

74 Davies, *Happiness Industry*.

75 Ashley Frawley, *Semiotics of Happiness: Rhetorical Beginnings of a Public Problem* (London and New York: Bloomsbury, 2015).

Chapter 2 Rekindling individualism

1 Cabanas and Illouz, 'Making of a "Happy Worker"'; Cabanas and Illouz, 'Fit fürs Glück'.

2 Jason Read, 'A Genealogy of Homo-Economicus: Neoliberalism and

the Production of Subjectivity', *Foucault Studies*, 6 (2009), 25–36; David Harvey, *A Brief History of Neoliberalism* (New York: Oxford University Press, 2007).

3 Michèle Lamont, 'Toward a Comparative Sociology of Valuation and Evaluation', *Annual Review of Sociology*, 38.2 (2012), 1–21 <https://doi.org/10.1146/annurev-soc-070308-120022>.

4 Jean Baudrillard, *The Consumer Society: Myths and Structures* (London: SAGE, 1998).

5 Ulrich Beck, *Risk Society: Towards a New Modernity* (London: SAGE, 2000); Luc Boltanski and Eve Chiapello, *The New Spirit of Capitalism* (London and New York: Verso, 2007) <https://doi.org/10.1007/s10767-006-9006-9>.

6 Eva Illouz, *Why Love Hurts: A Sociological Explanation* (Cambridge: Polity, 2012); Arlie Russell Hochschild, *The Managed Heart: Commercialization of Human Feeling* (Berkeley: University of California Press, 2003).

7 Illouz, *Saving the Modern Soul*; Illouz, *Cold Intimacies*.

8 Axel Honneth, 'Organized Self-Realization: Some Paradoxes of Individualization', *European Journal of Social Theory*, 7.4 (2004), 463–78 <https://doi.org/10.1177/1368431004046703>.

9 Nicole Aschoff, *The New Prophets of Capitalism* (London: Verso, 2015), p. 87.

10 Sara Ahmed, *The Promise of Happiness* (Durham, NC: Duke University Press, 2010).

11 Gilles Lipovetsky, *L'Ère du Vide: Essais sur l'Individualisme Contemporain* (Paris: Gallimard, 1983).

12 Michel Foucault, *The Birth of Biopolitics. Lectures at the Collège de France, 1978–1979* (Basingstoke: Palgrave Macmillan, 2008); Ulrich Beck and Elisabeth Beck-Gernsheim, *Individualization: Institutionalized Individualism and Its Social and Political Consequences* (London: SAGE, 2002); Anthony Giddens, *Modernity and Self-Identity* (Cambridge: Polity, 1991); Martin Hartmann and Axel Honneth, 'Paradoxes of Capitalism', *Constellations*, 2006 <http://onlinelibrary.wiley.com/doi/10.1111/j.1351-0487.2006.00439.x/full>.

13 Eduardo Crespo and José Celio Freire, 'La Atribución de Responsabilidad: De la Cognición al Sujeto', *Psicologia & Sociedade*, 26.2 (2014), 271–9.

14 Kenneth McLaughlin, 'Psychologization and the Construction of

the Political Subject as Vulnerable Object', *Annual Review of Critical Psychology*, 8 (2010), 63–79.
15 Cabanas, 'Rekindling Individualism'.
16 Foucault, *Birth of Biopolitics*.
17 Held, 'Tyranny of the Positive Attitude'; Ehrenreich, *Smile or Die*; Binkley, *Happiness as Enterprise*; Davies, *Happiness Industry*; Cederström and Spicer, *Wellness Syndrome*.
18 Frank C. Richardson and Charles B. Guignon, 'Positive Psychology and Philosophy of Social Science', *Theory & Psychology*, 18.5 (2008), 605–27 <https://doi.org/10.1177/0959354308093398>; Christopher and Hickinbottom, 'Positive Psychology, Ethnocentrism'; Christopher et al., 'Thinking'; Becker and Marecek, 'Positive Psychology: History in the Remaking?'; Louise Sundararajan, 'Happiness Donut: A Confucian Critique of Positive Psychology', *Journal of Theoretical and Philosophical Psychology*, 25.1 (2005), 35–60; Sam Binkley, 'Psychological Life as Enterprise: Social Practice and the Government of Neo-Liberal Interiority', *History of the Human Sciences*, 24.3 (2011), 83–102 <https://doi.org/10.1177/0952695111412877>; Jeff Sugarman, 'Neoliberalism and Psychological Ethics', *Journal of Theoretical and Philosophical Psychology*, 35.2 (2015) <https://doi.org/10.1037/a0038960>, 103–16; Ehrenreich, *Smile or Die*; Binkley, *Happiness as Enterprise*.
19 Cabanas, 'Rekindling Individualism, Consuming Emotions'; Cabanas, 'Positive Psychology and the Legitimation of Individualism'.
20 Nikolas Rose, *Inventing Our Selves: Psychology, Power and Personhood* (London: Cambridge University Press, 1998); Ron Roberts, *Psychology and Capitalism: The Manipulation of Mind* (Alresford: Zero Books, 2015).
21 Seligman, *Authentic Happiness*, p. 303.
22 Seligman, *Authentic Happiness*, p. 303.
23 Sundararajan, 'Happiness Donut'; Ahmed, *Promise of Happiness*.
24 Seligman, *Authentic Happiness*, p. 129.
25 Cabanas, 'Positive Psychology and the Legitimation of Individualism'.
26 William Tov and Ed Diener, 'Culture and Subjective Well-Being', in *Culture and Well-Being: The Collected Works of Ed Diener*, ed. by Ed Diener (London and New York: Springer, 2009), pp. 9–42; Ruut Veenhoven, 'Quality-of-Life in Individualistic Society', *Social Indicators Research*, 48.2 (1999), 159–88; Ruut Veenhoven, 'Life Is Getting Better: Societal Evolution and Fit with Human Nature', *Social Indicators Research*,

97.1 (2010), 105–22 <https://doi.org/10.1007/s11205-009-9556-0>; Seligman, *Flourish*; William Tov and Ed Diener, 'The Well-Being of Nations: Linking Together Trust, Cooperation, and Democracy', in *The Science of Well-Being: The Collected Works of Ed Diener*, ed. by Ed Diener (London and New York: Springer, 2009), pp. 155–73; Ed Diener, 'Subjective Well-Being: The Science of Happiness and a Proposal for a National Index', *American Psychologist*, 55 (2000), 34–43.

27 Robert Biswas-Diener, Joar Vitterso and Ed Diener, 'Most People Are Pretty Happy, but There Is Cultural Variation: The Inughuit, the Amish, and the Maasai', in *Culture and Well-Being: The Collected Works of Ed Diener*, ed. by Ed Diener (London and New York: Springer, 2009), pp. 245–60; Ed Diener, 'Introduction – The Science of Well-Being: Reviews and Theoretical Articles by Ed Diener', in *The Science of Well-Being: The Collected Works of Ed Diener*, ed. by Ed Diener (London and New York: Springer, 2009), pp. 1–10; Ulrich Schimmack, Shigehiro Oishi and Ed Diener, 'Individualism: A Valid and Important Dimension of Cultural Differences Between Nations', *Personality and Social Psychology Review*, 9.1 (2005), 17–31 <https://doi.org/10.1207/s15327957pspr0901_2>; Tov and Diener, 'Culture and Subjective Well-Being'.

28 Ed Diener, Marissa Diener and Carol Diener, 'Factors Predicting the Subjective Well-Being of Nations', in *Culture and Well-Being: The Collected Works of Ed Diener*, ed. by Ed Diener (London and New York: Springer, 2009), pp. 43–70, p. 67.

29 Ed Diener and Martin E. P. Seligman, 'Very Happy People', *Psychological Science*, 13 (2002), 81–84 <https://doi.org/10.1111/1467-9280.00415>; Seligman, *Flourish*; Veenhoven, 'Quality-of-Life in Individualistic Society'; Veenhoven, 'Life Is Getting Better', p. 120.

30 Shigehiro Oishi, 'Goals as Cornerstones of Subjective Well-Being', in *Culture and Subjective Well-Being*, ed. by Ed Diener and Eunkook M. Suh (Cambridge, MA: MIT Press, 2000), pp. 87–112.

31 Liza G. Steele and Scott M. Lynch, 'The Pursuit of Happiness in China: Individualism, Collectivism, and Subjective Well-Being During China's Economic and Social Transformation', *Social Indicators Research*, 114.2 (2013), 441–51 <https://doi.org/10.1007/s11205-012-0154-1>.

32 Aaron C. Ahuvia, 'Individualism/Collectivism and Cultures of Happiness: A Theoretical Conjecture on the Relationship between Consumption, Culture and Subjective Well-Being at the National

Level', *Journal of Happiness Studies*, 3.1 (2002), 23–36 <https://doi. org/10.1023/A:1015682121103>.

33 Ronald Fischer and Diana Boer, 'What Is More Important for National Well-Being: Money or Autonomy? A Meta-Analysis of Well-Being, Burnout, and Anxiety across 63 Societies', *Journal of Personality and Social Psychology*, 101.1 (2011), 164–84 <https://doi.org/10.1037/a0023663>, p. 164.

34 Navjot Bhullar, Nicola S. Schutte and John M. Malouff, 'Associations of Individualistic–Collectivistic Orientations with Emotional Intelligence, Mental Health, and Satisfaction with Life: A Tale of Two Countries', *Individual Differences Research*, 10.3 (2012), 165–75; Ki-Hoon Jun, 'Re-Exploration of Subjective Well-Being Determinants: Full-Model Approach with Extended Cross-Contextual Analysis', *International Journal of Wellbeing*, 5.4 (2015), 17–59 <https://doi.org/10.5502/ijw. v5i4.405>.

35 William Pavot and Ed Diener, 'The Satisfaction With Life Scale and the Emerging Construct of Life Satisfaction', *The Journal of Positive Psychology*, 3.2 (2008), 137–52 <https://doi.org/10.1080/17439760701756946>; Ed Diener, Robert A. Emmons, Randy J. Larsen and Sharon Griffin, 'The Satisfaction With Life Scale', *Journal of Personality Assessment*, 49.1 (1985), 71–5 <https://doi.org/10.1207/s15327752jpa4901_13>.

36 Seligman, *Authentic Happiness*.

37 Seligman, *Authentic Happiness*, p. 58.

38 Seligman, *Authentic Happiness*, p. 55.

39 Seligman, *Authentic Happiness*, p. 50.

40 Sonja Lyubomirsky, *The How of Happiness: A Scientific Approach to Getting the Life You Want* (New York: Penguin, 2007), p. 22, emphasis in the original.

41 Ehrenreich, *Smile or Die*, p. 172.

42 Layard, *Happiness: Lessons from a New Science*.

43 Layard, 'Happiness: Has Social Science a Clue?'

44 Daniel Kahneman and Angus Deaton, 'High Income Improves Evaluation of Life but Not Emotional Well-Being', *Proceedings of the National Academy of Sciences*, 107.38 (2010), 16489–93 <https://doi. org/10.1073/pnas.1011492107>.

45 Betsey Stevenson and Justin Wolfers, 'Subjective Well-Being and Income: Is There Any Evidence of Satiation?', *American Economic Review*,

103.3 (2013), 598–604 <https://doi.org/10.3386/w18992>, p. 604.

46 Betsey Stevenson and Justin Wolfers, 'Economic Growth and Subjective Well-Being: Reassessing the Easterlin Paradox', *Brookings Papers on Economic Activity*, 39.1 (2008), 1–102, p. 2.

47 Stevenson and Wolfers, 'Economic Growth and Subjective Well-Being', p. 2.

48 Stevenson and Wolfers, 'Economic Growth and Subjective Well-Being', p. 1.

49 Stevenson and Wolfers, 'Economic Growth and Subjective Well-Being', p. 29.

50 Dana Becker and Jeanne Marecek, 'Dreaming the American Dream: Individualism and Positive Psychology', *Social and Personality Psychology Compass*, 2.5 (2008), 1767–80 <https://doi.org/10.1111/j.1751-9004.2008.00139.x>, p. 1771.

51 Amir Mandel, 'Why Nobel Prize Winner Daniel Kahneman Gave Up on Happiness', *Haaretz*, 3 October 2018 <https://www.haaretz.com/israel-news/.premium.MAGAZINE-why-nobel-prize-winner-daniel-kahneman-gave-up-on-happiness-1.6528513?=&utm_campaign=newsletter-daily&utm_medium=email&utm_source=smartfocus&utm_content=htps%253A%252F%252Fwww.haaretz.com%252Fisrael-n>.

52 Lyubomirsky, *How of Happiness*, p. 21.

53 Carmelo Vázquez, 'El Bienestar de Las Naciones', in *La Ciencia Del Bienestar. Fundamentos de Una Psicología Positiva*, ed. by Carmelo Vázquez and Gonzalo Hervás (Madrid: Alianza Editorial, 2009), pp. 75–102, p. 131.

54 Seligman, *Authentic Happiness*.

55 Jason Mannino, 'How To Care for Yourself in Times of Crisis', *Huffpost*, 17 November 2011 <https://www.huffingtonpost.com/jason-mannino/how-to-care-for-yourself_b_170438.html>.

56 Heinrich Geiselberger, ed., *The Great Regression* (Cambridge: Polity, 2017).

57 Christopher Lasch, *The Minimal Self: Psychic Survival in Troubled Times* (New York and London: W. W. Norton, 1984), p. 174.

58 Isaiah Berlin, *Four Essays on Liberty* (Oxford: Oxford University Press, 1968), p. 139.

59 Jack M. Barbalet, *Emotion, Social Theory, and Social Structure: A Macrosociological Approach* (Cambridge: Cambridge University Press, 2004), p. 174.

60 Since 2008 the increasing worldwide presence of and interest in survivalism is another extreme, albeit symptomatic, example of this. Survivalism draws on a highly individualistic mentality of constant preparedness, full self-sufficiency and excessive self-concern for one's safety in a world where society is perceived as crumbling and the worst is expected to be around the corner, so everyone has to look out for themselves in order to survive. Although survivalism is not new, this social trend has in the last decade gone from a local hobby – especially in the United States – to a whole lifestyle fuelled by a fast-growing survivalist industry (Neil Howe, 'How Millennials Are Reshaping the Survivalism Industry', *Financial Sense*, 12 December 2016 <https://www.financialsense.com/neil-howe/how-millennials-reshaping-survivalism-industry>). Consumption of survivalist TV shows, Hollywood movies and self-help books has also grown globally and exponentially since 2008 – e.g., TV shows such as *Born Survivor*, which has reached an estimated 1.2 billion viewers worldwide, becoming one of the most-viewed TV shows on the planet, and the number of zombie/survival movies released in the 2010s has quadrupled in comparison to those released in the 1990s (Zachary Crockett and Javier Zarracina, 'How the Zombie Represents America's Deepest Fears', *Vox*, 31 October 2016 <https://www.vox.com/policy-and-politics/2016/10/31/13440402/zombie-political-history>. For instance, Daniel Nehring and colleagues have thoroughly analysed the extent to which survivalism has become a central topic in self-help literature in recent years. According to these authors, behind the notions of survivalism, adventure and advice, the survivalist self-help genre offers an individualistic vision that combines the insistence on personal fulfilment, introspection and the importance of pursuing one's dreams with the provision of easy 'strategies for simply getting by, surviving, or opting out of society's pressures altogether' (Daniel Nehring, Emmanuel Alvarado, Eric C. Hendricks and Dylan Kerrigan, *Transnational Popular Psychology and the Global Self-Help Industry: The Politics of Contemporary Social Change* (New York: Palgrave Macmillan, 2016), p. 4).

61 Michèle Lamont, 'Trump's Triumph and Social Science Adrift . . . What Is to Be Done?', *American Sociological Association*, 2016 <http://www.asanet.org/trumps-triumph-and-social-science-adrift-what-be-done>, p. 8.

62 Illouz, *Saving the Modern Soul*, p. 2.

63 Cabanas, 'Positive Psychology and the Legitimation of Individualism'.
64 Emma Seppälä, 'Secrets of a Happier Life', in *The Science of Happiness: New Discoveries for a More Joyful Life* (New York: TIME, 2016), pp. 11–17, p. 13.
65 Ellen Seidman, 'Fourteen Ways to Jump for Joy', in *The Science of Happiness: New Discoveries for a More Joyful Life* (New York: TIME, 2016), pp. 34–41, p. 37.
66 Seppälä, 'Secrets of a Happier Life', p. 16.
67 Kate Pickert, 'The Art of Being Present', in *The Science of Happiness: New Discoveries for a More Joyful Life* (New York: TIME, 2016), pp. 71–9, p. 77.
68 Traci Pedersen, 'Mindfulness May Ease Depression, Stress in Poor Black Women', *PsychCentral*, 2016 <https://psychcentral.com/news/2016/08/18/mindfulness-may-ease-depression-stress-in-poor-black-women/108727.html>.
69 Olga R. Sanmartín, '"Mindfulness" en el Albergue: Un Consuelo para los "Sintecho"', *El Mundo*, 7 January 2016 <http://www.elmundo.es/sociedad/2016/01/07/567d929a46163fa0578b465d.html>.
70 Cabanas, 'Positive Psychology and the Legitimation of Individualism'.
71 Jen Wieczner, 'Meditation Has Become a Billion-Dollar Business', *Fortune*, 12 March 2016 <http://fortune.com/2016/03/12/meditation-mindfulness-apps/>.
72 Miguel Farias and Catherine Wikholm, *The Buddah Pill: Can Meditation Change You?* (London: Watkins, 2015).
73 Cabanas, 'Positive Psychology and the Legitimation of Individualism'.
74 Ad Bergsma and Ruut Veenhoven, 'The Happiness of People with a Mental Disorder in Modern Society', *Psychology of Well-Being: Theory, Research and Practice*, 1.2 (2011), 1–6 <https://doi.org/10.1186/2211-1522-1-2>, p. 2.
75 Seligman, *Flourish*; Veenhoven, 'Life Is Getting Better'; Veenhoven, 'Quality-of-Life in Individualistic Society'; Diener and Seligman, 'Very Happy People'.
76 Brandon H. Hidaka, 'Depression as a Disease of Modernity: Explanations for Increasing Prevalence', *Journal of Affective Disorders*, 140.3 (2012), 205–14 <https://doi.org/10.1016/j.jad.2011.12.036>; Ethan Watters, *Crazy Like Us: The Globalization of the American Psyche* (New York and London: Free Press, 2010); Richard Eckersley, 'Is Modern Western Culture a Health Hazard?', *International Journal of Epidemiology*, 35.2

(2005), 252–8 <https://doi.org/10.1093/ije/dyi235>; Allan Horwitz and Jerome C. Wakefield, 'The Age of Depression', *Public Interest*, 158 (2005), 39–58; Robert Whitaker, *Anatomy of an Epidemic: Magic Bullets, Psychiatric Drugs, and the Astonishing Rise of Mental Illness in America* (New York: Crown, 2010); Lasch, *Minimal Self*; James L. Nolan, Jr., *The Therapeutic State: Justifying Government at Century's End* (New York: New York University Press, 1998); Ann Cvetkovich, *Depression: A Public Feeling* (Durham, NC: Duke University Press, 2012).

77 Robert D. Putnam, *Bowling Alone: The Collapse and Revival of American Community* (New York: Simon and Schuster, 2000).

78 Peter Walker, 'May Appoints Minister to Tackle Loneliness Issues Raised by Jo Cox', *The Guardian*, 16 January 2018 <https://www.theguardian.com/society/2018/jan/16/may-appoints-minister-tackle-loneliness-issues-raised-jo-cox>.

79 Anushka Asthana, 'Loneliness Is a "Giant Evil" of Our Time, Says Jo Cox Commission', *The Guardian*, 10 December 2017 <https://www.theguardian.com/society/2017/dec/10/loneliness-is-a-giant-evil-of-our-time-says-jo-cox-commission>.

80 Charles Taylor, *Sources of the Self: The Making of the Modern Identity* (Cambridge, MA: Harvard University Press, 1989).

81 Ashis Nandy, *Regimes of Narcissism, Regimes of Despair* (New Delhi: Oxford University Press, 2013), p. 176.

82 Cederström and Spicer, *Wellness Syndrome*; Frawley, *Semiotics of Happiness*; Barbara S. Held, 'The "Virtues" of Positive Psychology', *Journal of Theoretical and Philosophical Psychology*, 25.1 (2005), 1–34 <https://doi.org/10.1037/h0091249>; Alenka Zupančič, *The Odd One In* (Cambridge, MA: MIT Press, 2008).

83 Illouz, *Saving the Modern Soul*.

84 Iris B. Mauss, Maya Tamir, Craig L. Anderson and Nicole S. Savino, 'Can Seeking Happiness Make People Unhappy? Paradoxical Effects of Valuing Happiness', *Emotion*, 11.4 (2011), 807–15 <https://doi.org/10.1037/a0022010>.

85 Paul Rose and Keith W. Campbell, 'Greatness Feels Good: A Telic Model of Narcissism and Subjective Well-Being', *Advances in Psychology Research*, 31 (2004), 3–26; Hillary C. Devlin, Jamil Zaki, Desmond C. Ong and June Gruber, 'Not As Good as You Think? Trait Positive Emotion Is Associated with Increased Self-Reported Empathy

but Decreased Empathic Performance', ed. by Marco Iacoboni, *PLoS ONE*, 9.10 (2014), e110470 <https://doi.org/10.1371/journal.pone.0110470>; Joseph P. Forgas, 'Don't Worry, Be Sad! On the Cognitive, Motivational, and Interpersonal Benefits of Negative Mood', *Current Directions in Psychological Science*, 22.3 (2013), 225–32 <https://doi.org/10.1177/0963721412474458>; Jessica L. Tracy and Richard W. Robins, 'The Psychological Structure of Pride: A Tale of Two Facets', *Journal of Personality and Social Psychology*, 92.3 (2007), 506–25 <https://doi.org/10.1037/0022-3514.92.3.506>.

86 Marino Pérez-Álvarez, 'Reflexividad, Escritura y Génesis del Sujeto Moderno', *Revista de Historia de la Psicología*, 36.1 (2015), 53–90.

87 Frawley, *Semiotics of Happiness*; Frank Furedi, 'From the Narrative of the Blitz to the Rhetoric of Vulnerability', *Cultural Sociology*, 1.2 (2007), 235–54 <https://doi.org/10.1177/1749975507078189>; Frank Furedi, *Therapy Culture: Cultivating Vulnerability in an Uncertain Age* (London: Routledge, 2004).

88 Gilles Lipovetsky, *La Felicidad Paradójica* (Barcelona: Editorial Anagrama, 2007).

89 Robert A. Cummins and Helen Nistico, 'Maintaining Life Satisfaction: The Role of Positive Cognitive Bias', *Journal of Happiness Studies*, 3.1 (2002), 37–69 <https://doi.org/10.1023/A:1015678915305>; Adrian J. Tomyn and Robert A. Cummins, 'Subjective Wellbeing and Homeostatically Protected Mood: Theory Validation With Adolescents', *Journal of Happiness Studies*, 12.5 (2011), 897–914 <https://doi.org/10.1007/s10902-010-9235-5>.

90 Bergsma and Veenhoven, 'Happiness of People with a Mental Disorder'; Veenhoven, 'Life Is Getting Better'.

91 Vázquez, 'El Bienestar de las Naciones'; Seligman, *Flourish*; Seligman, *Authentic Happiness*.

92 Seligman, *Flourish*, p. 164.

93 Global Happiness Council, *Global Happiness Policy Report 2018* (New York: GHC, 2018) <https://s3.amazonaws.com/ghc-2018/GlobalHappinessPolicyReport2018.pdf>, p. 69.

94 Jack Martin and Anne-Marie McLellan, *The Education of Selves: How Psychology Transformed Students* (New York: Oxford University Press, 2013).

95 British Columbia Ministry of Education, 2008, *Career Planning*, as quoted in Sugarman, 'Neoliberalism and Psychological Ethics', p. 112.

96 http://www.ipositive-education.net/movement/
97 Global Happiness Council, *Global Happiness Policy Report*.
98 Richard Layard and Ann Hagell, 'Healthy Young Minds: Transforming the Mental Health of Children', in *World Happiness Report*, ed. by John Helliwell, Richard Layard and Jeffrey Sachs (New York: Sustainable Development Solutions Network, 2015), pp. 106–30.
99 Martin E. P. Seligman, Randal M. Ernst, Jane Gillham, Karen Reivich and Mark Linkins, 'Positive Education: Positive Psychology and Classroom Interventions', *Oxford Review of Education*, 35.3 (2009), 293–311 <https://doi.org/10.1080/03054980902934563>, p. 295.
100 Mark T. Greenberg, Roger P. Weissberg, Mary Utne O'Brien, Joseph E. Zins, Linda Fredericks, Hank Resnik and others, 'Enhancing School-Based Prevention and Youth Development through Coordinated Social, Emotional, and Academic Learning', *American Psychologist*, 58.6–7 (2003), 466–74 <https://doi.org/10.1037/0003-066X.58.6-7.466>.
101 Karen Reivich, Jane E. Gillham, Tara M. Chaplin and Martin E. P. Seligman, 'From Helplessness to Optimism: The Role of Resilience in Treating and Preventing Depression in Youth', in *Handbook of Resilience in Children*, ed. by Sam Goldstein and Robert B. Brooks (New York: Kluwer Academic/Plenum, 2005), pp. 223–37.
102 Lea Waters, 'A Review of School-Based Positive Psychology Interventions', *The Australian Educational and Developmental Psychologist*, 28.2 (2011), 75–90 <https://doi.org/10.1375/aedp.28.2.75>; Seligman, *Flourish*.
103 e.g., Kathryn Ecclestone and Dennis Hayes, *The Dangerous Rise of Therapeutic Education* (London and New York: Routledge, 2009).
104 Alison L. Calear, Helen Christensen, Andrew Mackinnon, Kathleen M. Griffiths and Richard O'Kearney, 'The YouthMood Project: A Cluster Randomized Controlled Trial of an Online Cognitive Behavioral Program with Adolescents', *Journal of Consulting and Clinical Psychology*, 77.6 (2009), 1021–32 <https://doi.org/10.1037/a0017391>.
105 Patricia C. Broderick and Stacie Metz, 'Learning to BREATHE: A Pilot Trial of a Mindfulness Curriculum for Adolescents', *Advances in School Mental Health Promotion*, 2.1 (2009), 35–46 <https://doi.org/10.1080/17547730X.2009.9715696>.
106 Cabanas, '"Psytizens", or the Construction of Happy Individuals'.
107 Ecclestone and Hayes, *Dangerous Rise*.

108 Ecclestone and Hayes, *Dangerous Rise*, p. 164.
109 Neil J. Smelser, 'Self-Esteem and Social Problems: An Introduction', in *The Social Importance of Self-Esteem*, ed. by Andrew M. Mecca, Neil J. Smelser and John Vaconcellos (Berkeley: University of California Press, 1989), pp. 1–23, p. 1.
110 Nathaniel Branden, 'In Defense of Self', *Association for Humanistic Psychology*, August–September (1984), 12–13, p. 12.
111 Roy F. Baumeister, Jennifer D. Campbell, Joachim I. Krueger and Kathleen D. Vohs, 'Does High Self-Esteem Cause Better Performance, Interpersonal Success, Happiness, or Healthier Lifestyles?', *Psychological Science in the Public Interest*, 4.1 (2003), 1–44 <https://doi.org/10.1111/1529-1006.01431>, p. 1.
112 Baumeister et al., 'Does High Self-Esteem Cause Better Performance', p. 3.
113 Neil Humphrey, Ann Lendrum and Michael Wigelsworth, *Social and Emotional Aspects of Learning (SEAL) Programme in Secondary School: National Evaluation* (London: Department for Education, 2010), p. 2.
114 Leslie M. Gutman and Ingrid Schoon, *The Impact of Non-Cognitive Skills on Outcomes for Young People: Literature Review* (London: Institute of Education, University of London, 2013) <https://educationendowmentfoundation.org.uk/public/files/Publications/EEF_Lit_Review_Non-CognitiveSkills.pdf>, p. 10.
115 Kathryn Ecclestone, 'From Emotional and Psychological Well-Being to Character Education: Challenging Policy Discourses of Behavioural Science and "Vulnerability"', *Research Papers in Education*, 27.4 (2012), 463–80 <https://doi.org/10.1080/02671522.2012.690241>, p. 476.
116 Kristján Kristjánsson, *Virtues and Vices in Positive Psychology: A Philosophical Critique* (New York: Cambridge University Press, 2013).
117 Sugarman, 'Neoliberalism and Psychological Ethics', p. 115.

Chapter 3 Positivity at work

1 Ehrenreich, *Smile or Die*.
2 Cabanas and Sánchez-González, 'Inverting the Pyramid of Needs'.
3 Kurt Danziger, *Naming the Mind: How Psychology Found Its Language* (London: SAGE, 1997); Roger Smith, *The Norton History of the Human Sciences* (New York: W. W. Norton, 1997).
4 Abraham H. Maslow, *Motivation and Personality* (New York: Harper & Row, 1970), p. 7.

5 Cabanas and Sánchez-González, 'Inverting the Pyramid of Needs.'.

6 Daniel Wren, *The Evolution of Management Thought* (Hoboken: John Wiley & Sons, 1994).

7 William G. Scott, *Organizational Theory: A Behavioral Analysis for Management* (Willowbrook: Richard D. Irwin, 1967).

8 Boltanski and Chiapello, *New Spirit of Capitalism*.

9 Maslow, *Motivation and Personality*.

10 Zygmunt Bauman, *The Individualized Society* (Cambridge: Polity, 2001); Beck, *Risk Society*.

11 Richard Sennett, *The Corrosion of Character: The Personal Consequences of Work in the New Capitalism* (New York: W. W. Norton, 1998).

12 Boltanski and Chiapello, *New Spirit of Capitalism* .

13 Bob Aubrey, quoted in Boltanski and Chiapello, *New Spirit of Capitalism*, p. 185.

14 Richard Sennett, *The Culture of the New Capitalism* (New Haven: Yale University Press, 2006); Boltanski and Chiapello, *New Spirit of Capitalism*.

15 Michael Daniels, 'The Myth of Self-Actualization', *Journal of Humanistic Psychology*, 28.1 (1988), 7–38 <https://doi.org/10.1177/0022167888281002>; Andrew Neher, 'Maslow's Theory of Motivation: A Critique', *Journal of Humanistic Psychology*, 31.3 (1991), 89–112 <https://doi.org/10.1177/0022167891313010>.

16 Edgar Cabanas and Juan Antonio Huertas, 'Psicología Positiva y Psicología Popular de la Autoayuda: Un Romance Histórico, Psicológico y Cultural', *Anales de Psicologia*, 30.3 (2014), 852–64 <https://doi.org/10.6018/analesps.30.3.169241>; Edgar Cabanas and José Carlos Sánchez-González, 'The Roots of Positive Psychology', *Papeles del Psicólogo*, 33.3 (2012), 172–82; García, Cabanas and Loredo, 'La Cura Mental de Phineas P. Quimby'.

17 Cabanas and Illouz, 'Making of a "Happy Worker"'; Illouz, *Saving the Modern Soul*.

18 Cabanas and Sánchez-González, 'Inverting the Pyramid of Needs'.

19 Cabanas and Sánchez-González, 'Inverting the Pyramid of Needs'.

20 Julia K. Boehm and Sonja Lyubomirsky, 'Does Happiness Promote Career Success?', *Journal of Career Assessment*, 16.1 (2008), 101–16 <https://doi.org/10.1177/1069072707308140>, p. 101.

21 Olivier Herrbach, 'A Matter of Feeling? The Affective Tone of Organizational Commitment and Identification', *Journal of Organizational*

Behavior, 27 (2006), 629–43 <https://doi.org/10.1002/job.362>; Remus Ilies, Brent A. Scott and Timothy A. Judge, 'The Interactive Effects of Personal Traits and Experienced States on Intraindividual Patterns of Citizenship Behavior', *Academy of Management Journal*, 49 (2006), 561–75 <https://doi.org/10.5465/AMJ.2006.21794672>; Carolyn M. Youssef and Fred Luthans, 'Positive Organizational Behavior in the Workplace: The Impact of Hope, Optimism, and Resilience', *Journal of Management*, 33.5 (2007), 774–800 <https://doi.org/10.1177/0149206307305562>.

22 Robert A. Baron, 'The Role of Affect in the Entrepreneurial Process', *Academy of Management Review*, 33.2 (2008), 328–40; Robert J. Baum, Michael Frese and Robert A. Baron, eds., *The Psychology of Entrepreneurship* (New York: Taylor & Francis, 2007); Ed Diener, Carol Nickerson, Richard E. Lucas and Ed Sandvik, 'Dispositional Affect and Job Outcomes', *Social Indicators Research*, 59 (2002), 229–59 <https://doi.org/10.1023/A:1019672513984>; Katariina Salmela-Aro and Jari-Erik Nurmi, 'Self-Esteem during University Studies Predicts Career Characteristics 10 Years Later', *Journal of Vocational Behavior*, 70 (2007), 463–77 <https://doi.org/10.1016/j.jvb.2007.01.006>; Carol Graham, Andrew Eggers and Sandip Sukhtankar, 'Does Happiness Pay? An Exploration Based on Panel Data from Russia', *Journal of Economic Behavior and Organization*, 55 (2004), 319–42 <https://doi.org/10.1016/j.jebo.2003.09.002>.

23 Timothy A. Judge and Charlice Hurst, 'How the Rich (and Happy) Get Richer (and Happier): Relationship of Core Self-Evaluations to Trajectories in Attaining Work Success', *Journal of Applied Psychology*, 93.4 (2008), 849–63 <https://doi.org/10.1037/0021-9010.93.4.849>.

24 Ed Diener, 'New Findings and Future Directions for Subjective Well-Being Research', *American Psychologist*, 67.8 (2012), 590–97 <https://doi.org/10.1037/a0029541>, p. 593.

25 Shaw Achor, *The Happiness Advantage* (New York: Random House, 2010), p. 4.

26 Michel Feher, 'Self-Appreciation; or, The Aspirations of Human Capital', *Public Culture*, 21.1 (2009), 21–41 <https://doi.org/10.1215/08992363-2008-019>.

27 Fred Luthans, Carolyn M. Youssef and Bruce J. Avolio, *Psychological Capital: Developing the Human Competitive Edge* (New York: Oxford University Press, 2007); Alexander Newman, Deniz Ucbasaran, Fei

Zhu and Giles Horst, 'Psychological Capital: A Review and Synthesis', *Journal of Organizational Behavior*, 35.S1 (2014), S120–38 <https://doi.org/10.1002/job.1916>.

28 Jessica Pryce-Jones, *Happiness at Work: Maximizing Your Psychological Capital for Success* (Chichester: John Wiley & Sons, 2010), p. ix.

29 Tim Smedley, 'Can Happiness Be a Good Business Strategy?', *The Guardian*, 20 June 2012 <https://www.theguardian.com/sustainable-business/happy-workforce-business-strategy-wellbeing>.

30 Pryce-Jones, *Happiness at Work*, pp. 28–9.

31 James B. Avey, Rebecca J. Reichard, Fred Luthans and Ketan H. Mhatre, 'Meta-Analysis of the Impact of Positive Psychological Capital on Employee Attitudes, Behaviors, and Performance', *Human Resource Development Quarterly*, 22.2 (2011), 127–52 <https://doi.org/10.1002/hrdq.20070>.

32 Youssef and Luthans, 'Positive Organizational Behavior in the Workplace'.

33 Cabanas and Illouz, 'Making of a "Happy Worker"'; Cabanas and Illouz, 'Fit fürs Glück'.

34 Eeva Sointu, 'The Rise of an Ideal: Tracing Changing Discourses of Wellbeing', *The Sociological Review*, 53.2 (2005), 255–74 <https://doi.org/10.1111/j.1467-954X.2005.00513.x>.

35 Arnold B. Bakker and Wilmar B. Schaufeli, 'Positive Organizational Behavior: Engaged Employees in Flourishing Organizations', *Journal of Organizational Behavior*, 29.2 (2008), 147–54 <https://doi.org/10.1002/job.515>; Thomas A. Wright, 'Positive Organizational Behavior: An Idea Whose Time Has Truly Come', *Journal of Organizational Behavior*, 24.4 (2003), 437–42 <https://doi.org/10.1002/job.197>.

36 Gerard Zwetsloot and Frank Pot, 'The Business Value of Health Management', *Journal of Business Ethics*, 55.2 (2004), 115–24 <https://doi.org/10.1007/s10551-004-1895-9>.

37 Joshua Cook, 'How Google Motivates Their Employees with Rewards and Perks', 2012 <https://hubpages.com/business/How-Google-Motivates-their-Employees-with-Rewards-and-Perks>.

38 Robert Biswas-Diener and Ben Dean, *Positive Psychology Coaching: Putting the Science of Happiness to Work for Your Clients* (Hoboken: John Wiley & Sons, 2007)., p. 190.

39 Biswas-Diener and Dean, *Positive Psychology Coaching*, pp. 195–6.
40 Micki McGee, *Self-Help, Inc.: Makeover Culture in American Life* (New York: Oxford University Press, 2005).
41 P. Alex Linley and George W. Burns, 'Strengthspotting: Finding and Developing Client Resources in the Management of Intense Anger', in *Happiness, Healing, Enhancement: Your Casebook Collection for Applying Positive Psychology in Therapy*, ed. by George W. Burns (Hoboken: John Wiley & Sons, 2010), pp. 3–14; Peterson and Seligman, *Character Strengths and Virtues*.
42 Angel Martínez Sánchez, Manuela Pérez Pérez, Pilar de Luis Carnicer and Maria José Vela Jiménez, 'Teleworking and Workplace Flexibility: A Study of Impact on Firm Performance', *Personnel Review*, 36.1 (2007), 42–64 <https://doi.org/10.1108/00483480710716713>, p. 44.
43 Gabe Mythen, 'Employment, Individualization and Insecurity: Rethinking the Risk Society Perspective', *The Sociological Review*, 53.1 (2005), 129–49 <https://doi.org/10.1111/j.1467-954X.2005.00506.x>.
44 Cabanas and Illouz, 'Making of a "Happy Worker"'; Cabanas and Illouz, 'Fit fürs Glück'.
45 Louis Uchitelle and N. R. Kleinfield, 'On the Battlefields of Business, Millions of Casualties', *The New York Times*, 3 March 1996 <http://www.nytimes.com>.
46 Eduardo Crespo and María Amparo Serrano-Pascual, 'La Psicologización del Trabajo: La Desregulación del Trabajo y el Gobierno de las Voluntades', *Teoría y Crítica de La Psicología*, 2 (2012), 33–48.
47 European Commission, *Towards Common Principles of Flexicurity: More and Better Jobs through Flexibility and Security*, COM(2007) 359 (Brussels: EC, 2007), p. 5.
48 Sennett, *Corrosion of Character*.
49 Fred Luthans, Gretchen. .R. Vogelgesang and Paul B. Lester, 'Developing the Psychological Capital of Resiliency', *Human Resource Development Review*, 5.1 (2006), 25–44 <https://doi.org/10.1177/1534484305285335>.
50 Debra Jackson, Angela Firtko and Michel Edenborough, 'Personal Resilience as a Strategy for Surviving and Thriving in the Face of Workplace Adversity: A Literature Review', *Journal of Advanced Nursing*, 60.1 (2007), 1–9 <https://doi.org/10.1111/j.1365-2648.2007.04412.x>.
51 https://www.bls.gov/

52 http://ec.europa.eu/eurostat/statistics-explained/index.php/Employme
nt_statistics
53 https://blog.linkedin.com/2016/04/12/will-this-year_s-college-grads-
job-hop-more-than-previous-grads
54 Alison Doyle, 'How Often Do People Change Jobs?', *The Balance*,
1 May 2017 <https://www.thebalance.com/how-often-do-people-cha
nge-jobs-2060467>.
55 Romain Felli, 'The World Bank's Neoliberal Language of Resilience', in
Risking Capitalism, ed. by Susanne Soederberg (Bingley: Emerald Group,
2016), pp. 267–95.
56 Salvatore R. Maddi and Deborah M. Khoshaba, *Resilience at Work: How
to Succeed No Matter What Life Throws at You* (New York: American
Management Association, 2005), p. 1.
57 Peter Greer and Chris Horst, *Entrepreneurship for Human Flourishing*
(Washington, DC: American Enterprise Institute for Public Policy
Research, 2014).
58 http://blog.approvedindex.co.uk/2015/06/25/map-entrepreneurship-ar
ound-the-world/
59 Cabanas and Illouz, 'Making of a "Happy Worker"'; Cabanas and Illouz,
'Fit fürs Gluck'.
60 Charles S. Carver, Michael F. Scheier and Suzanne C. Segerstrom,
'Optimism', *Clinical Psychology Review*, 30.7 (2010), 879–89 <https://
doi.org/10.1016/j.cpr.2010.01.006>; Robert Weis, 'You Want Me to
Fix It? Using Evidence-Based Interventions to Instill Hope in Parents
and Children', in *Happiness, Healing, Enhancement: Your Casebook
Collection for Applying Positive Psychology in Therapy*, ed. by George
W. Burns (Hoboken: John Wiley & Sons, 2012), pp. 64–75 <https://
doi.org/10.1002/9781118269664.ch6>; Shane J. Lopez, C. R. Snyder
and Jennifer Teramoto Pedrotti, 'Hope: Many Definitions, Many
Measures', in *Positive Psychological Assessment: A Handbook of Models and
Measures*, ed. by Shane J. Lopez and C. R. Snyder (Washington, DC:
American Psychological Association, 2003), pp. 91–106 <https://doi.
org/10.1037/10612-006>; Karen Reivich and Jane Gillham, 'Learned
Optimism: The Measurement of Explanatory Style', in *Positive
Psychological Assessment: A Handbook of Models and Measures*, ed. by Shane
J. Lopez and C. R. Snyder (Washington, DC: American Psychological
Association, 2003), pp. 57–74 <https://doi.org/10.1037/10612-004>.

61 Peterson and Seligman, *Character Strengths and Virtues*.
62 Michela Marzano, *Programados para Triunfar: Nuevo Capitalismo, Gestión Empresarial, y Vida Privada* (Barcelona: Tusquets, 2012).
63 Maria Konnikova, 'What Makes People Feel Upbeat at Work', *The New Yorker*, 30 July 2016 <http://www.newyorker.com/?p=3234730& mbid=nl_073016 Daily Newsletter (1)&CNDID=38849113&spMailing ID=9280546&spUserID=MTEwMTIzMzIyNTUzSo&spJobID=96243 2916&spReportId=OTYyNDMyOTE2So>.
64 Cabanas and Sánchez-González, 'Inverting the Pyramid of Needs'; Cabanas and Illouz, 'Making of a "Happy Worker"'; Cabanas and Illouz, 'Fit fürs Glück'.

Chapter 4 Happy selves on the market's shelves

1 http://possibilitychange.com/steps-to-change-my-life/
2 Illouz, *Emotions as Commodities*.
3 Cabanas, 'Rekindling Individualism, Consuming Emotions'; Cabanas, '"Psytizens", or the Construction of Happy Individuals'.
4 Christopher Lasch, *The Culture of Narcissism: American Life in an Age of Diminishing Expectations* (New York: W. W. Norton, 1979); Frank Furedi, *Therapy Culture*; Nolan, *Therapeutic State*; Ahmed, *Promise of Happiness*.
5 Binkley, *Happiness as Enterprise*, p. 163.
6 Wilhelm Hofmann, Maike Luhmann, Rachel R. Fisher, Kathleen D. Vohs and Roy F. Baumeister, 'Yes, But Are They Happy? Effects of Trait Self-Control on Affective Well-Being and Life Satisfaction', *Journal of Personality*, 82.4 (2014), 265–77 <https://doi.org/10.1111/ jopy.12050>; Derrick Wirtz, Juliann Stalls, Christie Napa Scollon and Karl L. Wuensch, 'Is the Good Life Characterized by Self-Control? Perceived Regulatory Success and Judgments of Life Quality', *The Journal of Positive Psychology*, 11.6 (2016), 572–83 <https://doi.org/10.10 80/17439760.2016.1152503>; Denise T. D. de Ridder, Gerty Lensvelt-Mulders, Catrin Finkenauer, F. Marijn Stok and Roy F. Baumeister, 'Taking Stock of Self-Control', *Personality and Social Psychology Review*, 16.1 (2012), 76–99 <https://doi.org/10.1177/1088868311418749>.
7 Peterson and Seligman, *Character Strengths and Virtues*, p. 38.
8 Heidi Marie Rimke, 'Governing Citizens through Self-Help Literature', *Cultural Studies*, 14.1 (2000), 61–78 <https://doi. org/10.1080/095023800334986>; Fernando Ampudia de Haro,

'Administrar el Yo: Literatura de Autoayuda y Gestión del Comportamiento y los Afectos', *Revista Española de Investigaciones Sociológicas (REIS)*, 113.1 (2006), 49–75; Sam Binkley, 'Happiness, Positive Psychology and the Program of Neoliberal Governmentality', *Subjectivity*, 4.4 (2011), 371–94 <https://doi.org/10.1057/sub.2011.16>; Rose, *Inventing Our Selves*.

9   Reivich and Gillham, 'Learned Optimism'.

10 Weis, 'You Want Me to Fix It?'

11 Lopez et al., 'Hope', p. 94.

12 Carver et al., 'Optimism', p. 1.

13 Lyubomirsky, *How of Happiness*, pp. 280–1.

14 Marc A. Brackett, John D. Mayer and Rebecca M. Warner, 'Emotional Intelligence and Its Relation to Everyday Behaviour', *Personality and Individual Differences*, 36.6 (2004), 1387–1402 <https://doi.org/10.1016/S0191-8869(03)00236-8>, p. 1389.

15 Illouz, *Cold Intimacies*; Lipovetsky, *La Felicidad Paradójica*.

16 https://my.happify.com/

17 https://my.happify.com/

18 Annika Howells, Itai Ivtzan and Francisco Jose Eiroa-Orosa, 'Putting the "App" in Happiness: A Randomised Controlled Trial of a Smartphone-Based Mindfulness Intervention to Enhance Wellbeing', *Journal of Happiness Studies*, 17.1 (2016), 163–85 <https://doi.org/10.1007/s10902-014-9589-1>.

19 Stephanie Baum, 'Happify Health Raises $9m to Expand Behavioral Health Research Business (Updated)', *MedCity News*, 15 August 2017 <https://medcitynews.com/2017/08/happify-health-raises-9m-expand-behavioral-health-research-business/?rf=1>.

20 Espeland and Stevens, 'Sociology of Quantification'; Nikolas Rose, 'Governing by Numbers: Figuring out Democracy', *Accounting, Organizations and Society*, 16.7 (1991), 673–92 <https://doi.org/10.1016/0361-3682(91)90019-B>.

21 Carl Rogers, *On Becoming a Person: A Therapist's View of Psychotherapy* (Boston: Houghton Mifflin, 1961), p. 166.

22 Rogers, *On Becoming a Person*, p. 33.

23 Carl Rogers, 'Some Observations on the Organization of Personality', *American Psychologist*, 2 (1947), 358–68, p. 362.

24 Maslow, *Motivation and Personality*, p. 46.

25 Peterson and Seligman, *Character Strengths and Virtues*, p. 29.
26 Timothy D. Hodges and Donald O. Clifton, 'Strengths-Based Development in Practice', in *Positive Psychology in Practice*, ed. by P. Alex Linley and Stephen Joseph (Hoboken: John Wiley & Sons, 2004), pp. 256–68, p. 258.
27 Kenneth Gergen, *The Saturated Self* (New York: Basic Books, 1991).
28 Isaiah Berlin, *Four Essays on Liberty* (Oxford: Oxford University Press, 1968).
29 Eugene Taylor, *Shadow Culture: Psychology and Spirituality in America* (Washington, DC: Counterpoint, 1999); Beril Satter, *Each Mind a Kingdom: American Women, Sexual Purity, and the New Thought Movement, 1875–1920*. (London: University of California Press, 1999).
30 Peterson and Seligman, *Character Strengths and Virtues*, p. 13.
31 Linley and Burns, 'Strengthspotting'.
32 Seligman, *Authentic Happiness*.
33 James H. Gilmore and Joseph B. Pine, *Authenticity: What Consumers Really Want* (Boston: Harvard Business School Press, 2007).
34 Guy Redden, 'Makeover Morality and Consumer Culture', in *Reading Makeover Television: Realities Remodelled*, ed. by Dana Heller (London: I. B. Tauris, 2007), pp. 150–64.
35 Linley and Burns, 'Strengthspotting', p. 10.
36 Bill O'Hanlon, 'There Is a Fly in the Urinal: Developing Therapeutic Possibilities from Research Findings', in *Happiness, Healing, Enhancement: Your Casebook Collection for Applying Positive Psychology in Therapy*, ed. by George W. Burns (Hoboken: John Wiley & Sons, 2010), pp. 303–14, p. 312.
37 Daniel J. Lair, Katie Sullivan and George Cheney, 'Marketization and the Recasting of the Professional Self: The Rhetoric and Ethics of Personal Branding', *Management Communication Quarterly*, 18.3 (2005), 307–43 <https://doi.org/10.1177/0893318904270744>.
38 Donna Freitas, *The Happiness Effect: How Social Media Is Driving a Generation to Appear Perfect at Any Cost* (New York: Oxford University Press, 2017), pp. 13–15.
39 Ehrenreich, *Smile or Die*.
40 Freitas, *Happiness Effect*, p. 71.
41 Freitas, *Happiness Effect*, p. 77.
42 Corey L. M. Keyes and Jonathan Haidt, eds., *Flourishing: Positive*

Psychology and the Life Well-Lived (Washington, DC: American Psychological Association, 2003).

43 Seligman, *Flourish*.

44 Seligman, *Flourish*.

45 Lahnna I. Catalino and Barbara L. Fredrickson, 'A Tuesday in the Life of a Flourisher: The Role of Positive Emotional Reactivity in Optimal Mental Health', *Emotion*, 11.4 (2011), 938–50 <https://doi.org/10.1037/a0024889>; Barbara L. Fredrickson, *Positivity* (New York: Crown, 2009); Judge and Hurst, 'How the Rich (and Happy) Get Richer (and Happier)'.

46 Seligman, *Flourish*, p. 13.

47 Sonja Lyubomirsky, Laura King and Ed Diener, 'The Benefits of Frequent Positive Affect: Does Happiness Lead to Success?', *Psychological Bulletin*, 131 (2005), 803–55 <https://doi.org/10.1037/0033-2909.131.6.803>; Fredrickson, *Positivity*.

48 Seligman, *Flourish*, p. 13.

49 Beck and Beck-Gernsheim, *Individualization*.

50 Carl Cederström and André Spicer, *Desperately Seeking Self-Improvement: A Year Inside the Optimization Movement* (New York and London: OR Books, 2017), p. 10.

51 John Schumaker, 'The Happiness Conspiracy', *New Internationalist*, 2 July 2006 <https://newint.org/columns/essays/2006/07/01/happiness-conspiracy>.

52 https://positivepsychologytoolkit.com/

53 Kennon M. Sheldon and Sonja Lyubomirsky, 'How to Increase and Sustain Positive Emotion: The Effects of Expressing Gratitude and Visualizing Best Possible Selves', *The Journal of Positive Psychology*, 1.2 (2006), 73–82 <https://doi.org/10.1080/17439760500510676>, pp. 76–7.

54 Sheldon and Lyubomirsky, 'How to Increase and Sustain Positive Emotion'.

55 Lyubomirsky, *How of Happiness*, p. 104.

56 Lyubomirsky, *How of Happiness*, p. 106.

57 Michel Foucault, *Technologies of the Self: A Seminar with Michel Foucault* (Amherst: University of Massachusetts Press, 1988).

58 Mongrain and Anselmo-Matthews, 'Do Positive Psychology Exercises Work?', p. 383.

59 Sheldon and Lyubomirsky, 'How to Increase and Sustain Positive Emotion', pp. 76–7, italics added.

60 Cabanas, 'Rekindling Individualism, Consuming Emotions'; Cabanas, '"Psytizens", or the Construction of Happy Individuals'.
61 Illouz, *Saving the Modern Soul*.

Chapter 5 Happy is the new normal

1 Gretchen Rubin, *The Happiness Project: Or, Why I Spent a Year Trying to Sing in the Morning, Clean My Closets, Fight Right, Read Aristotle, and Generally Have More Fun* (New York: HarperCollins, 2009), pp. 12–14.
2 Lyubomirsky, *How of Happiness*, p. 1.
3 Zupančič, *Odd One In*, p. 216.
4 Kennon M. Sheldon and Laura King, 'Why Positive Psychology Is Necessary', *American Psychologist*, 56.3 (2001), 216–17 <https://doi.org/10.1037/0003-066X.56.3.216>.
5 Marie Jahoda, *Current Concepts of Positive Mental Health* (New York: Basic Books, 1958) <https://doi.org/10.1037/11258-000>.
6 Boehm and Lyubomirsky, 'Does Happiness Promote Career Success?'; Catalino and Fredrickson, 'Tuesday in the Life'; Diener, 'New Findings and Future Directions'; Judge and Hurst, 'How the Rich (and Happy) Get Richer (and Happier)'; Lyubomirsky et al., 'Benefits of Frequent Positive Affect'.
7 Illouz, *Cold Intimacies*.
8 Barbara S. Held, 'The Negative Side of Positive Psychology', *Journal of Humanistic Psychology*, 44.1 (2004), 9–46, p. 12.
9 Seligman, *Authentic Happiness*, p. 178.
10 Seligman, *Authentic Happiness*, p. 129.
11 Lisa G. Aspinwall and Ursula M. Staudinger, 'A Psychology of Human Strengths: Some Central Issues of an Emerging Field', in *A Psychology of Human Strengths: Fundamental Questions and Future Directions for a Positive Psychology*, ed. by Lisa G. Aspinwall and Ursula M. Staudinger (Washington, DC: American Psychological Association, 2003), pp. 9–22, p. 18.
12 Laura A. King, 'The Hard Road to the Good Life: The Happy, Mature Person', *Journal of Humanistic Psychology*, 41.1 (2001), 51–72 <https://doi.org/10.1177/0022167801411005>, p. 53.
13 Barbara L. Fredrickson, 'Cultivating Positive Emotions to Optimize Health and Well-Being', *Prevention & Treatment*, 3.1 (2000) <https://doi.org/10.1037/1522-3736.3.1.31a>; Barbara L. Fredrickson and

T. Joiner, 'Positive Emotions', in *Handbook of Positive Psychology*, ed. by C. R. Snyder and Shane J. Lopez (New York: Oxford University Press, 2002), pp. 120–34.

14 Barbara L. Fredrickson, 'Updated Thinking on Positivity Ratios', *American Psychologist*, 68 (2013), 814–22 <https://doi.org/10.1037/a0033584>, p. 816.

15 Barbara L. Fredrickson and Marcial F. Losada, 'Positive Affect and the Complex Dynamics of Human Flourishing', *American Psychologist*, 60.7 (2005), 678–86 <https://doi.org/10.1037/0003-066X.60.7.678>, p. 678.

16 Fredrickson, 'Updated Thinking on Positivity Ratios', p. 816.

17 Fredrickson, 'Updated Thinking on Positivity Ratios'.

18 Barbara L. Fredrickson, 'The Role of Positive Emotions in Positive Psychology. The Broaden-and-Build Theory of Positive Emotions', *American Psychologist*, 56 (2001), 218–26 <https://doi.org/10.1037/0003-066X.56.3.218>, p. 221.

19 Fredrickson, 'Role of Positive Emotions in Positive Psychology', p. 221.

20 Fredrickson, *Positivity*.

21 Fredrickson, 'Role of Positive Emotions in Positive Psychology', p. 223.

22 Fredrickson, 'Updated Thinking on Positivity Ratios', p. 819.

23 Fredrickson, 'Updated Thinking on Positivity Ratios'.

24 Fredrickson, 'Updated Thinking on Positivity Ratios', p. 818.

25 Fredrickson, 'Updated Thinking on Positivity Ratios', p. 815.

26 Fredrickson and Losada, 'Positive Affect and the Complex Dynamics of Human Flourishing'.

27 Elisha Tarlow Friedman, Robert M. Schwartz and David A. F. Haaga, 'Are the Very Happy Too Happy?', *Journal of Happiness Studies*, 3.4 (2002), 355–72 <https://doi.org/10.1023/A:1021828127970>.

28 Fredrickson, *Positivity*, p. 122.

29 Barbara L. Fredrickson and Laura E. Kurtz, 'Cultivating Positive Emotions to Enhance Human Flourishing', in *Applied Positive Psychology: Improving Everyday Life, Health, Schools, Work, and Society*, ed. by Stewart I. Donaldson, Mihaly Csikszentmihalyi and Jeanne Nakamura (New York: Routledge, 2011), pp. 35–47, p. 42.

30 Nicholas J. L. Brown, Alan D. Sokal and Harris L. Friedman, 'The Complex Dynamics of Wishful Thinking: The Critical Positivity Ratio', *The American Psychologist*, 68.9 (2013), 801–13 <https://doi.org/10.1037/a0032850>, p. 801.

31 Brown et al., 'Complex Dynamics of Wishful Thinking', p. 812.
32 Fredrickson, 'Updated Thinking on Positivity Ratios', p. 814.
33 Fredrickson, 'Updated Thinking on Positivity Ratios.', p. 814.
34 Fredrickson, 'Updated Thinking on Positivity Ratios.', p. 819.
35 Jerome Kagan, *What Is Emotion? History, Measures, and Meanings* (New Haven: Yale University Press, 2007); Margaret Wetherell, *Affect and Emotions: A New Social Science Understanding* (London: SAGE, 2012).
36 Deborah Lupton, *The Emotional Self: A Sociocultural Exploration* (London: SAGE, 1998).
37 Ute Frevert, *Emotions in History: Lost and Found* (Budapest: Central European University Press, 2011); Richard S. Lazarus and Bernice N. Lazarus, *Passion and Reason: Making Sense of Our Emotions* (New York and Oxford: Oxford University Press, 1994); Michael Lewis, Jeannette Haviland-Jones and Lisa Feldman Barrett, eds., *Handbook of Emotions* (New York and London: Guilford Press, 2008); Barbara H. Rosenwein, 'Worrying About Emotions in History', *The American Historical Review*, 107.3 (2002), 821–45; Wetherell, *Affect and Emotions*.
38 Catherine Lutz and Geoffrey M. White, 'The Anthropology of Emotions', *Annual Review of Anthropology*, 15.1 (1986), 405–36 <https://doi.org/10.1146/annurev.an.15.100186.002201>.
39 Catharine A. MacKinnon, *Are Women Human? And Other International Dialogues* (Cambridge, MA, and London: Harvard University Press, 2007); Lauren Berlant, *Cruel Optimism* (Durham, NC: Duke University Press, 2011).
40 Illouz, *Why Love Hurts*; Eva Illouz, 'Emotions, Imagination and Consumption: A New Research Agenda', *Journal of Consumer Culture*, 9 (2009), 377–413 <https://doi.org/10.1177/1469540509342053>.
41 Jack M. Barbalet, *Emotion, Social Theory, and Social Structure: A Macrosociological Approach* (Cambridge: Cambridge University Press, 2004); Arlie Russell Hochschild, *The Outsourced Self: Intimate Life in Market TImes* (New York: Metropolitan Books, 2012).
42 Horace Romano Harré, *Physical Being: A Theory for a Corporeal Psychology* (Oxford: Blackwell, 1991).
43 Ehrenreich, *Smile or Die*; Sundararajan, 'Happiness Donut'; Cabanas and Sánchez-González, 'Roots of Positive Psychology'.
44 Lazarus, 'Does the Positive Psychology Movement Have Legs?'
45 Kagan, *What Is Emotion?*, p. 8.

46 Lazarus, 'Does the Positive Psychology Movement Have Legs?'

47 Forgas, 'Don't Worry, Be Sad!'; Hui Bing Tan and Joseph P. Forgas, 'When Happiness Makes Us Selfish, but Sadness Makes Us Fair: Affective Influences on Interpersonal Strategies in the Dictator Game', *Journal of Experimental Social Psychology*, 46.3 (2010), 571–6 <https://doi.org/10.1016/j.jesp.2010.01.007>.

48 Marino Pérez-Álvarez, 'Positive Psychology: Sympathetic Magic', *Papeles del Psicólogo*, 33.3 (2012), 183–201.

49 Anthony Storr, *Human Aggression* (Harmondsworth: Penguin, 1992).

50 Svetlana Boym, *The Future of Nostalgia* (New York: Basic Books, 2001).

51 Jens Lange and Jan Crusius, 'The Tango of Two Deadly Sins: The Social-Functional Relation of Envy and Pride', *Journal of Personality and Social Psychology*, 109.3 (2015), 453–72 <https://doi.org/10.1037/pspi0000026>.

52 Marino Pérez-Álvarez, 'Positive Psychology and Its Friends: Revealed', *Papeles del Psicólogo*, 34 (2013), 208–26; Mauss et al., 'Can Seeking Happiness Make People Unhappy?'; Pérez-Álvarez, 'Science of Happiness.'

53 Tan and Forgas, 'When Happiness Makes Us Selfish', p. 574.

54 Devlin et al., 'Not As Good as You Think?'; Joseph P. Forgas and Rebekah East, 'On Being Happy and Gullible: Mood Effects on Skepticism and the Detection of Deception', *Journal of Experimental Social Psychology*, 44.5 (2008), 1362–7 <https://doi.org/10.1016/j.jesp.2008.04.010>; Jaihyun Park and Mahzarin R. Banaji, 'Mood and Heuristics: The Influence of Happy and Sad States on Sensitivity and Bias in Stereotyping', *Journal of Personality and Social Psychology*, 78.6 (2000), 1005–23 <https://doi.org/10.1037/0022-3514.78.6.1005>.

55 Joseph P. Forgas, 'On Being Happy and Mistaken: Mood Effects on the Fundamental Attribution Error', *Journal of Personality and Social Psychology*, 72.1 (1998), 318–31; Forgas, 'Don't Worry, Be Sad!'.

56 Peterson and Seligman, *Character Strengths and Virtues*.

57 Daniel Lord Smail, 'Hatred as a Social Institution in Late-Medieval Society', *Speculum*, 76.1 (2001), 90–126 <https://doi.org/10.2307/2903707>.

58 Barbalet, *Emotion, Social Theory, and Social Structure*.

59 Spencer E. Cahill, 'Embarrassability and Public Civility: Another View of a Much Maligned Emotion', in *Social Perspectives on Emotions*, ed. by

David D. Franks, Michael B. Flaherty and Carolyn Ellis (Greenwich, CT: JAI, 1995), pp. 253–71.

60 Arlie Russell Hochschild, 'The Sociology of Feeling and Emotion: Selected Possibilities', *Sociological Inquiry*, 45.2-3 (1975), 280–307 <https://doi.org/10.1111/j.1475-682X.1975.tb00339.x>.

61 Axel Honneth, *The Struggle for Recognition: The Moral Grammar of Social Conflicts* (Cambridge, MA: MIT Press, 1996).

62 Tim Lomas and Itai Ivtzan, 'Second Wave Positive Psychology: Exploring the Positive–Negative Dialectics of Wellbeing', *Journal of Happiness Studies*, 17.4 (2016), 1753–68 <https://doi.org/10.1007/s10902-015-9668-y>.

63 Seligman, 'Building Resilience'.

64 Luthans et al., 'Developing the Psychological Capital of Resiliency'; Ann S. Masten and Marie-Gabrielle J. Reed, 'Resilience in Development', in *Handbook of Positive Psychology*, ed. by C. R. Snyder and Shane J. Lopez (Oxford: Oxford University Press, 2002), pp. 74–88; Reivich et al., 'From Helplessness to Optimism'.

65 Michele M. Tugade and Barbara L. Fredrickson, 'Resilient Individuals Use Positive Emotions to Bounce Back From Negative Emotional Experiences', *Journal of Personality and Social Psychology*, 86.2 (2004), 320–33 <https://doi.org/10.1037/0022-3514.86.2.320>, p. 320.

66 Michael Rutter, 'Psychosocial Resilience and Protective Mechanisms', *American Journal of Orthopsychiatry*, 57.3 (1987), 316–31 <https://doi.org/10.1111/j.1939-0025.1987.tb03541.x>; Ann S. Masten, Karin M. Best and Norman Garmezy, 'Resilience and Development: Contributions from the Study of Children Who Overcome Adversity', *Development and Psychopathology*, 2.4 (1990), 425–44 <https://doi.org/10.1017/S0954579400005812>.

67 Lawrence G. Calhoun and Richard G. Tedeschi, eds., *Handbook of Posttraumatic Growth: Research and Practice* (Mahwah: Lawrence Erlbaum Associates, 2006).

68 Keyes and Haidt, *Flourishing*.

69 P. Alex Linley and Stephen Joseph, 'Positive Change Following Trauma and Adversity: A Review', *Journal of Traumatic Stress*, 17.1 (2004), 11–21 <https://doi.org/10.1023/B:JOTS.0000014671.27856.7e>; Richard G. Tedeschi and Lawrence G. Calhoun, 'Posttraumatic Growth: Conceptual

Foundations and Empirical Evidence', *Psychological Inquiry*, 15.1 (2004), 1–18 <https://doi.org/10.1207/s15327965pli1501_01>.

70 Linley and Joseph, 'Positive Change Following Trauma and Adversity', p. 17.

71 Enric C. Sumalla, Cristian Ochoa and Ignacio Blanco, 'Posttraumatic Growth in Cancer: Reality or Illusion?', *Clinical Psychology Review*, 29.1 (2009), 24–33 <https://doi.org/10.1016/j.cpr.2008.09.006>; Patricia L. Tomich and Vicki S. Helgeson, 'Is Finding Something Good in the Bad Always Good? Benefit Finding Among Women With Breast Cancer', *Health Psychology*, 23.1 (2004), 16–23 <https://doi.org/10.1037/0278-6133.23.1.16>.

72 Seligman, *Flourish*, p. 159

73 Seligman, 'Building Resilience', n.p., paras.1–2.

74 Martin E. P. Seligman and Raymond D. Fowler, 'Comprehensive Soldier Fitness and the Future of Psychology', *American Psychologist*, 66 (2011), 82–6 <https://doi.org/10.1037/a0021898>; Seligman, *Flourish*.

75 Seligman, *Flourish*, p. 181.

76 Nicholas J. L. Brown, 'A Critical Examination of the U.S. Army's Comprehensive Soldier Fitness Program', *The Winnower*, 2 (2015), e143751 <https://doi.org/10.15200/winn.143751.17496>.

77 Roy Eidelson and Stephen Soldz, 'Does Comprehensive Soldier Fitness Work? CSF Research Fails the Test', *Coalition for an Ethical Psychology Working Paper*, 1.5 (2012), 1–12.

78 Eidelson and Soldz, 'Does Comprehensive Soldier Fitness Work?', p. 1.

79 Thomas W. Britt, Winny Shen, Robert R. Sinclair, Matthew R. Grossman and David M. Klieger, 'How Much Do We Really Know About Employee Resilience?', *Industrial and Organizational Psychology*, 9.02 (2016), 378–404 <https://doi.org/10.1017/iop.2015.107>; John Dyckman, 'Exposing the Glosses in Seligman and Fowler's (2011) Straw-Man Arguments', *American Psychologist*, 66.7 (2011), 644–5 <https://doi.org/10.1037/a0024932>; Harris L. Friedman and Brent Dean Robbins, 'The Negative Shadow Cast by Positive Psychology: Contrasting Views and Implications of Humanistic and Positive Psychology on Resiliency', *The Humanistic Psychologist*, 40.1 (2012), 87–102 <https://doi.org/10.1080/08873267.2012.643720>; Sean Phipps, 'Positive Psychology and War: An Oxymoron', *American Psychologist*, 66.7 (2011), 641–2 <https://doi.org/10.1037/a0024933>.

80 Brown, 'Critical Examination', p. 13 (para. 66).
81 Angela Winter, 'The Science of Happiness. Barbara Fredrickson on Cultivating Positive Emotions', *Positivity*, 2009 <http://www.positivi tyratio.com/sun.php>.
82 Martha Nussbaum, *The Fragility of Goodness: Luck and Ethics in Greek Tragedy and Philosophy* (New York: Cambridge University Press, 2001).
83 Ruth Levitas, *Utopia as Method: The Imaginary Reconstruction of Society* (Basingstoke and New York: Palgrave Macmillan, 2013).
84 Jean Baudrillard, *Simulations* (New York: Semiotext(e), 1983).
85 Veenhoven, 'Life Is Getting Better'.
86 Bergsma and Veenhoven, 'Happiness of People with a Mental Disorder'; Ad Bergsma, Margreet ten Have, Ruut Veenhoven and Ron de Graaf, 'Most People with Mental Disorders Are Happy: A 3-year Follow-Up in the Dutch General Population', *The Journal of Positive Psychology*, 6.4 (2011), 253–9 <https://doi.org/10.1080/17439760.2011.577086>.
87 Veenhoven, 'Life Is Getting Better', p. 107.
88 Veenhoven, 'Life Is Getting Better', p. 120.
89 Seligman, *Authentic Happiness*, p. 266.
90 Emmanuel Levinas, *Entre Nous: Thinking-of-the-Other* (London and New York: Continuum, 2006).
91 Sidney Hook, *Pragmatism and the Tragic Sense of Life* (New York: Basic Books, 1974).

Conclusion

1 Julio Cortázar, *Cronopios and Famas* (New York: New Direction Books, 1999), pp. 23–4.
2 Terry Eagleton, *Hope without Optimism* (New Haven: Yale University Press, 2015).
3 Robert Nozick, *Anarchy, State, and Utopia* (New York: Basic Books, 1974).